In *Rebirth of the Goddess*, Carol P. Christ co ... . philosophical reflections to create a new model of embodied thinking. This first systematic thealogy of the Goddess argues that the shift from God to Goddess signals a transformation of Western theology, philosophy, and ethics, offering the hope that we can create a different world.

"We Christian males did not understand the full implications of process theology until feminists showed them to us. Carol Christ carries that process further, and I am grateful."
—John B. Cobb Jr., author of over thirty books including *Christ in a Pluralistic Age* and *A Christian Natural Theology*

"I am deeply moved by Carol Christ's vision of love at the heart of the universe. Though I cannot share it, yet I also cannot easily dismiss it, because she recognizes the inescapability of loss and grief and cruelty—she has never forgotten the Holocaust."
—Christine Downing, author of *The Goddess*, *Women's Mysteries*, and *Psyche Sisters*

"One of feminist spirituality's founding mothers here offers a thealogy—a way of understanding the diverse, often divergent ways in which modern women use the image of the goddess . . . . a charged testimonial to the power of the feminine divine in her own life . . . . weav(ing) autobiography, anthropology, comparative religion, and history into a seamless garment of impassioned thought."
—Patricia Monaghan, author of *The New Book of Goddessess and Heroines*

"Carol Christ articulates clear reasons for regarding the Goddess movement as an important strand of contemporary religious activity, and she has convinced me that contemporary theologians *of all persuasions* would benefit from reflecting seriously on the implications of her sort of thealogy. *Rebirth of the Goddess* is a fine example of what I call 'constructive theology,' a sort of theology much needed today, as we seek to re-orient our lives in face of the mammoth problems (ecological, social, political, economical, moral, religious) that humanity now faces."
—Gordon Kaufman, author of *In Face of Mystery: A Constructive Theology*

"A timely 'systematic thealogy' that beautifully incorporates the embodied, embedded sensibilities of a distinguished scholar and pioneer of the spiritual journey into Goddess religion . . . . a valuable contribution to the field of religious studies . . . . this book both clarifies and inspires."
—Charlene Spretnak, author of *States of Grace*

"*Rebirth of the Goddess* is a wonderful book, full of information, easy to read, and it gives us, for the first time, an articulate thealogy—something the women's spirituality movement has been missing. It fills a tremendous need."
—Donna Read, Director and Producer of "Goddess Remembered" and "The Burning Times"

Selected by *New Age Journal* for summer reading

Other books by Carol P. Christ

Diving Deep and Surfacing
Laughter of Aphrodite
Odyssey with the Goddess
Womanspirit Rising (with Judith Plaskow)
Weaving the Visions (with Judith Plaskow)

Rebirth of the Goddess

*Finding Meaning
in Feminist Spirituality*

Carol P. Christ

Routledge

New York · London

Published in 1997 by
Routledge
Taylor & Francis Group
711 Third Avenue
New York, NY 10017

Published in Great Britain by
Routledge
Taylor & Francis Group
2 Park Square
Milton Park, Abingdon
Oxon OX14 4RN

© 1997 by Carol P. Christ
Routledge is an imprint of Taylor & Francis Group

International Standard Book Number 0-415-92186-4 (Softcover)
Library of Congress Card Number 98-37858

Library of Congress Cataloging-in-Publication Data

Christ, Carol P.
  Rebirth of the goddess : finding meaning in feminist spirituality
/ Carol P. Christ.
      p.   cm.
      Originally published: Reading, Mass. : Addison-Wesley, c1997.
  Includes bibliographical references and index.
  ISBN 0-415-92186-4 (pbk. : alk. paper)
  1. Women—Religious life.   2. Goddess religion.   3. Feminism—
Religious aspects.   I. Title.
  [BL625.7.C47   1998]
  291.2'082—dc21   98-37858

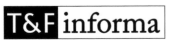

Taylor & Francis Group
is the Academic Division of T&F Informa plc.

Visit the Taylor & Francis Web site at
http://www.taylorandfrancis.com

and the Routledge Web site at
http://www.routledge-ny.com

In memory of
Jane Ellen Harrison,
Gertrude Rachel Levy,
and Marija Gimbutas,
ancestors,
mentors.

Contents

List of Illustrations

Prologue:
Before the Beginning

Evrynome—A Story of Creation
by Christine Lavadas

Long, long in the past, far, far in the future,
At that point, before the beginning, after the end,
Where time and space do not exist,
Where all colors and forms are lost in the blackness of void,
There was a heavy vast silence,
A profound eternal motionlessness,
And nothingness and everything were the same.

And then Evrynome, Gaia, Goddess of a thousand names,
Mother of all,
Sighed.

And the sound of her breath echoed pleasingly in her ears.
As if it were a foreseeing
And yet as if it were remembrance,
She heard summer breezes ruffling tall green grasses,
And winter hurricanes howling through deep valleys,
And the pounding of the sea,
And the calling voices of all creation.
And so Evrynome, Gaia, Goddess of a thousand names,

Mother of all,
Pursed her lips and whistled for the wind.

Then slowly, smoothly, with perfect sensuality
She rose up from the timeless bed of her infinite rest
And caught up the wind
In her cupped hands,
In her streaming hair,
In the billows of her skirts,
And in the warm secret places of her body,
And she danced.

She danced delicately, she danced frenziedly,
She danced in staccato rhythm and liquid movement,
She danced with pure precision and orgiastic abandon,
She danced gloriously,
She danced holding the wind in her close embrace,
She danced the love and the joy of creation.
She danced and she danced.

And from the arch of her foot leapt the circles of time,
And from the curve of her spine, the spirals of life,
Day and night,
Black and white,
Absorption, reflection,
Birth, death, resurrection.
And as ecstasy grew, as the beat increased,
The wind blew wild and her belly swelled round.
And from the rivers of her sweat, oceans flowed,
And with each heave of her breast, mountains rose.
And when she threw back her hair and opened her hands,
Life teemed around her and harmony reigned.
Creation now danced in her perfect time
And she smiled.

Preface:
Rebirth of the Goddess

One of the most unexpected developments of the late twentieth century is the rebirth of the religion of the Goddess in western cultures. Though we were taught that the Gods and Goddesses died with the triumph of Christianity, the reemergence of the Goddess is not as surprising as it might seem. When Christian emperors outlawed the worship of the Goddess,

> the Goddess' religion went underground. Some of those old traditions, particularly those connected with birth, death, and earth fertility rituals, have continued to this day without much change in some regions; in others, they were assimilated.[1]

In America, Europe, Australia, and New Zealand, hundreds of thousands of women and increasing numbers of men brought up in the biblical religions are rediscovering the language, symbols, and rituals of the Goddess.[2] For me and for many others, finding the Goddess has felt like coming home to a vision of life that we had always known deeply within ourselves: that we are part of nature and that our destiny is to participate fully in the cycles of birth, death, and renewal that characterize life on this earth.[3] We find in the Goddess a compelling image of female power, a vision of the deep connection of all beings in the web of life, and a call to create peace on earth. The return of the Goddess inspires us to hope that we can heal the deep rifts between women and men, between "man" and nature, and between "God" and the world, that have shaped our western view of reality for too long.[4]

The rebirth of the Goddess raises many questions. Who is the Goddess, and what does She mean? Is She God in female form? The feminine face of the God of biblical traditions? Or is She everything He was not? Is Goddess yet another deity *out there*? Or is Goddess *in us*? Is She Mother Earth or Mother Nature? Is She loving and tender? Or brutal and blind? What does She have to do with familiar Goddesses like Athena and Aphrodite? Is She born from the head of Zeus, fully armed and ready for battle? Does She brazenly expose herself, then simper and cower like Marilyn Monroe? Can the image of the Goddess affirm women's minds as well as our bodies? Is She white? Is She black? Yellow? Or brown? Is She a creation of female fantasy? Or male fear? Does She herald a return to primitive superstition? Is She bloodthirsty and orgiastic? A pagan idol? Does She symbolize tribal loyalties to blood and land? Is the image of the Goddess as oppressive to men as the image of God has been to women? Does the Goddess romanticize women and nature, leaving culture and politics to men? Is She the Goddess or Goddesses? One or many? What about the Gods? Can She provide an end to suffering? Does She answer the questions we have about death? Is She yet another "opiate of the people"? An image that makes women feel good but turns us away from the world in which we live? Can ethics be found in Goddess religion?

All of these and many other questions will be answered in this book. But, as we shall see, few of the questions raised by the Goddess can be answered with a simple "yes" or "no" because these questions arise out of traditional understandings of Goddess and God. As we explore the meaning of the Goddess, we must change the questions we ask as well as the ways we answer them. This means rethinking many of the most deeply held and unrecognized assumptions of our culture. I will argue that neither the history nor the contemporary meaning of the Goddess can be understood unless we develop holistic modes of thinking, abandoning the categorical distinctions between "God," "man," and "the world" and transforming the classical dualisms of spirit and nature, mind and body, rational and irrational, male and female, that have structured the worldview we know as western thought.

From *thea*, "Goddess," and *logos*, "meaning," this book is a *thea-logy*,[5] a reflection on the meaning of the Goddess. For those who wonder about the meaning of the Goddess who has touched their lives, *Rebirth of the Goddess* provides a clear understanding of the radical implications of the Goddess for cultural transformation and a way of explaining their worldview to others. For those who know little about the Goddess except her name—for women and men, atheists and agnostics, Christians and Jews, scholars and students in many fields, all who are curious—it offers a challenging new interpretation of human history and culture; another, and possibly more satisfying, way of understanding the world and our place in it; and perhaps even a greater hope for the future of life on earth. Finally, *Rebirth of the Goddess* challenges theologians and historians of religion to reformulate foundational theories about the nature of divinity and the origins of religion.

In developing a systematic thea-logy of the Goddess it is important to be as clear, coherent, and consistent as possible. To be clear means that after thinking long and hard, I will express the meaning I have discovered in the simplest language I can find. Much philosophical and theological language is unnecessarily difficult and inaccessible. To be coherent means that the insights must hold together and create a paradigm or interpretive framework that helps us make sense of the world and our lives. To be consistent means that ideas developed in reflection on one issue are carried over into the discussion of others so that the thea-logy as a whole can be seen to be governed by an internal logic and a number of basic insights.

In the vision developed in this book, the Goddess is the power of intelligent embodied love that is the ground of all being. The earth is the body of the Goddess. All beings are interdependent in the web of life. Nature is intelligent, alive, and aware. As part of nature, human beings are relational, embodied, and interdependent. The basis of ethics is the feeling of deep connection to all people and all beings in the web of life. The symbols and rituals of Goddess religion bring these values to consciousness and help us build communities in which we can create a more just, peaceful, and harmonious world.

Since many of the readers of this book will not be familiar with the Goddess, the first chapter depicts my own and several other representative journeys to the Goddess and introduces many of the most familiar images, symbols, and rituals of the Goddess movement. Readers acquainted with theology will recognize that from there on, the structure of the book follows a traditional pattern. Chapter 2 reflects on how we know what we claim to know about the Goddess (*epistemology*) and considers the sources and norms for writing thea-logy (*method*). Chapter 3 provides arguments for the interpretation of the *history* of the Goddess that has inspired the contemporary movement, and Chapter 4 probes the assumptions that shape the writing of history (*historiography*). Chapters 5 through 8 discuss themes that in classical theology are called "God," "The Universe," "Man," and "Ethics."

Though it is increasingly recognized that a new religion of the Goddess is being created,[5] some resist the word *religion*, identifying it with a God who is outside the self and an authoritarian system of dogma, law, or ritual. However, the word *religion* comes from the Indo-European *leig*, "to bind," and *re*, "to turn" or "to turn back."[6] Since the symbols and rituals of the Goddess bring to consciousness (remind us of) our sense of deep connection (or binding) to all people and all beings in the web of life, I find the word *religion* appropriate.[7]

Because the theology we have known has all too often told us what to think, stifled questions, and denied experience, a thea-logy of the Goddess will be viewed with suspicion by some. This opinion was expressed nearly a century ago by the classicist Jane Harrison, who studied the earliest Greek Goddesses.

> For theology . . . [is] not a starting-point, but a culmination, a complete achievement, an almost mechanical accomplishment, with scarcely a hint of origines, an accomplishment moreover, which is essentially literary rather than religious, skeptical and moribund in its very perfection.[8]

Harrison's depiction of theology as a way of distancing oneself from religious experience accurately describes much of the theology I encountered in graduate school. I frequently felt that theology as "rational reflection" was dead and deadening. Yet at its best, theology attempts to make sense of the questions that we ask in the living of our lives. Who are we? Why are we here? What is the meaning of life? What is the meaning of death? Why do we suffer? How should we live? What should we do?[9]

Because questions do arise in our experience of the Goddess and because I think it is important to reflect on them, I have dared to write a thea-logy. For a long time I hesitated, not wanting to distance myself or others from the beauty and deep feeling of Goddess imagery and ritual. I started several times, completed a draft, set it aside—all the while asking myself whether it was possible to write a thea-logy that opened doors rather than closed them. The five years in which an earlier version of this book sat untouched were years in which I was forced to ask basic questions again, confronting the powers of life and death, wondering if there was a place for me in the universe. Toward the end of that time, I wrote about my spiritual quest in *Odyssey with the Goddess*.[10] In that book, I chose narrative form because it seemed closer to the shape of experience.

It was not until after I emerged from my own underworld with deeper knowledge that I could begin again to try to write the kind of a thea-logy I longed to read as a student. A thea-logy honed in struggle, a thea-logy in which the life that inspired its conceptions is not hidden. A thea-logy in which the voice of experience and the voice of reflection come together. This book proposes and models *embodied thinking* as an alternative to objective thought. My goal is that readers not only know what I think but also who I am and why I think the way I do. This will make it easier to understand the relevance (or lack of relevance) of my ideas to their own lives.

Thea-logy can never provide final answers to all the questions we have. Nor do I expect readers of this book to agree with everything I say. What I write has emerged in my reflection on my experience. I hope others will be inspired to think about the meanings that arise in *their* experience.

1

In Search of Her

Though I never heard the word *Goddess* spoken when I was a child, I felt her power in the eerie calls of the peacocks that nested on the roof of my grandmother's house as my brother and I fell asleep in the yellow bedroom; in the waves that crashed over me as we played at Huntington Beach; in the oaks and scrub brush along hillside trails I hiked in the San Gabriel Mountains; in the liquid eyes of black-tailed deer as they turned to look at me in Calaveras State Park; in the pouring rain that filled my rubber boots as I walked home from school.

I was more interested in religion than my parents, often convincing them to take me to church to sing hymns when they would have preferred to sleep late on Sunday mornings. The God I met in church was, like my father and grandfathers, wise and powerful, the ultimate judge in whose eyes I hoped to find favor. In college, I identified with the Israel of the Bible whom God defined as a "stiff-necked child" who must be severely punished, but who would ultimately be forgiven. I suppose I decided to major in religion in the hope that I could understand God well enough to make myself acceptable to him.

When I began to study the Hebrew Bible in college, I was drawn to the prophets' images of the trees of the field clapping their hands on the day of redemption, of mountains and hills resounding in song. I did not understand when my professors said that this was an example of the pathetic fallacy, which they defined as attributing feelings to inanimate objects. I thought the prophets' words spoke of the deep communion we share with nature. I sensed what Jewish theologian Martin Buber meant when he spoke of having an "I-Thou" relation with a tree, a piece of mica, a horse, because I too had felt a special connection to stones, plants, and animals. I was terribly disappointed when my professors said they never understood this aspect of Buber.

Several years of graduate study in theology convinced me that there was something wrong with the traditional image of God. My questioning began with theologians' words about women. Woman was body, man was soul; woman was flesh, man was spirit. Because of her lesser rational capacity, woman was persuaded by the serpent; because she could not control her passions, woman was seduced. I was a woman, and try as I might, I did not see myself in this picture. I knew my mind was as good as anyone's, and I did not view my body as a source of temptation. Gradually, it began to dawn on me that the image of God as Father, Son, and Spirit was at the root of the problem. No matter what I did, I would never be "in his image." While I had hoped to find in God a father who would love and accept my female self, it seemed that "he," like my father and most of my professors, liked boys better. I decided that unless we could call God Mother as well as Father, Daughter as well as Son, women and girls would never be valued.

As I became increasingly alienated from God as Father, I found myself unable to attend church, sing hymns, or pray. With no new images to replace the ones I could no longer accept, I felt empty. Late one night, the anger that had been building up inside me spilled out. I cried out to God, "I want you to know how much I have suffered because you let yourself be named in man's image as God of the fathers, as the man of war, as king of the universe." I sobbed in pain and rejection, until my tears were gone. In the silence that followed, a voice said, "In God is a woman like yourself. She shares your suffering."[1]

A year later, when I heard the name of the Goddess in a workshop led by a woman called Starhawk, I felt the experience of my entire life affirmed. Starhawk describes the Goddess as

> *Mother Earth, who sustains all growing things, who is the body, our bones and cells. She is air—the winds that move in the trees and over the waves, breath. She is the fire of the hearth, the blazing bonfire and the fuming volcano; the power of transformation and change. And she is water—the sea, original source of life; the rivers, streams, lakes and wells; the blood that flows in the rivers of our veins. She is mare, cow, cat, owl, crane, flower, tree, apple, seed, lion, sow, stone, woman. She is found in the world around us, in the cycles and seasons of nature, in mind, body, spirit, and emotions within each of us.*[2]

Images of the Goddess depict female power as creative and vital. Images of the Goddess tell us that we participate in the mysteries of nature, in the cycles of birth, death, and renewal. She was the one I intuited when I responded to nature imagery in the prophets and Buber's I-Thou relation with a tree. She was the one I sought when I expressed my anger at God. She was the one I had not known. She was the one I had always known.

Hunger for a female image of God was awakened in me by the rebirth of the women's movement. Consciousness-raising provided a model of a woman's space where we could share our stories, "hear each other into speech,"[3] allow the Goddess to reemerge in our midst. We discovered books written decades earlier that had rarely been checked out of libraries: M. Esther Harding, Jane Ellen Harrison, G. Rachel Levy, Helen Diner. We read about the Goddess in journals and newsletters, in books just being published: Jean Mountaingrove, Ruth Mountaingrove, Z. Budapest, Hallie Mountain-Wing, Merlin Stone, Elizabeth Gould Davis, Marija Gimbutas, Charlene Spretnak, Starhawk.[4] We created study groups and ritual circles. "The Goddess is alive. Magic is afoot," we chanted gleefully.[5]

The road from that initial awakening to the writing of this book has not always been easy. Though discovering the Goddess affirmed my female self and my sense of connection to nature, it set me apart from inherited religious communities, my culture, my family, some of my friends, and many of my closest colleagues. The journey of a dissident daughter is sometimes lonely.[6]

My experiences of the power of the Goddess were confirmed by the friends with whom I formed a women's spirituality group, Rising Moon, which met regularly for more than a decade, by many of my students, and by those who heard me speak or read my work. A series of mystical experiences in places where the Goddess had been worshiped in ancient Greece convinced me that I had chosen the right path.[7] Yet the more I listened to my deepest intuitions, the less comfortable I felt teaching and writing in academia in the required objective voice. My classes often provoked deep transformations in my students, yet this could not be graded. I felt drawn to write about the relation of my experience and my thinking, but this was not acceptable to most other scholars. Eventually the tensions in my life became so great that I resigned a tenured full professorship and moved to the Greek island where I had spent summers swimming in the sea and teaching in an experimental program.

I found what I was looking for in Greece, but not immediately. First I had to go through what I now see as a dark night of the soul, a time of initiation in which I felt very alone, doubted the presence of the Goddess in my life, lost my ability to write, and came very close to giving up my will to live. Those times are past now, but when I was living them I could see no way out of the deep isolation I felt.

My mother's dying[8] brought me to the gates of death in a very literal way. I knew that I wanted to be with my mother as she died. My friends told me I would help her make the transition. I sensed only that I had to be with her. During my mother's illness, I came to understand that my love for her was deeper than any I had ever felt. When I opened my heart to her in a letter, she called me to her. Soon after I arrived, my mother abandoned herself to the process of dying. Death came quickly and easily, perhaps because she ceased to struggle against it. As my mother drew her last breaths, I felt the room flooded with what I can only describe as a great power of love. A revelation had been given to me. Until that moment, I had always felt that I had not been loved enough. I began to understand that a great matrix of love had always surrounded and sustained my life. Since then, I have come to experience love as the gift of the abundant earth. It truly is the power of all being, the power I know as a Goddess.

Many Journeys to the Goddess

Though my story of coming to the Goddess is unique, as all stories are, it depicts a journey that has been shared by many women and increasing numbers of men.[9] Those to whom the Goddess has spoken come from all walks of life. Some are young, some are old; some are white, some are black, yellow, or brown; some are Christians, some are Jews, and some were raised without any religion at all. The Goddess has made her presence felt to many in dreams and in visions, to others through reading and meditation. Experience is much valued as a source of knowledge in Goddess spirituality. Most have found her because they sought within, though some are now learning about the Goddess from parents or family. The stories that follow give a sense of the diverse lives the Goddess has touched and of the many ways she has made her presence felt.

Christine Downing was led to the Goddess through a dream that signaled a major change in her life. At the beginning of the dream, Downing drove into the desert alone, her car had a flat tire, and she began to walk in the dark. A kindly old man[10] offered to help her, but to her own surprise, Downing responded, "This time I need to go in search of Her." Eventually she found herself at the edge of a sandstone cliff and climbed up to a small cave.

I prepare myself to sleep there, as though to fall asleep were part of my way to Her.
While I sleep there in the cave I dream that within the cave I find a narrow hole leading into an underground passage. I make my way through that channel deep, deep into another cave well beneath the earth's surface. I sit down on the rough un-

even floor, knowing myself to be in her presence. Yet, though She is palpably there, I cannot discern her shape. I wait and wait, expecting to be able to see Her once my eyes grow accustomed to the darkness, that does not happen.[11]

Downing's search for the Goddess led her through other dreams, reflection on her life, much reading, and the writing of her first book as she approached her fiftieth year.

Luisah Teish discovered the Goddess in a profound experience of despair. She describes a time in her life when the contradictions of being black and female drove her to consider suicide: "I wanted to be an asset to my community, to contemplate the meaning of existence and produce beauty. But literally everything in the society told me I was a useless nigger wench."[12] Wishing to die, Teish left her body. Her sister tried to rouse her from what seemed like a deep sleep, to no avail. And then, "Without warning a voice—quite [my] own yet more lovely—rose from the breast of the carcass and spoke, saying, 'Get back in yo' body, Girl, you have work to do.'"[13] Later a cowrie-shell reading given by a *voudou* priest helped Teish to understand that the voice speaking was Oshun, African Goddess of love, art, and sensuality. "In short, he said that my Goddess was speaking *to* and *through* me and that I should 'listen to my head' and do whatever She told me to do."[14] Teish understood that "She was the *me* I hid from the world."[15] The Goddess challenged her to transform her life, change her friends, and become a spiritual teacher.[16]

Nelle Morton was already an older woman when she first felt the power of the Goddess. Active for years in the women's movement in the Presbyterian Church and in the Commission on Women of the National Council of Churches, she was drawn to participate in a nondenominational worship service created by and for women. There she heard a woman speak the words, "Now SHE is a new creation." At that moment, Morton was transformed:

It was as if intimate, infinite, and transcending power had enfolded me, as if great wings had spread themselves around the seated women and gathered us into a oneness. . . . That is the first time I experienced a female deity. . . . It was also the first time I realized how deeply I had internalized the maleness of the patriarchal God and that in so doing I had reneged on my own woman identity.[17]

Only in experiencing the Goddess did Morton recognize that the image she had of God was male and how deeply she had been wounded by it.

Lynn Gottlieb was a young Jewish woman pursuing rabbinic studies when she found the Goddess during a meeting of feminist theologians. That night several women spoke about discovering the Goddesses. At first Gottlieb was frightened and retreated into her mind, where she heard one of her professors decrying paganism as antithetical to Judaism. But the calm presence of one of the women who spoke enabled Gottlieb to listen. As this woman finished, Gottlieb sensed a voice within her saying, "My body is the mountain, My birth waters are the parting seas. Speak these words and you will not be consumed."[18] At the end of the evening, Gottlieb understood that "yes, I need the Goddess. I need her to midwife the spirit that sings with a woman's voice inside me."[19] Eventually ordained as a rabbi, Gottlieb fashioned a place for herself on the radical edge of Jewish reform, imagining and creating a renewed Judaism that celebrates women's experiences through the image of divine power as "She Who Dwells Within."

Jess Hayden is a young Australian woman who grew up with the Goddess. When she was a teenager, her mother and several other women organized ritual performances for the seasonal holidays. Hayden and the other children wore costumes and played the parts of nymphs, elves, and fairies while learning about the Goddesses. Hayden has a deeply intuitive sense of the presence of the Goddess in natural cycles and in her body. She says that the Goddess "triggered an age-old knowledge within myself."[20] Yet she is often frustrated because she has not yet found the language to express what she feels and knows to friends brought up in different traditions.[21]

For another young woman, Caz Love, the Goddess has been an inspiration for art. After participating in a Goddess pilgrimage to Crete, she wrote,

I feel like I have really experienced the Goddess and that she has touched the deepest place in me. When I returned home from Greece, I felt high. I felt I had found the meaning in my life, the center from which I could operate. All the feelings I had felt from looking at images of the Goddess, reading about her, painting her—those glimpses of connection, of finding a lifeline, of seeing my heart reflected—all exploded into glorious fruition in Crete. Upon returning I felt my truth was deeper than before.

Love was inspired by her experience to show her paintings of the Goddess for the first time. But her high was soon modulated by anger and sadness:

What I did not expect was how profoundly the pilgrimage would affect my perceptions of our culture—especially since I was already a feminist, anti-violence, pro-earth woman. But experiencing the beauty and reverence for life in Minoan culture and the huge presence of the Goddess in the sites, the land, in all of us, has magnified my feelings so intensely that I feel angry! So angry at the way our culture is. And I feel overwhelmingly, despondently sad.

I am sad and angry that I will never grow up in a society that reveres nature and the feminine, with a mother who grew up in beauty and love and equality. I am angry that I don't know if I will ever live on a peaceful planet. I want to scream! . . . Sometimes I feel like the patriarchy is choking me, has been choking me my whole life and every time I try to cough up whatever is in my throat, it gets pushed back again. . . .

I am experiencing the light and darkness both more intensely.[22]

Love eloquently articulates the feelings the Goddess evokes in many other women. Knowing that the world was once different than it is now can be a source of enormous hope and great despair. Holding the two together is not easy.

Ralph Metzner is one of a growing number of men who have discovered in the civilization of the Goddess a vision of a culture that affirms his search for a "nonwarring, nondominating social system."[23]

It was a revelation when I heard Marija Gimbutas describe, in her Lithuanian accent and calm, deliberate voice, the peaceful, matricentric (not matriarchal), egalitarian, artistic, aboriginal Europeans and saw her slides of the almost overwhelming profusion of Goddess figurines that remain from those cultures.[24]

For Metzner, learning about the Goddess cultures of Old Europe was more than an intellectual exercise:

Some days later, while meditating on what [Gimbutas] had related, I received this image: a wise, friendly, scholarly woman walks into my house and calmly informs me that underneath the basement of my house is another house, one much larger, much older, and much better furnished and appointed than the one in which I lived. This image profoundly altered my sense of my ancestral heritage.[25]

The image of the Goddess transformed Metzner's sense of who he was and who he could become. Like many of the women whose stories are told here, Metzner's discovery of the Goddess led him to write a book.

Images of the Goddess

As these stories indicate, symbolism, both visual and verbal, has played a primary role in the reemergence of the Goddess. Powerful images of the Goddess, rather than stories, myths, or rituals, often spark the moment of awakening. Pictures of statues of Goddesses that are up to 25,000 years old have been reproduced over and over in books and in slide shows to evoke a feeling for a female God.

For Anne Barstow, seeing the image of the Goddess was a "remembering," a recollection of something she already knew about her own power, as well as a "re-membering," that gave her a new relation to her body, to female sexuality.[26] Like many other women, Barstow was driven by a sense of her exclusion from the Christian tradition to begin research that eventually led her to the Goddess. As she says, "I became interested in the prehistoric Goddess when I first asked myself, 'What would a religion created, at least in part, by women be like? What values did it express? What needs would it meet?'"[27] Motivated by her desire, Barstow began to study the Neolithic religion of Çatal Hüyük in Anatolia (modern Turkey). The images of the Goddess she discovered were profoundly moving to her:

> I know what I felt when I first saw the ruins of a shrine at Çatal Hüyük: the goddess figure above the rows of breasts and bulls' horns, her legs stretched wide, giving birth, was a symbol of life and creativity such as I had not seen in a Western church.[28]

Barstow felt a profound validation of her femaleness in the images of the Goddess from Çatal Hüyük.

Poet Adrienne Rich vividly describes the impact ancient Goddess images can have on modern women. At first repulsed by images that did not fit our culture's ideals of female beauty, Rich gradually came to see that

> she is beautiful in ways we have almost forgotten, or which have become defined as ugliness. Her body possesses mass, interior depth, inner rest, and balance. She is not smiling; her expression is inward-looking or ecstatic and sometimes her eyeballs seem to burn through air. . . . She is not particularly young, or rather she is absolutely without age. . . . She exists, not to cajole or reassure man, but to assert herself.[29]

The Goddess is woman whole in herself. She speaks to us of a power that is our birthright.

The images of the Goddess also evoke the sacredness of nature. This confirms a deep intuition that has been denied in our culture: that we are nature and that nature is holy. As we look at ancient images, we see that

> the Goddess in all her manifestations was a symbol of the unity of all life in Nature. Her power was in water and stone, in tomb and cave, in animals and birds, snakes and fish, hills, trees, and flowers. Hence the holistic and mythopoeic perception of the sacredness and mystery of all there is on Earth.[30]

Those who are moved by images of the Goddess feel as strongly about the Goddesses's connection to nature as they do about her image as female: A sense of the connection of the female body to nature's powers of transformation and regeneration is affirmed.

The ancient images of the Goddesses that follow have inspired the experience of the divine as female in the contemporary Goddess movement. Turn the pages slowly. Let the images speak to you.[31] Perhaps you too will feel as my friend Sue Camarados did when she first saw them and exclaimed: "They are so strong, so powerful, and so sensual!"

FIGURE 1. *Carved of soft, reddish brown stone, she could fit easily into the palm of a hand. Pendulous breasts lie against her swelling belly; thin arms rest on them. Her sacred triangle is clearly outlined. Tight braids circle her head. If she has a race, it must be African. In the beginning, she was. Ana, Nana, Grandmother, Ground of All Being. Goddess of Willendorf, c. 25,000 B.C.E.*

FIGURE 2. *Her body is a bunch of grapes, small oval head, sloping shoulders, two stem-like arms on two swelling breasts, two bulging hips, round belly, two oval thighs narrowing over tiny calves, two swelling buttocks echoing her breasts. She is the power of two doubling again and again. Fertile Source. Goddess of Lespugue, France, c.* 23,000 B.C.E.

FIGURE 3. *The curves of her heavy breasts, full belly, wide hips, and generous thighs were carved into the soft walls of a limestone cave, center of mysteries. With one hand she points toward her vulva. In the other she holds the horn of a bison, crescent moon marked with thirteen lines, months of the lunar year. Traces of red ochre, blood of life and renewal, are still visible on her body. Womb of Darkness and Transformation. Goddess of Laussel, France, c. 25,000 B.C.E.*

FIGURE 4. *Her swollen pregnant belly and round knees bear the sign of the moon. Her pendulous breasts point to the two leopards that flank her, guardians and companions. From between her legs, life emerges. Birth. Rebirth. Ma, Mama, Giver of Life. Goddess with Leopards of Çatal Hüyük, c. 6500–5600 B.C.E.*

FIGURE 5. *She is seated on substantial hips and buttocks. Thick, snakelike arms and legs encircle her sacred center. Her face is beaked, her body marked with flowing lines of energy or water. Fashioned of clay burnished to look like stone, she is solid as rock, small enough to set on an altar. Eternal, Ever-renewing Earth. Goddess of Kato Chorio, Ierapetra, Crete, c. 5800–4800 B.C.E.*

FIGURE 6. *White as bone, stiff as death, her face is a mask. Two dots, two seeds, her piercing eyes; four dots, her teeth. Her life-renewing triangle is outlined with seeds of rebirth. Goddess of Death and Regeneration. Stiff White Lady of Stara Zagora, Bulgaria, c. 4500–4300 B.C.E.*

FIGURE 7. *She tenderly cradles her child in her arms. Red spirals of creation and renewal mark her belly and protruding buttocks; horizontal bands of energy decorate her slender arms and legs. Nurturing Mother. Goddess of Sesklo, Greece, c. 4800–4500 B.C.E.*

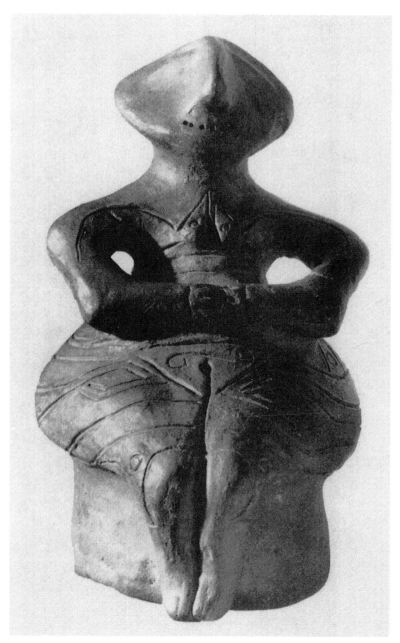

FIGURE 8. *Her center of gravity is her sacred triangle, encircled by full hips and joined to the ground by the line that begins in her cleft and ends at her feet. She is masked and decorated with symbols of life, triangles and flowing lines. Mother Earth. Goddess of Pazardzik, Bulgaria,* c. *4000 B.C.E.*

FIGURE 9. *She is a bird poised for flight. Her chest is incised with chevrons, ending in stumps of arms becoming wings. She bends forward slightly, her lovely full buttocks thrust out like the tail of a bird. Her legs are wound with snake coils, moving upward. Goddess of Renewal, Energy Rising. Bird Goddess of Moldavia, c. 4000 B.C.E.*

FIGURE 10. *She is a vessel shaped like a mountain. Like living rock, her body is marked with zigzags, combs, meanders, and flowing lines. Her face is beaked, her arms barely indicated as wings. Her eyes stare at us, liquid pours from her breasts. Filling up and spilling over. Water of life. Nourishing Mother. Goddess of Mallia, Crete, c. 2000 B.C.E.*

FIGURE 11. *Her full breasts are accentuated by a tight bodice; her sacred womb is covered by an embroidered apron. She holds two writhing snakes in her outstretched arms. Her eyes stare in trance. She sees in the darkness. Ariadne, Dictynna, Skoteini, Guardian of Mysteries. Snake Goddess of Knossos, Crete, c. 1600 B.C.E.*

FIGURE 12. *Her body is the tree of life. Her egg breasts nourish the world. Her arms reach out in blessing. She is garlanded with fruits of the earth. Heads of wild and domestic animals decorate her body. Her beautiful temple by the sea was one of the seven wonders of the ancient world. Mother of All the Living. Artemis of Ephesus, Roman copy of destroyed ancient statue, second century C.E.*

Goddess Images as Transformative

Visual images of the Goddesses stand in stark contrast to the image of God as an old white man, jarring us to question our culture's view that all legitimate power is male and that female power is dangerous and evil. The image of the naked Eve brazenly taking the apple from the serpent, then cowering in shame before a wrathful male God, tells us not only that female will is the source of all the evil in the universe, but also that the naked female body is part of the problem. This image communicates to the deep mind the message that female will and female nakedness must be controlled and punished by male authority. In contrast, the Goddesses show us that the female can be symbolic of all that is creative and powerful in the universe. The simplest and most profound meaning of the image of the Goddess is the *legitimacy and goodness of female power, the female body, and female will*.[32]

The image of the Goddess is transformative because the image of God as male has been deeply internalized in western culture. "He big and old and tall and grey-bearded and white" is how novelist Alice Walker's character Celie described God to her friend Shug, adding that his eyes are "sort of bluish-grey."[33] Feminist thealogians and theologians argue that most of us have similar images somewhere in our minds, even though we may protest that we no longer believe in the biblical God or insist that we think of God as spiritual and genderless. The image of God as a powerful old white man has been communicated to us in many ways.

Though one of the Ten Commandments forbids making images of God, this prohibition has not been adhered to in the Roman Catholic and Christian Orthodox traditions. Following artistic conventions that both preceded and followed him, Michelangelo painted God on the ceiling of the Sistine Chapel in the Vatican (the seat of the papacy) as a large old white man with blue eyes and a silver beard, dressed in flowing lavender robes. Fig leaves and fabric were later added to cover the genitals of Christ and other figures on the walls of the Sistine Chapel, but no pope ever found the image of God as an old white man to be heretical and ordered it painted over. In Christian Orthodox tradition, the image of a bearded Christ as Pantocrator (Ruler of All) is traditionally found on the highest dome in the center of the church, while the familiar icon of the Holy Trinity pictures a white-bearded God the Father and a brown-bearded Christ seated on thrones with a white dove hovering above. The museums, cathedrals, and churches in western and eastern Europe and in Latin America are filled with images of God the Father as old, gray-bearded, white, and male.

In much of Protestantism and in Judaism, such images are not found. But as Jewish feminist theologian Marcia Falk argues, "If as Jews we decline to make theological images out of clay or canvas, we must realize that we make them just as surely—perhaps more effectively—out of words."[34] When we call God "Lord" and "King" or "Father" and "Son," and refer to the world as "his" creation, we designate "his" gender just as clearly and definitively as when we paint "him" as an old white man.

The God we have known in the Jewish and Christian traditions is not only a male but also a judgmental "dominating other."[35] This God has "dominion" over the earth, and his power is proved through his victories over his enemies. In Exodus, God is "a man of war" who casts Pharaoh's chariots and his army into the sea.[36] When his will is not obeyed, he sends floods, earthquakes, and armies as his agents of destruction.[37] Christianity became the official religion of the Roman Empire only after the emperor Constantine saw a vision of a cross in the sky with the inscription "in this sign conquer."[38] God and Christ led the crusaders of the Roman Catholic church into battle to conquer lands held by Orthodox Christians and Muslims.[39] The military might of God is celebrated in the popular Protestant hymns "A Mighty Fortress Is Our God" and "Onward Christian Soldiers." The notion that America is a "promised land" given by God (to civilized white Europeans) is an essential part of the American national ethos that must be acknowledged by every president.[40] Soldiers die around the world "for God and country." Some Christians and Jews await the final establishment of God's will through apocalyptic destruction that will create "a new heaven and a new earth."[41] And many Christians fear the day of judgment when God will consign some to heaven and some to hell for all eternity. Feminists view the judgmental, dominating other as an integral part of the image of God as a patriarchal male.

Despite the verbal and visual images of God as a dominant white male, theologians frequently assert that God has no body, no gender, no race, and no age. Many state that the God they worship is neither female nor male. Surely it is true that we do not all understand God as literally as Celie did. However, most people become flustered, upset, and even angry when it is suggested that the God they know as "Lord" and "Father" might also be called "God the Mother" or "Goddess." This shows that they unconsciously accept the familiar image of God as male. Similarly, though few would assert that God has a race, most people (including some people of color) have difficulty imagining God as black. The power of conventional imagery is effectively unmasked in the words of a bumper sticker that reads, "God is coming and She is black!"

Some believe that we can break the hold of the white male God on the deep mind by replacing the male language of Christian and Jewish liturgy with neuter or neutral imagery: "God the Father" could be invoked as "Our Parent" or as "Creator," while the ubiquitous "he" and "his" could be excised. This solution has been proposed in the revised liturgies of liberal synagogues and churches.[42] But many feminist theologians and thealogians insist that the masculine images of God will not be transformed unless we can (also) imagine God as "she."[43] Jewish feminist theologian Judith Plaskow argues that we must learn to speak the name of the Goddess: "The deep resistance called forth by her naming indicates that the needs she answered are still with us. It is precisely because she is not distant that the Goddess needs to be recognized as a part of God."[44] Unless and until the God we have known can (also) be called "Goddess," the specter of the male God will still be with us.

In our culture, *Goddess* is a powerfully transformative metaphor, as Goddess thealogian and priestess Starhawk writes:

> *The mystery, the paradox, is that the Goddess is not "she" or "he"—or she is both—but we call her "she" because to name is not to limit or describe but to invoke. We call her in and a power comes who is different from what comes when we say "he" or "it." Something happens, something that challenges the ways in which our minds have been shaped in images of male control.*[45]

Images of the Goddess help to break the hold of "male control" that has shaped our images not only of God, but of all significant power in the universe. This insight may come in a flash. But it can also take years of living with images of the Goddess, both verbal and visual, before it settles fully into the body and mind.

On the first day of a class, I showed several hundred slides of the Goddesses. Afterward, one of the women came to me and told me that she was a survivor of incest. When she was a child, her body had been violated by an uncle every Sunday afternoon for years in an upstairs room of her grandmother's house during family gatherings. Later, more than half of the women in the class told me similar stories. It is not surprising that women who have been sexually abused are led by a (false) sense of sin and guilt to the study of religion. Nor is it surprising that images of sacred female power provoke them to cry out against the violation of their bodies and their souls.

As the "good" daughter of a controlling father and a self-sacrificing mother, both of whom gave more attention to the boys in the family, I was made to feel that something was wrong with me simply because I was female. I learned that girls are to be seen and not heard, suppressing myself and my feelings to the point that I became painfully shy and awkward. As my body grew to be over six feet tall, I realized that there was something particularly shameful about my size. When my father's friends remarked sarcastically about my height, I ran to my room and cried. I garnered praise for doing well in school, yet I was also told that girls should not be too smart, or boys would be afraid of them. When I first heard a tall black woman in Ntozake Shange's moving play *for colored girls who have considered suicide/when the rainbow is enuf* cry out, "i found god in myself/and i loved her/i loved her fiercely,"[46] I felt chills up and down my spine. I was beginning to accept my own tall female body, my own intelligent self. But it would be many years before I could love myself fiercely.

Rituals of the Goddess

While images and metaphors inspire the rebirth of the Goddess, rituals bring her power into our lives. Ritual, including song, dance, and physical gesture, involves the senses of taste, touch, sight, smell, and hearing. Over time rituals take root in the body, shaping a body wisdom, so that acting in light of the conceptions they express becomes second nature. When shared, rituals create and confirm community. Rituals thus create powerful, pervasive, and long-lasting moods and motivations.[47]

For many, the first ritual act is to make a home altar. Creating a sacred space brings the Goddess to consciousness and provides a place to offer thanks for the gifts of life, health, and love and to pray for guidance, protection, and healing. Home altars are a very ancient tradition. Roman Catholic and Orthodox Christian grandmothers who light candles or oil lamps in front of images or icons of the Mother of God, like Jewish women who light the Sabbath candles, reenact practices with roots far older than Judaism and Christianity. Home altars have proliferated in contemporary Goddess spirituality, drawing on the artistic impulses and love for beauty of the women who make them.

As I write, I gaze at a small altar on my desk for inspiration. A copy of the seated Neolithic Goddess from Kato Chorio, Ierapetra (Figure 5) sits under a lamp, reminding me of my journeys to Crete. In the Goddess's lap is a small hand-stitched triangle filled with leaves from the Agia Myrtia, the Sacred Myrtle Tree in the Paliani Convent of Crete, where I received healing. A bouquet of seven purple and white anemones begins to drop petals and seeds. A piece of rock crystal found near the cave of Trapeza in Crete, three greenish stones from the sea, and an amethyst heart remind me that the Goddess is earth.

A next step might be to gather with friends to invoke the power of the Goddess. Charlene Spretnak participates in spring in a ritual that is celebrated in the San Francisco Bay area. It shares a focus on the renewal of the earth and the human body and soul in springtime with many other Goddess rituals that differ in detail. This ritual begins with a procession from the parking lot of a local park. Men and women carry flowers and greens, while children create a trail of flower petals. Arriving at a known place, they make a beautiful flower garland on the earth, a foot wide and six inches high. Inside it, an image of the Goddess, a bowl of water, sprays of flowers, and bird feathers are placed, along with food offerings. When the wreath is complete, the group stands quietly, breathing together, breathing in the beauty of the earth. Then each takes flowers from the garland and weaves a flower crown for her- or himself. The ritual continues with storytelling, singing, dancing, feasting.[48] Participants in such rituals acknowledge that the rhythms of a healthy human life echo the rhythms of the universe. They affirm that we are not alone, but part of a great communion of being that includes plants, animals, other humans, the earth itself.

Sometimes Goddess rituals are simple and solitary. I recently received a letter from a friend, Patricia Allott Silbert, who wrote:

I am in a gardening mode—looking at gardening magazines, walking around in my garden checking the small green tips of leaves sticking up through the snow and earth. Green beginnings of daffodils, crocuses, and snow drops out already. . . .

I want to be one of those eccentric older women who are known for their gardens, and for their dedication to their own little patch of the earth. Everywhere we have lived, I have made it my business to leave the land in better shape, planted with flowers, trees, and shrubs. . . . My garden is my own creation of paradise. It is one thing I can do to add to the sacrality of the earth. Caring for Her, Gaia.[49]

Allott Silbert performs the timeless ritual of tending her garden, following in the footsteps of her mother and grandmother, my mother and grandmother, and thousands and thousands of women before them.

Creating a thing of beauty with nature is a shared bond of women across cultures. In my adopted Greece, women who work in the fields, take goats and sheep up into the mountains, and work inside the home, fill balconies and courtyards with geraniums, roses, and jasmine, which they plant in gaily painted empty olive oil cans. Alice Walker recalled that "my mother adorned with flowers whatever shabby house we were forced to live in. . . . It is only when my mother is working in her garden that she is radiant, almost to the point of being invisible . . . ordering the universe in the image of her personal conception of Beauty."[50] Rachel Bagby's mother, Rachel Edna Samiella Rebecca Jones Bagby, founded the Philadelphia Community Rehabilitation Corporation to reclaim vacant inner-city lots for people to grow food and flowers.[51] The religion of the Goddess provides a language to name an activity that women have always known to be sacred.

Starhawk describes a seemingly different, but deeply related, set of rituals that were enacted as part of the Diablo Canyon Blockade, a nonviolent action aimed at stopping the opening of the Diablo Canyon nuclear power plant in northern California. The participants in these rituals believed that their commitment to the Goddess required them to oppose nuclear power plants, which generate electrical power at the risk of poisoning the earth, the sea, the air, and the bodies of all living beings. At the beginning of the blockade, a large group of demonstrators moving in a circle began a Native American chant:

> *The earth, the water, the fire, the air*
> *returns, returns, returns, returns.*

This affirms the knowledge that nuclear power plants destroy the balance of the earth's elements and the group's commitment to work to restore the balance. At another time, they chanted

> *She changes everything she touches,*
> *and everything she touches, changes.*

followed by

> *We are changers.*
> *Everything we touch can change.*

This celebrates the Goddess as the power of transformation and our participation in that power. It was important for Starhawk and others to name their participation in the blockade not only as a political act, but also as a deeply spiritual commitment. After the blockade was over, Starhawk reflected:

> *The ritual, the magic, spins the bond that can sustain us to continue the work over years, over lifetimes. Transforming culture is a long-term project. . . . If we cannot live to see the completion of that revolution, we can plant its seeds in our circles, we can dream its shape in our visions, and our rituals can feed its growing power.*[52]

Goddess rituals sometimes involve pilgrimages to sacred places. Nonnative North Americans are beginning to recognize the deep loss we suffered when our ancestors were uprooted or uprooted themselves from lands that held memories stretching back through the generations. The earth holds the energies of the beings who have lived upon it. Sacred places hold the dreams, visions, and hopes of all the people who have visited them. The idea of pilgrimage stems from this fact. A pilgrimage can be as simple as returning each year to a favorite park at a specific season, as in the ritual described by Charlene Spretnak. Some nonnative Americans have also begun to visit the places known as sacred by Native Americans.[53] Many from European-based cultures gain sustenance from visiting sacred places in Europe.

One group of women traveled together to Crete to contact the energies of ancient cultures that celebrated the Goddess. During their pilgrimage, they hiked together up the side of a mountain to a small cave called Trapeza. Archaeologists say this cave was inhabited in Neolithic times, six to eight thousand years ago. The women were aware that caves were once viewed as the womb of the Goddess, the opening to the center of the earth, the place of mysteries.

The Trapeza cave has two small enfolding rooms. The women gravitated to the smaller one, placing candles and a terracotta image of a Neolithic Goddess on a stone in its center. Libations of milk and honey were poured on the rock, and a song was sung. Then each woman spoke all the names she could remember of her motherline. "I am Carol, daughter of Janet, daughter of Lena, daughter of Dora, who came to the United States from Germany, granddaughter of Mary Rita, daughter of Elizabeth who came from Ireland," and so on around the circle. This was followed by the naming of female mentors and friends. As hundreds of female names echoed off the walls of the cave, the group sensed its connection to Neolithic women who may have sat in a circle in that same cave, remembering ancestors.[54] This ritual strengthens women by giving us a sense of connection to a history of female energy and creativity stretching from the present back into the distant past.

Perhaps because they articulate a deeply familiar sense of our connection to natural rhythms and processes, Goddess rituals do not require a specific form of "belief" or "faith" in the Goddess. Participants in Goddess rituals differ widely in their ideas about the Goddess. Some view the Goddess as a personality who can be invoked in prayer; others see the Goddess as nature or the energy within nature; while others think of her as a metaphor for the deepest aspects of "self." Starhawk expressed a common refusal to choose between interpretations when she said, "When I feel weak, [the Goddess] is someone who can help and protect me. When I feel strong, she is the symbol of my own power. At other times I feel her as the natural energy in my body and the world."[55] Since many have come to the Goddess from Catholic or Protestant traditions where specific beliefs were required on threat of eternal damnation, there is very little inclination to require belief as a condition of entry into a ritual circle.

Goddess rituals have no set form. Though there are groups that follow established ritual protocols, in the Goddess movement as a whole there is no accepted "order of worship" or "liturgy." Many groups celebrate at set times; others come together when the spirit wills. Most Goddess rituals embody a sense of playfulness and invention. Individuals and groups experiment with different forms, sometimes following a pattern described in a book, at other times allowing spontaneity to reign. Some enjoy reenacting the same ritual again and again, while others prefer to allow each ritual to evolve anew.

Goddess rituals are often held on the new or full moon, in recognition of the connection of women's cycles with those of the moon. Moon celebrations are held at night, reclaiming the darkness as a source and symbol of deep wisdom. Other shared celebrations are of seasonal transitions: at the spring and fall equinoxes (March 21 and September 21); the summer and winter solstices (June 21 and December 21); and the holidays that fall exactly in between, dividing the year into eight seasons, February 2 (sometimes called Candlemas or Brigid's Day); May 1 (or May Day); August 1 (sometimes called Lammas); and October 31 (All Hallow's Eve or Halloween).[56] In the southern hemisphere, the seasonal holidays are the same, but the month of celebration differs. Books by Z. Budapest and Starhawk have been used as inspiration for the creation of rituals by groups around the world.[57]

Rituals geared to the phases of the moon and to the changes of the seasons remind us that we are part of nature, depending on and participating in its cycles of growth, death, and renewal. The dark of the moon is a time of reflection and insight, whereas the full moon is a time of energy and manifestation. Each season is honored for its distinctive quality. Spring is rebirth; summer is harvest; fall is transformation; winter is hibernation. Every season harbors the mystery of its opposite. Summer is abundant life, but also death, for fruit is picked and the sun dries out the soil. Winter is death, but in deepest winter, seeds sprout beneath the earth, and the days begin to get longer.

Goddess rituals are familiar, celebrating feelings we already have and deepening our understanding of folk holidays, such as May Day and Halloween. Through Goddess rituals, we recognize that Christian and Jewish holidays incorporate elements of prebiblical seasonal festivals. The Easter and Passover eggs and the Paschal Lamb are ancient symbols of rebirth, while Christmas trees, mistletoe, yule logs, and Hanukkah candles bring light and life into the year's darkest days. Eggs, flowers, candles, and other familiar elements are often incorporated into Goddess rituals, providing a sense of continuity with the past.

But Goddess rituals, like the Goddess herself, are also unfamiliar, challenging the pervasive dualisms of western culture, insisting that death be honored equally with life, darkness equally with light, woman equally with man. The simple act of invoking the Goddess reveals how deeply we have internalized and accepted the notion that all significant and beneficial power in the universe is male. And rather than putting us in touch with a "changeless" God who stands above the world, Goddess rituals connect us to a divinity who is known within nature and who personifies change. Instead of portraying God primarily as the "light shining in the darkness," Goddess rituals value the darkness as a place of transformation. Not focused on life after death, Goddess religion calls us to hallow the cycles of birth, death, and regeneration in this life.

Thealogy Begins
in Experience

Those whose journeys to the Goddess were described in the previous chapter would agree that they found the Goddess in experience. But to say that thealogy is rooted in experience is to risk having it dismissed as "merely confessional," a code word in the intellectual and scholarly worlds for "not worthy of serious consideration." Thus it is important to demystify the mythos and the ethos of objectivity, which lead us to discount works that are written from a personal point of view.

Questioning Objectivity

The ethos of objectivity, a product of the Enlightenment, is a worldview that is rooted in the myth that objective thought is possible and desirable.[1] The mythos behind the ethos of objectivity is the story that "mankind's" route out of the "mire" of "superstition," "ignorance," and "barbarism" is "rational" thinking guided by "universal" principles. According to this tale, "ignorant" people, including children, women, and "savage" or "lesser" races, act out of passion and personal interest, whereas educated "civilized" (white) men act out of universal rational principles. This mythos shapes the ethos of the system of "higher" education, defining "rationality," "objectivity," and "universality" as the criteria for intelligent thought. The ethos of objectivity is the root of the "scientific" method, in which the researcher aspires to "dispassionate," "disinterested" "control" and "analysis" of data. This worldview requires the masking of the interests, feelings, and passions that inspire thinking.

The ethos of objectivity tells us that dispassionate, rational analysis is the bulwark of civilization, whereas subjectivity and passion open the floodgates of irrationality and chaos. This idea can be traced back to the myths of the slaying of the primordial Goddesses by male Gods and heroes like Marduk and Apollo in stories that define nature and the primordial female power that rises from it as chaos. Such myths shaped the thinking of Plato, who identified the rational and the good with that which transcends the changeable, the finite, and the so-called "animal" passions. The ethos of objectivity grew out of the tradition of philosophy as rational thought that Plato began.

A friend once told me a story that illustrates the passionate and not entirely rational hold that the ethos of objectivity has on its defenders. She and a male colleague had a long-lasting argument that always began with his insisting that there must be a rational basis for ethics. Like psychologist Carol Gilligan, who wrote a book about women's different modes of ethical thinking,[2] my friend always responded that feeling was an important factor in ethical decision making. One day, in the midst of the usual argument, my friend's colleague broke down and began to stammer, "But, but . . . if we don't have a rational basis for ethics . . . we'll have, we'll have . . . irrationality . . . Nazi Germany." "Now at least," my friend said, "I understand the stake he had in this argument. Isn't it amazing that we argued about this subject for years before he revealed why he felt so passionately about the need for a rational basis for ethics?"

The failure to name the fear that lurks beneath the ethos of objectivity means that the myth that underlies it cannot be discussed, criticized, or deconstructed. When exposed to the light of day, the belief that objectivity protects us against irrationality and chaos does not seem to be true. While it can be argued (for example) that the genocide practiced in Nazi Germany resulted from an outpouring of "irrational" hatred, it is just as plausible to say that excessive "rationality" was its cause. The Nazi state was overly organized and bureaucratized, leading its servants to forget or ignore the compassion they might otherwise have had for its victims. Thus it can reasonably be asserted that the Nazis were not overly emotional, but overly dispassionate in carrying out the tasks assigned to them by the war machine.

As philosopher Alfred North Whitehead states in a different context, many of the most important assumptions that shape thinking are implicit rather than explicit:

> *When you are criticizing the philosophy of an epoch, do not chiefly direct your attention to the intellectual positions which its exponents feel it necessary explicitly to defend. There will be some fundamental assumptions which adherents of all the*

varied systems within the epoch unconsciously presuppose. Such assumptions appear so obvious that people do not know what they are assuming because no other way of putting things has occurred to them.[3]

While presented under the guise of "objective fact," the view of the world taught in the universities is based on a number of unnamed and unexamined assumptions. One of these is the notion that rational men have always held the power in the civilized world and always will.

Since women were excluded from the notion of "rational man" in the first place, it is not surprising that as we have entered "higher" education in significant numbers, women are challenging the mythos and the ethos of objectivity. Feminist scholars begin with the assumption that women and nonelite men are as intelligent and valuable as elite men, and that our contributions to history must have been as significant as those of elite men. But questions such as "What have women contributed to history?" and "How has culture functioned to oppress women?" are not considered significant within the male-centered scholarly world. Similarly, the data that would be necessary to answer such questions have not been preserved or have been purposely destroyed, and where they exist, they have not (until recently) been studied. Thus feminist scholars are asking "non-questions about non-data," as philosopher Mary Daly writes with characteristic wry wit.[4]

The paradigm shift (or shift in assumptions) implicit in making women both questioners and data is profound. Feminists challenge unquestioned notions of canon: Was Homer a better poet than Sappho? And if not, then why isn't Sappho studied as frequently as Homer? And ideas: Is war a more important human endeavor than love? And if not, then why does the history that is told focus on war? And value: Does the literary tradition from Homer to Dostoyevski from which Sappho and so many others were excluded, in fact embody the highest ideals of humankind? And authority: Can we trust the values and judgments of men who created a literary tradition from which the works of Sappho were excluded, and in which the fact and the reasons for the burning of Sappho's works (and the preservation of Homer's) are rarely discussed?

If criticism of the scholarly tradition stopped here, the changes required would be far-reaching. But the paradigm shift called for by feminist scholarship applies not only to the content, but also to the form of scholarly work. We not only ask "non-questions" about "non-data," but we also use a "non-method," as Mary Daly notes. We question the most unquestioned assumption of all, the notion that scholarship is or should be objective.

Feminist analysis reveals that scholarship that has been presented to us as objective, rational, analytical, dispassionate, disinterested, and true, is rooted in the passion to honor, legitimate, and preserve elite male power. Feminists understand that the ethos of scholarly objectivity is in fact mythos. We know that there is no dispassionate, disinterested scholarship. We admit that our scholarship is passionate, is interested, is aimed at transforming the world we have inherited.

Yet it remains difficult to demystify and disavow the ethos of objectivity. As long as universities remain controlled by patriarchal interests, and feminists seek employment in them, we will be pressured to make our work conform to patriarchal norms. And if the alternative to objective scholarship is portrayed as "non-scholarship" (to continue Daly's play on words), then not all who have been trained as scholars will be comfortable in embracing it.

Many schools of scholarly thought, including Marxist theory (which argues that historical action is motivated by economic interests), hermeneutical theory (which argues that we understand and create theory on the basis of previously held conceptions), and deconstructionism (which argues that all claims about truth reflect power interests), have challenged the ethos of objectivity, arguing that there is no thought that can be divorced from the body and history of the thinker. According to such theories, we all view the world through the perspective of our personal experiences, our ethnicity, our race, our sex, our class, our nationality, our history. Though we may attempt to be objective, our perspectives enter into the way we phrase questions (and fail to ask non-questions) and into the choice of data (and the ignoring of non-data). Even scientific discoveries come about only when the presuppositions, the paradigms, exist through which data can be noticed, connections made, theory developed.[5]

Though theories critical of objectivity are widely understood and discussed, *objectivity remains the predominant model of intellectual and scholarly knowledge.* The ethos of objectivity is so deeply embedded in the structures and ideological commitments of the university and the culture it creates that it is nearly impossible to challenge it successfully. The reasons for this are complex and have to do not only with the desires of those who have power to retain it, but also with the irrational fear that ways of thinking not firmly rooted in so-called rational principles will lead us straight back to the chaos monster—in other words, to woman and nature. The folly of this point of view is the subject of this book.

Embodied Thinking

Embodied thinking is an alternative to objective thought.[6] When we think through the body, we reflect upon the standpoints embedded in our life experiences, histories, values, judgments, and interests. Not presuming to speak universally or dispassionately, we acknowledge that our perspectives are finite and limited. Rather than being "subjective," "narrowly personal," "merely confessional," "self-referential," or "self-indulgent" (discrediting terms taken from the ethos of objectivity), embodied thinking enlarges experience through empathy. Empathy is the act of putting ourselves in another's place, attempting to feel, to know, to experience the world from standpoints presented in a text, in an artifact, in the lives of a group of people from a different place or time. Empathy reaches out to others, desiring to understand the world from different points of view. Empathy is possible because we have the capacity to make connections between our lives and those of others and the ability to connect imaginatively with experiences different from our own.

When I first read black American novelist Alice Walker's reflection on her mother's garden,[7] memories of my mother's garden helped me to enter into the world Walker depicted. Through reading Walker's story I came to a new appreciation of the creativity my mother and grandmother invested in their gardens. However, black feminists argue that white feminists must learn not only to identify with black women's stories, affirming experiences of joy and pain that are shared, but also to understand that for black women in racist societies, these very human experiences are often bound and shaped by poverty, violence, and discrimination. Though Alice Walker's mother and my mother both created beautiful gardens, Walker's mother grew flowers in front of sharecroppers' shacks in poor "Negro" areas, while my mother planted her garden in the yards of tract homes in "white" suburbia. White women's empathy with Walker's mother must not stop at understanding her love for nature and beauty, but must include comprehension of the structures of racial injustice that made it likely that Walker and her mother would live in poverty and fear of racial violence, while my mother and I lived in relative comfort and freedom from fear. As white women recognize difference, our empathy must embrace the outrage that can motivate us to fight the structures of oppression. Still, difference is rarely absolute. While I can never know what it is like to be taunted for being black, I can remember exactly what it felt like to be called names nearly every day for years and to shrivel in shame because I was taller than all the other kids. This helps me empathize with being seen as inferior because of color.

Empathetic scholarship draws on all the standard tools of research, including gathering historical data, careful attention to detail, analysis, criticism, concern for truth. But as we use the tools of traditional scholarly research, we transform them. We unmask the biases and the passions that are hidden in traditional scholarship, and we freely admit our own. We are beginning to write "in a different voice," one that interweaves scholarly analysis with a personal standpoint.[8]

Yet the best scholarship always has been empathetic and embodied. Education, study, and research can move us to see and feel the world in new ways, transforming us through enlarging our vision. Not only feminists, but all scholars would be more true to the real aims and visions of scholarship if we named our work as embodied thinking rather than objective thought.

Acknowledging that the judgments we make are finite, we can overcome personal bias by situating our work in a community of discourse in which it can be affirmed, amplified, and criticized from standpoints that are both similar and different from our own. If we do not pretend that our standpoints are universal, then we do not claim to present universal truth. This means that criticism of the limitations of our perspectives is no longer a mark of failure, but an expected, accepted, and welcomed part of scholarly dialogue.[9]

My conviction that thealogy begins in experience means that I, like many other feminist scholars, can no longer write in an impersonal voice. I believe that I must not only acknowledge and admit that my views are rooted in my life, but that I must also show how this is true. When I read theology, I often ask myself, why does he or she assert that . . . ? Traditionally, theologians mask the personal experiences that lead them to think as they do. For them, personal experience is irrelevant to the truth of their argument. As we recognize the limitations of the impersonal voice, we often replace it with an exclusively or primarily personal and subjective voice. In my earlier book, *Laughter of Aphrodite*,[10] I argued for the integration of personal experience with reflective thinking. But the essays in that book were written in two voices: one the objective scholarly voice intended to gain recognition in my field; the other the emerging voice of my experience. Putting the two together is not easy, but this is what I have attempted to do in this book. On virtually every topic I discuss, I explain why I think as I do. But I also set the opinions rooted in my experience in a larger context, developing them into a consistent and coherent explanation of the world and our place in it. *This book is an experiment in fully embodied thinking.*

Experience

The thinking in this book is based in experience. Yet experience can be defined in different ways. Materialists limit experience to sense data, while idealists define experience as the thought processes of the isolated rational ego. Those working within the ethos of objectivity argue that the inclusion of personal experience "narrows" the scope of a work, making it less than "universal."

When I use the word *experience*, I assume that it is embodied, relational, communal, social, and historical. My experience includes everything I have ever tasted, touched, heard, seen, or smelled. It encompasses everything I have thought, felt, or intuited, as well as everyone I have ever met, everything I have ever read or heard about, and everything I have ever done or suffered. It is shaped by the history of my times, including the family ethos of suburban white America in the post World War II period, the explosion of energy in protests against racism, poverty, and war in the sixties and seventies, the counterculture and women's movement, the increasing conservatism of the eighties and nineties.

All experiences are shaped by the lens through which we view them. The lens of interpretation includes factors of which we are aware, as well as those of which we are not aware, the "fundamental assumptions," which are unconsciously presupposed. These assumptions are embedded in language, linguistic conventions, habits of thought, and cultural symbols that provide us with notions of what is possible, real, and valuable. They are reinforced by educational, economic, religious, political, and other institutional structures that reward those who agree with prevailing cultural norms while punishing those who disagree with them.

On the other hand, some of a culture's fundamental assumptions can be challenged when they fail to provide adequate interpretation of the experience of a group of people. The consciousness-raising groups that gave birth to the women's liberation movement in the late seventies and early eighties are one example of a group that challenged assumptions. In them, women came together to question conventional views about sexuality and sex roles and to create new frameworks for naming and understanding women's experience.

Interpretation of experience involves an element of choice. For example, many women have had the experience of feeling excluded by masculine language for God, but they have interpreted this experience differently. One woman perceives the experience of being excluded by male language and symbolism as threatening to her faith, so she tries to suppress it. Another decides to work from within her religion to create change. A third concludes that all religions are patriarchal plots against women and becomes an atheist. A fourth explores Buddhism. The last seeks the Goddess.

To write of experience and interpretation suggests that there are discrete moments of pure experience, followed by discrete moments of interpretation.

But most of the time, experience and interpretation are an ever-shifting but seamless web. Both experiences and interpretations are built up out of other experiences and interpretations. Though there are times when we reflect consciously, and others when we react impulsively or intuitively, and even times when we change our worldviews, there is no moment of pure experience, no moment of pure interpretation.

Throughout this book, I share experiences that have given rise to my understanding of the Goddess and her relation to human and other forms of life. Some of these experiences could be called revelatory or mystical. My understanding of the Goddess is deeply shaped by experiences of connection to nature and to other people that I have had since childhood and that now have become a part of my daily experience. My relation to the Goddess began in an argument with God during which I heard a voice saying, "In God is a woman like yourself." A revelation of the presence of love that occurred as my mother died is the source of my understanding that we are surrounded by what I call a great matrix of love.[11] These experiences play a crucial role in my thealogy, leading me to make claims about the nature of reality and the Goddess that I would not otherwise make.

The ethos of objectivity would deny mystical or revelatory experience as a valid source of information, dismissing it as subjective psychological projection, perhaps even labeling it "irrational" and "dangerous." Though I am aware that others might view my experiences as arising from nothing more than a vivid imagination, I choose to interpret them as revelation of the nature of being. To do otherwise would be to deny what poet, philosopher, and mystic Audre Lorde has taught me to call my "deepest and nonrational knowledge."[12] It would also be to deny some of the most important ways women and men have gained knowledge of the Goddess in our time.

But this does not mean that I unthinkingly accept mystical revelation as a source of knowledge. In the mystical tradition of the Catholic church, there was a practice of "testing" mystical experience. This usually meant submitting to a (male) confessor who would decide if a vision or voice indeed came from God. Women did not always fare well under this system. Joan of Arc was burned at the stake; Hildegard of Bingen narrowly escaped the same fate; but Teresa of Avila's confessor encouraged her to write her visions in what has become one of the most widely read books in the world.

I have developed my own methods of testing my deepest nonrational knowledge. I find that when I want something desperately, I can sometimes convince myself that my deepest intuition (or even the Goddess) is telling me it will become so. I have learned to be suspicious of nonrational "knowledge" that seems like a way of assuring myself that I can have what I want. I am also aware that people have committed great wrongs in the name of mystical knowledge. I would not do anything on the authority of mystical experience that my reflective mind told me was harmful to myself or others. On the other hand, if mystical or revelatory experience makes my life richer and more meaningful and helps me better understand the world and my place in it, I am willing to accept it as valid even though it cannot be proved to someone who is skeptical. Of course, insights based in mystical experience, like all other experiential knowledge, find confirmation or disconfirmation in communities.

The idea that we are interdependent in the web of life is open to scientific investigation, but the experience of deep connection to all beings in the web of life, which plays an important role in my understanding of the human place in the world, is not. Nor is there proof that the Goddess exists. No rational argument can convince a determined atheist to change her or his mind. My good friend and colleague Naomi Goldenberg finds the Goddess a psychologically meaningful metaphor yet rejects the idea of divinity. She is quite willing to admit that experiences of "the Goddess" affirm the body and help women gain self-esteem, but she finds the idea that the Goddess exists outside the human psyche implausible. I respond to her that it makes more sense of my experience and that of others to understand the Goddess as the ground of being,[13] the sustainer of life, and as a power with whom I am in relation. I base my thealogy on this conviction. There is also no proof that the ground of being is love. My other good friend and colleague Judith Plaskow insists that the ground of being is awesome yet ambiguous power that often seems indifferent to human moral struggles. Before my mother died, I was inclined to agree with her. But the revelation that occurred as my mother died has opened me to experiencing the power of love more fully and more deeply in my life. This insight has become foundational in my understanding of the Goddess.

Experience is not only a resource; it can also be a limitation. I am a white, middle class, heterosexual woman of a certain age, background, and experience. Acknowledging my history, I do not claim that the thealogy I write is universal or definitive. People from the East Coast of North America may note that my understanding of nature is shaped by having lived much of my life in California and Greece, where the climate is moderate and nature is, for the most part (except for the occasional earthquake and drought), a warm and nurturing power. Those who are Jewish may feel that my Christian background influences my understanding of the Goddess. Lesbians may find the image of the Goddess I invoke insufficiently critical of the heterosexual norm. Europeans may find my ability to reject inherited religious traditions and to discover alternative spiritual perspectives peculiarly American. People of color will note that my understanding of the Goddess draws on sources from Europe, the Near East, and North America, but not Latin America, Africa, or South or East Asia. Some Americans may find the perspectives I have gained by living in Greece bewildering.

There are a number of possible responses to the recognition of limitation. I believe the healthiest is affirmation of ourselves in our finitude, particularity, and uniqueness, coupled with openness to learning from others. A common, but not very helpful, response is to feel guilty and powerless to speak, particularly if the limitation one recognizes is membership in a dominant (and oppressive) culture, race, sex, or class. For white middle class women, whose egos have frequently been damaged by the dynamics of sex, class, and religion and for whom self-hatred is a familiar emotion, the temptation to guilt is particularly strong. White women often use guilt feelings as an excuse to retreat from examining our own experience, denying the (relative) validity of our own standpoints as white (middle-class) (heterosexual) women. We may feel that we have a "right" to speak only when we are speaking "for" those more oppressed than ourselves, but this stance can be patronizing and often reflects false universalism in yet another form. Recognizing these dangers, I have chosen to write with honesty and self-love about the particularities of my experience and perspective. I expect my work to be enlarged, expanded, and criticized.

Community

My experiences of the Goddess, like everything else in my life, are inspired and shaped by the experiences of others. When I speak with other women or read their words, I often find myself saying, "Yes, that explains what happened to me." In this book, I draw on the words of others as I attempt to articulate the meaning of the Goddess. So, besides being personal, this thealogy is, in the deepest sense, communal. If my understanding of the Goddess were not confirmed and challenged by the experiences of others, I would probably be in a mental hospital, rather than sitting at my pine desk in Athens on a hot summer day writing this book.

In thinking about the Goddess, I count as my closest community those friends, colleagues, and others who, like me, recognize that women have been disparaged and denied full participation in the world's "great" religions and who are working to understand women's spiritual experience, to transform existing religions, and to create alternatives. Many of these women are scholars I have known through the Women and Religion section of the American Academy of Religion. I have met others through the grass-roots women's spirituality movement or through women's groups in the churches and syna-gogues. Some have felt the power of the Goddess reemerging in their lives, while others have stayed within traditional religious communities. I will be quoting the insights of these spirit sisters throughout this book. For me the voices of women are a lifeline. The research, experience, and questions of others have sparked, shaped, and modulated my own. I hope the readers of this book will not find these many voices distracting, but will hear them as I do, as testifying to the depth and breadth of women's spiritual vision.

Greece and the Greek people have also had a deep influence on my un-derstanding of the Goddess. In America, I often felt that we were "creating" the Goddess as we called her into our lives. We said we believed in the power of the Goddess, but deep down we were not sure. This is understandable given that our emerging vision was not widely accepted in our culture. I think that is why many of us are drawn to ceremonial magic: opening and closing the circle, calling the directions, raising the cone of power, casting spells, ex-perimenting with tarot and other forms of divination. Yet the psychic effort required to "create" the Goddess often left me feeling ungrounded.

What had been a vague uneasiness became clarified during a retreat with a group of activists and leaders in the women's spirituality movement. After a long day, much of it spent arguing about difference, the group gathered out-side under a full moon. I remember that the energy was high and that there was drumming. I soon developed a splitting headache and pulled away from the circle. American Indian teacher Carol Lee Sanchez had done the same. "You white women know how to raise the energy," she commented as we sat together by the pool, "but you don't know how to ground it. We Indians are part of the land. I get tired of grounding the energy for all of you," she con-cluded. Sanchez helped me to name and understand what was missing in my experience of the Goddess at that time. Like many other white women, I had learned how to "raise energy" through concentration and chanting, with rat-tles and drums. This created a feeling of excitement, intensity, heightened awareness. But I had not fully understood that all life energy, including en-ergy "raised" in a circle, comes to us from the earth, rises through the body, and through the body returns to earth. Because I lived more in my mind than in my body, the energy I raised "got stuck" in my head (giving me a headache) rather than enlivening my body and returning to earth. That night, I prom-ised myself that I would never again raise power I could not ground. In time I would understand that in order to be grounded, we must feel ourselves to be part of the land.

Like the Native Americans, the Greek people are part of the land. In Greece, I feel the presence of the Goddess in places once sacred to her.

Wherever an ancient temple was, there is almost always a church. Greek Christians' devotion is focused by lighting a candle in front of an icon (an image painted on wood) of the Mother of God, a saint, the Holy Trinity. If a prayer is answered, a gift is brought to the icon in thanksgiving. Greek icons are surrounded by votive offerings of flowers, large candles, lamps, and precious jewelry, testifying to the power of the divine to intervene in human life. At first, I rejected Greek piety as an expression of the patriarchal Christianity I desired to leave behind. But gradually it dawned on me that Greek practice is rooted in simple and meaningful gestures that are far more ancient than Christianity. Modern Greeks who speak their deepest needs to the Mother of God after making a pilgrimage to a beautiful place are not much different from their ancient ancestors, who brought offerings to Goddess Mother. I began to light candles and open my heart in places filled by other pilgrims. *As I did so, I realized that the Goddess had never died! She could not die because she was in the land, she was the land.*

Now, instead of coming into my head, the Goddess rises through my feet. She surrounds me in the air I breathe. I don't have to create her. She is. My ritual practice has become simplified. Like the Greeks, I light candles, kiss the icon of the Mother, and tell her what is in my heart. Or I pour a libation of milk or honey, water or wine, on a stone I have set beneath a myrtle tree growing in a pot on my balcony, sing to the image of the Goddess that nestles beneath the tree, and tell her what I need. Because the Goddess has entered into my bones and because I see her in my home and in nature, I no longer feel the need to follow elaborate ritual procedures to call her into my life.

This explains why the practice of magic as defined in feminist Wicca (witchcraft) is not central in my understanding of the Goddess. Though I was introduced to the modern practice of Goddess worship by Starhawk and Zsuzsanna Budapest and continue to find their work on ritual inspiring, I no longer identify with "magic" as they defined it in their earlier works.[14] I look back with nostalgia and gratitude to the time when my Goddess circle, Rising Moon, used their books as "cookbooks," deriving great inspiration and insight from them. And I still find meaning in attuning myself to the rhythms of the moon and celebrating the seasons of the year. But as my experience of the Goddess becomes rooted in the Greek land, I find my practice more and more inspired by nature itself and by my growing knowledge of the ancient history of the Goddesses. Spell casting, tarot card reading, and other forms of divination often were, for me, yet another head-trip, a very American way of trying to control reality and achieve individual desire.[15] I now find that my needs are better met by my remaining open to what life has to offer than by trying to mold reality to my will.

Goddess History

Goddess history is an important source and resource for Goddess thealogy. If we did not know anything at all about the ancient Goddesses, it is very unlikely that symbols and images of the Goddess would be emerging in our lives today. The more deeply I immerse myself in the history of the Goddess, the more important it becomes to me. Twenty years ago, I often felt alone and vulnerable when I spoke the name of the Goddess. Now my experience and ideas are firmly grounded in history. I not only have studied Goddess history intensively, I have also brought this history to life through descending into the darkness of sacred caves, climbing to the tops of sacred mountains, and feeling the power of images of the Goddesses in my home. The history of the Goddess, not surprisingly, is controversial in the scholarly world. My understanding of Goddess history is shaped by the feminist perspective that gives me the tools to criticize conventional views of the past.

My knowledge is limited by the nature of the sources, mainly Greek, European, and Near Eastern, on which I draw. For a long time, I thought I could not write a Goddess thealogy unless I incorporated insights and images from the history of the Goddess in Far Eastern, African, and American traditions. Some North American followers of the Goddess have been introduced to her through non-European traditions. Others, in a spirit of inclusiveness, have been careful to include discussions of non-European images of the Goddess in their work.

My decision to focus on Goddesses in Europe and the Near East derives from my history and from my understanding of the integrity of my work. My early interest in the Hebrew Bible provided me with a perspective from which to approach the history of the Goddesses in Near Eastern religion. My studies of Christian history gave me a starting point for exploring the pre-Christian religions of Europe and the survival of paganism in folk practice and within Christianity. Living in Greece has caused me to devote most of my attention to the Goddesses of the Greek land. But unlike many other interpreters of Greek religion, including classicists and Jungians, my understanding of Greek religion is not based exclusively or even primarily on literary sources.

The more I become familiar with the Goddesses of Greece and Crete, the more I recognize that extremely complex histories must be unraveled before they can be understood. Layers upon layers of prejudice that is only partly conscious shroud the history of the Goddesses. These prejudices are philosophical, religious, social, and political. They are deeply and emotionally held even by scholars who claim to be objective. The nature of these prejudices must be understood and challenged if we are to understand how the earliest Goddesses survived and were transformed in the written records of patriarchal myth. Then we must painstakingly sift and reevaluate the information that has come to us through patriarchal sources, searching for pieces of a story that has been hidden from us. This means that we cannot easily gain knowledge of Goddess traditions by consulting a few classic texts. In addition, the longer I live in Greece, the more I understand that the history of the Goddesses is intimately involved with particular landscapes.[16] Thus I do not feel I am able to speak with integrity about Goddesses from traditions I have not studied deeply and whose lands I do not know.

Nonetheless, the model of a feminist critical approach to the history of the Goddess that I propose can be useful in unraveling the histories of the Goddesses in cultures I do not discuss. The research of others on the Goddesses of Asia, Africa, and Latin America confirms that we must everywhere distinguish the Goddesses of earlier (possibly) prepatriarchal Paleolithic or Neolithic cultures from the Goddesses who appear in the written records of later patriarchal myth and religion. And it is always important to ask what the Goddesses mean or may have meant to women and how they correlate with women's social roles.

Goddess history, for me, is the ground on which I stand. But Goddess religion is not wedded to a text or defined by a particular history. It makes a great deal of difference to me to know that the Goddess has a history, that feminists in the twentieth century did not make her up out of whole cloth. But this history cannot provide a specific blueprint for the future. The Goddess who manifests in our lives today speaks in our languages and suggests courses of action suitable to our times. And, as the small voice told me years ago, she too has suffered and had her history stolen from her. This has affected her, as it has affected all of us.

Nature

Another important source for a Goddess thealogy is the web of life or nature. The power of the Goddess is present in the earth and in all beings in the universe. We can learn a great deal from attending to the lessons plants and animals, stones and sea, have to teach us.

Modern people can also learn from the attitudes of traditional peoples toward nature. For North Americans, the Native American worldview is an important resource because it is a living tradition rooted in the particularities of the land where we were born or live by choice.[17] Australians and New Zealanders can derive similar insights from Aboriginal cultures. Because the experience of nature is never abstract, but always shaped by the geography and climate of a particular place, an authentic American or Australian spirituality must be rooted in the lands where we live, just as an authentic Greek spirituality must be rooted in the Greek land.

In Europe, a sense of the sacredness of nature was not fully lost when Christianity became the dominant and only officially sanctioned religion because Christian churches were built in places known as holy from time immemorial. In contrast, the Protestants, Catholics, and Jews who settled North America, Australia, and New Zealand did not adapt their inherited European- and Mediterranean-based spirituality to the geography of the lands they claimed. Americans have a civil religion that celebrates God and country,[18] and many of us love the parts of the American land we know, but our religious traditions do not help us understand or celebrate our spiritual connection to the earth. Australians and New Zealanders have in addition lost the seasonal basis of their religious traditions: Christmas and Hanukkah are celebrated at midsummer; Easter and Passover in the fall. Because I believe that spirituality must be rooted in connection to a particular place, I refer to my experiences in Greece and draw extensively on the spirituality of Native American writers in articulating my understanding of the human relation to nature.

The use of native traditions by those of us whose ancestors were born elsewhere has become a hotly debated subject. Some Native Americans and Aboriginals fear that the new interest in their spiritual traditions will become another form of exploitation by their conquerors. Carol Lee Sanchez, whose roots are both Native American and Lebanese, reflects on this question in ways I find helpful. Sanchez distinguishes between the reverence for the American land and the sense of the sacredness of all beings in the web of life found in Native American traditions and the concrete practices of various Native American tribes. She states that it is appropriate for all Americans to learn from the Native Americans to approach our lives in a "sacred manner." This understanding does not "belong" to the Native Americans and cannot be "stolen" from them. What would be inappropriate is for non-Native Americans to sing sacred songs in Native American languages, to dance the sacred dances as they have been handed down in traditional cultures, and especially to pretend that we are the new experts on Native American traditions.[19] The same would be true when Australians and New Zealanders learn from Aboriginal cultures.

Christianity and Judaism

Though presenting a different view, this book is very much in conversation with Christian and Jewish understandings of God. This is not only because I was raised Christian (with influences from Protestantism, Catholicism, and Christian Science) and identified strongly with Judaism at one point in my life (my college thesis was on nature imagery in the Hebrew prophets; one of my doctoral exams was on the theology of Martin Buber; and my dissertation was on Elie Wiesel). Nor is it only because I studied the Christian and Jewish Bibles and the theologies based on them. Biblical images of God and their Christian and Jewish interpretations are an integral part of western culture. It is difficult to speak of the Goddess without comparing her positively or negatively to the images of God in our inherited religious traditions. And even when we do not do so consciously, we interpret the Goddess against the background provided by the God we have known.

Because I think it is important to reflect upon the ways the emerging Goddess challenges traditional understandings of God, I often compare and contrast the meaning of the Goddesses with traditional views. Since it would be impossible to take account of the entire histories of Christianity and Judaism, I isolate those aspects of traditional verbal and visual symbolism ("our Father," "the Holy One blessed is he," "Lord of All") and theology (God as all-powerful, God as judge) that I believe have played the most important roles in shaping our culture's understanding of God, humanity, and nature.

I am aware that many Christians and Jews (feminists and others) have concerns similar to those expressed in this book. The Christianity and Judaism they envision is quite different from the "traditional views" I describe. Indeed, I often refer positively to the ideas of Jews and Christians (including Martin Buber, Paul Tillich, Judith Plaskow, Marcia Falk, Elisabeth Schüssler Fiorenza, Beverly Harrison, Delores Williams, Gordon Kaufman, John Cobb) in developing my understanding of the meaning of the Goddess. Yet the traditional images of God found in the Bible and expressed in prayers, chants, and hymns and the interpretations given in traditional theologies continue to provide the primary access to God for the vast majority of Christians and Jews. Until and unless these sources of religious experience and knowledge are transformed, traditional understandings will still be with us, no matter what liberal and radical theologians say.

Anti-Judaism is deeply rooted in western (Christian and secular) cultures. When I first realized this, I was still a Christian, and I felt devastated.[20] Based in the struggles of the early Christian church with the synagogue, anti-Judaism forms part of the texture of the New Testament and thus influences Christian liturgy and Christian practice. The negative images of the scribes and Pharisees, the notion that "Judas" (from the Hebrew word for Judah and the Greek word for Jew) and "the Jews" betrayed Christ, and the idea that Judaism is a religion of "law" rather than "spirit" have deeply influenced the way many of us think about the world. Such images portray Jews and Judaism as "the other" and create a climate in which Jews and Judaism can be blamed for a variety of problems. This in turn legitimates acts of discrimination and violence against Jews. I view Christian anti-Judaism as one of the sources of the Nazi program of genocide. As long as the biblical stories that blame the death of Jesus on the Jews form the basis of Christian celebrations of Easter, the attitudes created by these stories will continue to shape culture and politics. I believe it is incumbent on all of us who come from Christian backgrounds to work to eradicate anti-Judaism.

Because of my own work with Judaism and because some of my closest friends and colleagues are Jewish, I am sensitive to the Jewish feminist critique of anti-Judaic elements in both Christian feminist theology and Goddess thealogy.[21] Anti-Judaism is expressed in the image of Jesus as completely at odds with the Judaism of his time. In this picture, Judaism is defined as a religion of patriarchal law, and its God is presented as a wrathful dominating other, while Jesus is said to have challenged the law and proclaimed a God of love. This understanding discounts the richness and vitality of the Judaism from which Jesus and other Jewish religious innovators emerged. It ignores the images of a loving God in the Hebrew Bible and the images of a wrathful God in the New Testament, not to mention the vengeful God portrayed in Christian doctrines of last judgment and hell. Law is found in Christianity as well as Judaism, as traditions of Roman Catholic and Protestant morality attest.

Anti-Judaism is also expressed when the "Old Testament" is blamed for the rise of patriarchal attitudes, patriarchal religion, and the suppression of the Goddesses. Neither Jews nor Judaism are responsible for the development of patriarchy. Patriarchy existed in the Near East and in Europe long before the time of the writing of the Hebrew Bible. The myths of the slaying of the Goddess did not originate in the Bible. The transformation of the Goddesses to support the values of ancient Mediterranean warrior cultures happened independently of the Bible. The values of the ancient Hebrews were a product of and contributed to processes of cultural change that were occurring all over the ancient world. If anyone is to be "blamed" for the suppression of the Goddesses in western culture, it should be the Christian emperors whose edicts outlawed all "pagan" religions.

It is also important to distinguish clearly between Christianity and Judaism and not to blame the Old Testament or Judaism for ideas and attitudes that are either unique to Christianity or are found in both traditions. While the image of Eve is used to define female roles in Judaism, the most well known verbal and visual understandings of the Genesis story depicting Eve as the origin of sin and evil are a product of Christianity. Painted and sculpted images of God as an old white man were made by Christians, not Jews. The images of God as Lord and King are common in both Christian and Jewish liturgies, but the image of God as Father is far more prominent in Christianity.

We must be careful not to repeat prejudices that are consciously and unconsciously assumed in our culture. We must base our telling of the history of the Goddesses on a careful and nuanced understanding of the past. Only then do we have the right to be critical of ideas and attitudes found in the Jewish or Christian Bibles or in Judaism or Christianity.

Mythos and Ethos

Finally, in thinking about the meaning of the Goddess in an embodied way, we must remember that religious symbols shape the way we see ourselves and the world. Those attracted to Goddess religion make this connection intuitively, rejecting exclusively masculine images of God as serving the interests of male dominance and control. Many are also drawn to the images of the Goddesses because they provide an orientation that can help us save the planet from ecological destruction.

Anthropological theory helps us understand how religious symbols are connected to the lives of individuals and cultures. According to anthropologist Clifford Geertz, a religion is a "system of symbols which act to produce powerful, pervasive, and long-lasting moods and motivations." A religious symbol like God or Goddess is both a "model of" the divine reality and a "model for" human behavior. Religious symbols set the tone of a culture, defining some things as real and important and suggesting (or decreeing) how we should live. Religious symbols and rituals give rise to "moods," psychological attitudes or deep feelings, that make us accept some things and reject others, attend to some things and not to others. Religious symbols thus "motivate" us to act in certain ways and not others. A "mythos" or symbolic worldview, and an "ethos" or way of life of a community or society are integrally related.[22]

Recognizing that religious symbols shape our understanding of the world and suggest patterns of action, Christian theologian Gordon Kaufman proposes that we must ask if our religious symbols are compatible with our ethical concerns. If they are not, he argues, we must be prepared to discard them.[23] Kaufmann finds that inherited religious symbols have often helped to sanction the human enterprise of "exploiting—and often destroying—the capacities of planet earth to sustain life, including human life."[24] I agree with

Kaufman that we must judge our religious symbols in terms of their ability to help us preserve and enhance life in this time of crisis for planet earth.

Though we can analyze religious symbols in light of our ethical concerns, we cannot create symbols through our rational intellect alone. Theologian Paul Tillich recognized this when he stated that "symbols cannot be produced intentionally" because "they grow out of the individual or collective unconscious and cannot function without being accepted by the unconscious dimension of our being."[25] There would be no reason to be critical of patriarchal or warlike images of God if such images did not still speak to people within religious communities. Nor would there be a need to understand the function of the symbols of the Goddess if they had not emerged in the dreams, visions, meditations, prayers, rituals, songs, poetry, and visual art of contemporary women. Thealogians and theologians must be sensitive to the complex ways symbols arise, are sustained, and fall out of use.

Still, contemporary experience of the process of discovering and creating new symbols of God the Mother and Goddess suggests that the process of symbol creation is partly conscious. Though we cannot in any simple way invent new symbols to accord with our ethical visions, we can reflect on the inadequacy of old symbols, thus opening ourselves to recognizing new symbols as they arise in our experience. We can experiment with unfamiliar symbols, knowing that some will take root and others will not, and we can examine the symbols that rise up from dreams or the unconscious from the perspective of our ethical visions, deciding whether we want to affirm them in ritual practice and in life.

3

The History
of the Goddess

"In the beginning, people prayed to the Creatress of Life. . . . At the very dawn of religion, God was a woman. Do you remember?"[1] So wrote Merlin Stone in a book that inspired many to seek to uncover the history of the Goddess.[2] When I first read those words, my flesh tingled. Goddess religion is far more ancient than Judaism and Christianity. The new story about the Goddess is not the story told in major and well-accepted texts in the history of religion, archaeology, and classics. Nor is it a restatement of the outdated theory of "primitive matriarchy." The rediscovery of the Goddess has provoked a reconsideration of the roles of women and Goddesses in the origin and history of religion. Based on several decades of re-searching the sources, a new interpretive framework I call the "Goddess hypothesis" draws together archaeological, historical, and anthropological evidence and theory. In it, both women and Goddesses play important roles in human history.

The Mother of the Living and the Dead in the Paleolithic Era

The first evidence of religious ritual comes several million years after the famed "Lucy" and her ancestors, who are thought to be the first humans, appeared in Africa.[3] As far back as 70,000 to 50,000 B.C.E., Neanderthal peoples carefully buried their dead, often in a fetal position. Some Neanderthals apparently also placed or planted flowers around the body at the time of burial.[4] Burial in a fetal position suggests that Neanderthals may have thought that we are returned to the body of the Mother of the Living and the Dead. Perhaps Neanderthals believed as well that we would be reborn, individually or communally, from the womb of the Mother.[5]

From the Upper Paleolithic, or late Old Stone Age (c. 32,000–10,000 B.C.E.) come the many Paleolithic Goddesses, small carved female statues and reliefs, full of figure, and usually unclothed, including the Goddesses of Willendorf, Lespugue, and Laussel. (See Figures 1 to 3.) Most of these images are small enough to have been held and easily carried by the nomadic peoples who made them.

The great paintings of bison, wild oxen, horses, deer, ibex, and mammoth found deep in the darkest recesses of the well-known caves at Lascaux and Altamira and more recently at Chauvet come from the same time period as the Goddess images. The symbolism of the Paleolithic caves is generally interpreted as hunting magic.[6] Man the hunter, it is said, communed with the spirit of the great beast before going out to kill it. This interpretation, while it may be partially correct, does not tell us why the paintings are located deep within the caves nor why pregnant beasts (which no hunter would kill) are also portrayed. It does not tell us what part, if any, women might have played in the cave rituals, and it fails to connect the symbolism of the caves to the Paleolithic Goddesses.

Historian G. Rachel Levy proposes that Paleolithic people understood the cave to be the womb of the Creatress, the Great Mother, the Earth. Rituals performed in her center would have reflected people's desire to participate in the creativity of the Mother of the Living and the Dead and to align themselves with the power of the great beasts that emerged from her womb.[7] Levy's theory is unexpectedly supported by art historian Andre Leroi-Gourhan's finding that abstract symbols of the female are found either in the most prominent chamber of a cave or in the "central position" in a painted grouping.[8]

The idea that the cave is the womb of the Earth Mother, the place of transformation, and that the darkness within the cave is the site of mysteries, the place of deep nonverbal communication with her, is also found in Neolithic and Bronze Age Crete, where rituals were celebrated in caves.[9] Echoes of this understanding are found in cave shrines to the Goddesses and to Pan and the Nymphs in Greek and Hellenistic religion. It was carried over into Christianity in the traditional Orthodox icon that shows Mary giving birth to Jesus in a cave.[10] Throughout the centuries, the Virgin Mary has frequently appeared in caves, such as at Lourdes in France.

If the cave is the womb of the Goddess, then the two major symbols of Paleolithic art, the painted caves and the images of the Goddesses, are deeply connected. Could it be that in the Paleolithic era, those whose rituals took them deep into the darkest chambers of caves were searching for her, Mother of Mysteries, Great Womb of Life and Death?

Poet, philosopher, and mystic Susan Griffin imagines a spiritual journey into the womblike darkness of a cave:

> The shape of a cave, we say, or the shape of a labyrinth. The way we came here was dark. Space seemed to close in on us. We thought we could not move forward. We had to shed our clothes. We had to leave all we brought with us. And when we finally moved through this narrow opening, our feet reached for ledges, under us was an abyss, a cavern stretching farther than we could see. Our voices echoed off the walls. We were afraid to speak. This darkness led to more darkness, until darkness leading to darkness was all we knew. . . .
>
> We see nothing. We are in the center of our ignorance. Nothingness spreads around us. But in this nothing we find what we did not know existed. With our hands we begin to trace faint images etched into the walls. And now, beneath those images we can see the gleam of older images. And these peel back to reveal the older still. The past, the dead, once breathing, the forgotten, the secret, the buried, the once blood and bone, the vanished, shimmering, now like an answer from these walls, bright and red. Drawn by the one who came before. And before her. And before. Back to the beginning.[11]

The journey into a cave is a journey into the great womb of life and death. In the darkness, the mystery is revealed. We are reborn.

In the popular imagination, Paleolithic society is seen as dominated by male hunters who went out and clubbed wild beasts, then came home to their caves and clubbed their wives and children. In fact, the human communities that produced the cave paintings and statues of the late Upper Paleolithic were made up of gatherers and hunters who lived in small family groups or clans of probably not fewer than twenty individuals.[12] These people were deeply in tune with nature, moving from place to place as the seasons shifted, in search not only of the great beasts, but also of water to drink and wild greens, fruits, nuts, seeds, vegetables, insects, reptiles, fish, and small animals to eat.

Feminist scholarship has challenged the image of early man as a savage hunter who dominated his women and children, arguing that "woman the gatherer" made important contributions to the Paleolithic clan. Woman the gatherer provided up to 80 percent of the food of the clan in the form of edible plants. She probably also "hunted" small animals, such as snails, lizards, turtles, fish, and birds.[13] Women no doubt played a primary role in food preparation, as they have in all known cultures. Studies of small-scale societies suggest that though roles are usually divided by sex, elders of both sexes are respected, and anyone with a good idea can be heard.

From this perspective, the Paleolithic Goddesses would have symbolized not only the birth-giving powers of women, but also the status of women as food providers and the respect given to grandmothers within the clan. These images must have given the women who probably made some of them and certainly held and carried them "a sense of participation in essential mysteries."[14]

The Neolithic "Revolution"

Between 10,000 and 8000 B.C.E., the last ice age ended. As the ice caps receded from Europe and the Near East, the conditions were ripe for the Neolithic, or New Stone Age, revolution that began about 9000 B.C.E. in the Near East.[15] The Neolithic "revolution," which probably was a long evolution, is defined by the discovery of agriculture, followed by stock breeding. During the Neolithic period, the arts of pottery making and weaving were created.

As anthropologist Ruby Rohrlich has noted, most anthropologists will "concede" that women probably were the inventors of agriculture.[16] Because women were the primary food gatherers and food preparers in Paleolithic societies, they are the most likely ones to have noticed the relation between dropped seeds and the green plants that come up. Because women had responsibility for the care of human babies, they may also have been the ones to feed and care for the abandoned young of wild animals and thus the first to domesticate animals.[17] Women's role in the creation of weaving is suggested by the fact that spinning and weaving are part of woman's traditional roles in nearly all agricultural societies.[18] Women are also the potters in many, though not all, traditional cultures. Women probably invented pottery because the earliest pots were made to aid women's work of food storage and preparation.[19] If women were the creators of all of these new developments of the Neolithic age, or even of some of them, it is not hard to imagine that their status would have been high.

Anthropological research and contemporary experience in much of the world show the important role of women in small-scale agriculture and stock breeding. In contemporary traditional societies around the world, women still perform a large share of farm labor. Even in urban settings, women unconsciously continue their traditional roles as cultivators of living things when they work in their gardens. Men come to play dominant roles in agricultural production when the animal-drawn (iron) plow and geographical conditions permit the cultivation of larger fields (making it harder to farm and watch children at the same time) and in stock breeding when large herds are taken far from the home.[20]

The agricultural revolution has long been celebrated as one of the great revolutions in human history because it enabled humans to settle in one place and begin to develop society and culture as we know them today. But the role of women in the invention of agriculture[21] and in the rapid, almost miraculous, hybridization of grain,[22] in the domestication of animals, and in the creation of pottery and weaving is given cursory (or no) attention by conventional scholars.

All of the new discoveries of the Neolithic era were probably understood to be "mysteries" whose secrets were revealed by the Goddess. Seed into plant into edible food, abundant and good to eat. Flax or wool into thread into cloth, carpets, blankets, and other items of use and beauty. Earth, water, and fire into well-crafted pots to hold food and water. Though all of these processes begin with raw materials found in nature, the secrets of their transformation are by no means self-evident. Later mythology connects all of these mysteries to women and Goddesses. In Greece, the mysteries of agriculture were given by the Goddesses Demeter and Persephone, whose most ancient rites, the Thesmophoria, were celebrated exclusively by women. To three ancient women, the Fates, was attributed the "weaving" of human destiny. Vessels molded with eyes and breasts or in the image of a Goddess (Figure 10) suggest that the secrets of the making of pottery may also have been understood as entrusted to women by the Goddess. The primacy of the Goddess in the Neolithic religion was a reflection of the important roles of women in Neolithic culture.

Old Europe

Archaeologist, mythographer, and historian of religion Marija Gimbutas coined the term *Old Europe* to differentiate the Neolithic and Chalcolithic, or Copper Age, cultures of southern and eastern Europe, 6500 to 3500 B.C.E., from the more familiar patriarchal warrior societies that succeeded them.

[The Old European] culture took keen delight in the natural wonders of this world. Its people did not produce lethal weapons or build forts in inaccessible places, as their successors did, even when they were acquainted with metallurgy. Instead, they built magnificent tomb-shrines and temples, comfortable houses in moderately-sized

villages, and created superb pottery and sculptures. This was a long-lasting period of remarkable creativity and stability, an age free of strife. Their culture was a culture of art.[23]

Gimbutas summed up the difference between the two cultural systems: "The first was matrifocal, sedentary, peaceful, art-loving, earth- and sea-bound; the second was patrifocal, mobile, warlike, ideologically sky oriented, and indifferent to art."[24] It is very difficult for those from modern European-based cultures to understand the religion and culture of Old Europe because we "are still living under the sway of that aggressive male invasion and only beginning to discover our long alienation from our authentic European Heritage—gylanic, nonviolent, earth-centered culture."[25]

In Neolithic Old Europe, as in the Paleolithic societies that preceded it, the Goddess was worshiped as the Giver, Taker, and Renewer of Life.

The Great Mother Goddess who gives birth to all creation out of the holy darkness of her womb became a metaphor for Nature herself, the cosmic giver and taker of life, ever able to renew Herself within the eternal cycle of life, death, and rebirth.[26]

The Goddess was celebrated in the symbolism of Old European art, which Gimbutas named "the language of the Goddess." The language of the Goddess can be compared to the symbolic world of medieval Christianity, sometimes called the great chain of being. In the medieval worldview, all of creation testified to the glory of God, and everything within nature was symbolic (often in very specific ways) of Creation and Redemption. In the language of the Goddess, all of nature was part of her body and symbolic of her power.

The Goddess as Giver of Life was symbolized as birds, chevrons, and v's; as water, zigzags and m's; as meanders and water birds; as breasts, streams, eyes, mouth and beak; as spinner, metalworker, and music maker; as ram, as net, as the power of three, as vulva and birth giver, as deer and bear, as snake. The Goddess as Taker and Regenerator of Life was symbolized as vulture, owl, cuckoo, hawk, dove, boar; as the stiff white lady (bone), the stiff nude, the egg, the column of life, the regenerative vulva, the triangle, the hourglass, the bird claw, the ship of renewal, the frog, the hedgehog, the fish, the bull, the bee, and the butterfly. As Renewing and Eternal Earth, she was Earth Mother, pregnant Goddess, lozenge and triangle with dots, sow, sacred bread, hill and stone as omphalos (belly), tomb as womb, holed stones, the power of two, and doubling. As Energy and Unfolding, she was spiral, lunar cycle, snake coil, hook and axe, opposed spiral, caterpillar, snake head, whirls, comb and brush, standing stone, and circle.[27] Two of the most important symbols in Old European religion were the bird and the snake.[28] The bird represented life and death and the power of flight, while the snake represented death and regeneration and connection to earth. Often the Goddess was pictured as a woman with bird or snake characteristics. (See Figures 5 to 9.)

Gimbutas believed that women played central roles in the religion and society of Old Europe. Grave evidence shows no great disparities among individuals or between women and men. This stands in sharp contrast to the royal graves of later periods and suggests that not only women and men, but all members of the society, were equal. The most clear marks of patriarchal societies—implements of war and the celebration of warriors and the warrior God—are lacking.[29] Gimbutas interpreted the civilization of Old Europe as "matristic," worshiping the Mother and honoring women, and "matrilineal," with family ties being traced through the female line. Because of the centrality of the symbol of the Goddess, from evidence of cult scenes found in shrines and also from burials of women with ritual objects, she hypothesized that women played central roles in the creation of Old European religion and probably also the leading roles in its rituals. Though clear evidence is lacking, she suggested that the towns of Old Europe may have been organized around a "theacratic, communal temple community . . . guided by a highly respected elder—Great Mother of the clan and her brother or uncle, with a council of women as a governing body."[30] Gimbutas did not call Old Europe "matriarchal," for this would imply that women dominated men. She insisted that men played important and valued roles within the culture, perhaps especially in trade.

Çatal Hüyük

Archaeologist James Mellaart found a culture similar to that of Old Europe in the Neolithic town of Çatal Hüyük (c. 6500–5650 B.C.E.) in Anatolia (central Turkey). Like the towns of Old Europe, Çatal Hüyük was prosperous and peaceful. As in Old Europe, there is no evidence of warfare or the kind of centralized authority and class division associated with patriarchal kingship. Mellaart believed that women played central roles in the agricultural and religious life of the village. Goddess symbolism was preeminent: "The supreme Deity was the Great Goddess."[31] (See Figure 4.)

Mellaart hypothesized that the "Neolithic religion of Çatal Hüyük (and of [nearby] Hacilar) was created by women."[32] In the burials of women and children (but not men) under sleeping platforms in the homes, he saw evidence of both matriliny, with family line and inheritance (where it existed) being passed through the mother, and matrilocality, with women remaining in their mothers' homes and towns. Though Mellaart theorized that women were not subordinate at Çatal Hüyük, the revolutionary implications of this theory to transform our understanding of religious and cultural origins are not developed in his work. In the work of feminist scholars, the role of women at Çatal Hüyük becomes central.[33]

Female Power versus Male Dominance

It is often argued that women can play important economic roles in agricultural societies and yet still be subordinated symbolically or in fact.[34] This evidence must be carefully evaluated.

My observation and study of the lives of traditional farm women in Greece and Crete suggests that even though they lived in religiously and politically patriarchal cultures, women could still have a good deal of power, especially prior to the introduction of a money-based economy.[35] Women were economically indispensable to the home economy: They not only were primarily responsible for child care, household maintenance, and cooking, they also worked in the fields, planted fruits and vegetables, picked and processed olives, spun, wove, sewed clothing, embroidered incredibly beautiful dowry items, tended sheep and goats, made cheese, and baked bread. Men did not, for the most part, derive status from work outside the home. The home was the primary workplace for both women and men, and status was ascribed to the (patrilineal) family as a whole. Though the traditional village was symbolically patriarchal, women exercised great control within the home and also over their sons, even after they married. It has even been argued that the familiar picture of Greek men sitting in public spaces while their wives and daughters stay home might be interpreted to mean that men were not really welcome in the home.[36]

But traditional Greek society differs in several important ways from the culture of Old Europe. Though the Mother of God has an important place in Greek Christianity, the Father and Son take theological priority, and the religious hierarchy is exclusively male. Women are relegated to the left side of the church and are forbidden to take communion or kiss the icons when they are "unclean" (menstruating or after childbirth), and in baptism, a female child is not taken behind the iconostasis, the screen that separates the community from the altar, because she cannot become a priest. The structures of marriage and family, as defined by the church, are patriarchal, requiring wives and daughters to be obedient to husbands and fathers. Traditionally, marriages were arranged, and girls were often married against their will. The political structures of the village and the more distant (often foreign) government were also dominated by men. Moreover, men were greatly celebrated for their roles as fighters in the ongoing struggle against foreign domination. Since we do not have evidence that any of these patriarchal structures existed in Old Europe, it seems probable that women there had greater power than their counterparts in traditional Greece.

The work of anthropologist Peggy Reeves Sanday sheds further light on this question. In a survey of sex roles and power based on information from 150 different societies, Sanday found a strong contrast between societies that celebrated "female power" and those organized in terms of "male dominance." To her surprise (because this was not her original hypothesis), Sanday discovered that "symbolism played a key role in channeling secular power roles."[37] She found that "in societies where the forces of nature are sacralized . . . there is a reciprocal flow between the power of nature and the power inherent in women."[38] In such societies, women have considerable power, but they are not dominant because they mix freely with men and share power with them. Sanday noted a strong correlation between Goddesses or female Creators, participation of women in sacral roles, and female power in society. Other variables correlated with female power were a positive view of nature, connection to the land (a settled rather than migratory lifestyle), lack of environmental stress such as prolonged drought, and the absence of external threat such as warfare. Societies characterized by female power were usually focused around gathering, fishing, and the early stages of agriculture.

In contrast, Sanday found that male dominance is correlated with societies organized around hunting, animal husbandry, and advanced (larger-scale) agriculture. Male dominance often arose in response to environmental stress or warfare. Male dominance is correlated with symbolic changes in the way women and nature are viewed, with male Gods and a male priesthood. Whereas societies organized around female power are egalitarian, male-dominant societies are not.

Though Sanday did not consider Paleolithic or Neolithic Europe, it is easy to see that Old Europe, especially in the Neolithic, fits her model of the kind of society that honors female power, while the Indo-Europeans are typical of male-dominant cultures.

Not a Matriarchy

Many feminist scholars view Paleolithic and Neolithic societies as prepatriarchal, matrifocal, probably matrilineal, and in the Neolithic, often matrilocal. The term *matriarchy* is not used by scholars who are aware of its contro-

versial history. Matriarchy literally means rule of the mother or mother principle and has often been understood to mean a society that is the opposite of
a patriarchy, a society ruled by the fathers or the father principle. The idea
that matriarchy preceded patriarchy was proposed by historian J.J. Bachofen
in his influential *Das Mutterrecht* [The Mother Right], published in 1861.[39]
Bachofen uncovered important data, but his theories are flawed by his con-
flation of matrilineal inheritance with rule by women and by his assumption
that patriarchy represents a higher stage of civilization.

Contemporary feminists have noted that most known patriarchal societies
are characterized not only by the rule of men within family and society, but
also by central organization, hierarchy, class division, and slavery. Frequent
and organized warfare is characteristic of patriarchy, and patriarchal societies
are most usually ruled by men who are warriors or who control the military.[40]
Since widespread warfare and centralized large-scale hierarchical social organization (including class division and slavery) are not characteristic of all societies, then by this definition prepatriarchal societies must have existed. But
if matriarchy is the opposite of patriarchy, then these societies should not be
called matriarchies, since this would imply that there were large-scale class-
and slave-based societies in which groups or classes of women ruled through
control of the military.

Women and Goddesses in Neolithic Cultures

Putting the work of Marija Gimbutas and James Mellaart together with anthropological theories about female power, a picture begins to emerge of
prosperous, settled, Neolithic villages and towns where women played central roles in farming, weaving, and the making of pots. The primary religious symbol, the Goddess, celebrated women's roles not only as birth
givers, but also as transformers of seed to grain to bread, of clay to pot, of
wool or flax to thread to cloth. Given the important social roles of women
and the predominance of Goddess symbolism, there is no reason not to believe that women created and played central roles in Neolithic religion and
culture.

If, as seems likely, women were the primary actors in the Neolithic revolution wherever it occurred, then it makes sense to look for evidence of the
high status of women and for symbolism connecting women, nature, and female divinities in other early agricultural societies. And indeed, anthropologist Daniel McCall suggests that West African religions may best be understood through a "two culture" model (similar to that proposed by Gimbutas
for Europe):

The various Earth Mother cults among the Akan, Yoruba, and Ibo (and other West African peoples) are remnants of Neolithic religion, truncated and modified by later influences. . . . It was only later, after the "urban revolution," that as male rulers and priests became powerful, "the status of the goddess in all her manifestations" was lowered. . . . [Before that,] the basic social institution was the matriclan, and the "land would generally have descended in the female line."[41]

Other scholars believe that the Neolithic stratum of the Indus Valley civilization may have shared many characteristics with Neolithic Old Europe. The powerful Goddesses of patriarchal Hindu society would be explained as survivals of an earlier religious consciousness not completely eradicated by the Indo-Europeans.[42]

The Rise of Patriarchy and War

The peaceful and egalitarian matrifocal societies of the Neolithic period came to an end as agriculture began to be transformed through the invention of technologies such as the iron plow and centrally organized irrigation techniques, that over time allowed some individuals to control large plots of land that were worked by others. This process was hastened by the invention of more deadly (bronze and iron) weapons and by the establishment of marauding and warfare as ways of life. It is likely that in some areas, internal developments prepared the way for the dominance of warriors, while in others, relatively peaceful agricultural societies were attacked by warlike pastoral nomadic groups, such as the Indo-Europeans who invaded southern and eastern Europe and progressed as far into Asia as the Indus valley.[43]

Yet many scholars argue that Neolithic societies generally developed into warlike patriarchal Iron Age urban city-states by a process of internal evolution, rather than by violent overthrow. Feminist anthropologist Margaret Ehrenberg, for example, correlates patrilineal descent and land ownership with the development of the iron plow, which allowed larger plots to be farmed by one individual; with the herding of larger numbers of animals for milk (rather than exclusively for wool and meat), which took the shepherd farther and farther from the home; and, ironically, with the increasing occupation of women's time with their new invention, weaving.[44]

Ehrenberg notes that large herds seem to call for raiding (called "rustling" in the American West) and that this could be the beginning of warfare.[45] We can imagine that land disputes might develop as farming and herding begin to require larger and larger areas. This conflict has been immortalized in the well-known song from the American musical *Oklahoma!* which exhorts, con-

trary to well-known fact, that "the farmer and the cowboy can be friends." Yet
Ehrenberg does not postulate warfare (either internally developed or exter-
nally imposed) as a major factor in the rise of patriarchy.

Gimbutas's argument that Old Europe was overthrown by successive waves
of invasion by Indo-European warrior groups has been attacked as being "simplistic" by historians who favor evolutionary theories of cultural change. Yet
we know from recent history in the Americas that indigenous cultures can be
overthrown and nearly extinguished by better-armed, horse-riding invaders.
Few would argue, for example, that the matrifocal Pueblo culture of the American southwest simply "evolved" peacefully into the patriarchal urban cultures
of Santa Fe, Phoenix, and Tucson. It seems to me that there is an element of
(self-serving) denial in theories that discount invasion as one of the primary
modes of effecting cultural change. Surely historian of religion Mircea Eliade
was correct when he wrote that conquests carried out by Indo-European
groups "did not end until the nineteenth century of our era."[46]

While evolutionary factors no doubt played a role in the cultural changes
that occurred in Europe between 4400 and 2000 B.C.E., evolutionary theory
alone fails to account for the marked differences in burial practices and language between what Gimbutas has called the "two cultures" of Europe. In addition, scientist L. Luca Cavalli-Sforza has discovered genetic evidence for a
population expansion into Europe from a place that "almost perfectly
matched Gimbutas' projection for the center of Kurgan [early Indo-Euro-
pean] culture."[47] Geographer Robert DeMao confirms a massive migration
out of the Middle East and Eurasia about 4000 B.C.E. by what he called "pa-
tristic" cultures.[48] It is unlikely that such major population shifts occurred
without conflict. If the "emigrants" were better armed, riding horses, and
more culturally attuned to fighting, the resultant destruction of indigenous
cultures is not hard to imagine.

In my opinion, the institutionalizing of warfare as a way of life (however
it occurs) is the single most important factor leading to the subordination of
women. Warfare brings with it major changes in society, including kingship,
large-scale land ownership and resultant class division, slavery, concubinage,
and the subordination of women. The first kings were military leaders who,
when they were not conducting wars of aggression or defense, used their
armies to control the people who had become their subjects on the land they
conquered. The first slaves were prisoners of war, brought back to serve their
conquerors. The first concubines were captured women.[49] When warfare becomes a part of life, boys and men are trained to become aggressive, violent,
and dominant. The "spoils" of war, offered to men as a reward for killing, are
the wealth of other cultures and the right to rape and capture "enemy"

women.[50] Patterns of dominance are transferred to local cultures when soldiers come home. And as history has shown, when warfare begins, it often seems that the only way to survive is to adopt the methods of the attacker. Warfare then becomes a way of life, even for those who initially resist it.

Though women have supported warfare in a variety of ways, sometimes even taking up arms, women as a group have not participated in warfare on the same scale as men. Different explanations have been proposed to explain this historical fact. Some point to the relatively lesser physical strength of women; others note that women stay home to take care of children. Peggy Reeves Sanday argues that warfare grew out of the hunt, which was a primarily male endeavor, and posits a symbolic opposition between giving birth and killing that made it seem wrong for women to participate in large-scale activities that involved the taking of life.[51] Whatever the reasons, it was men who became the warriors in most cultures, and the rise of the warrior to social power inevitably led to the decline in the social power of women as a group.

Slaying the Goddesses

Most people are more familiar with the Goddesses from classical Greek and Near Eastern mythology than with the Goddesses of earlier times. These Goddesses, including Athena, Aphrodite, Artemis, Inanna, and Ishtar, come from the warrior societies of the Bronze and Iron Ages. In the mythologies of these cultures, the Goddesses of the Neolithic and Paleolithic eras are slain or made subordinate to the new Gods of the patriarchal warriors, such as Zeus and Marduk. As classicist Jane Harrison points out, the writers of patriarchal mythologies are motivated by a "theological animus."[52] Their goal is to dethrone the Goddess and to legitimate the new culture of the patriarchal warriors.

The Babylonian creation myth, the *Enuma Elish* (first complete text, c. 668–626 B.C.E.) is one example of this genre.[53] In it, the primordial Creatress of Sumerian religion, Tiamat, the Goddess of the Salty Sea, is slain by the new God Marduk. As is common in such "epics," the Goddess is vilified so that her murder can be justified. The Creator Goddess is alleged to have given birth to a race of evil monsters who wreak havoc upon the earth: "She spawned enormous serpents with cutting fangs, chockfull of venom instead of blood, snarling dragons wearing their glory like Gods. (Whoever sees this thing receives the shock of death.)"[54] Even though Tiamat gives birth to these monsters in order to fight the God Marduk who plans to usurp her, the hearers of the tale are implored to agree that the Creatress of such creatures must be destroyed. Note the sadistic violence against the female body that characterizes Marduk's victory:

> *The Lord [Marduk] shot his net to entangle Tiamat, and the pursuing tumid wind,*
> *Imhullu, came from behind and beat her in the face. When the mouth gaped open*
> *to suck him down he drove Imhullu in, so that the mouth would not shut but wind*
> *raged through her belly; her carcass blown up, tumescent, she gaped—And now he*
> *shot the arrow that split the belly, that pierced the gut and cut the womb.*
>
> *Now that the Lord [Marduk] had conquered Tiamat he ended her life, he flung*
> *her down and straddled the carcass; the leader was killed, Tiamat was dead.*[55]

The writer (or writers) of this epic does not cringe from stating that Marduk cuts open the swelling (pregnant?) womb of the primordial Goddess. In celebrating the violence done to the Goddess, the *Enuma Elish* legitimates the violence done to the women of the "enemy" in war and to "evil" women at home.

The *Enuma Elish* employs several tactics to discredit the Goddess that are also used in other versions of the myth of the slaying of the Goddess. First, it discredits the Goddess as Birth, Death, and Regeneration by stating that she creates evil monsters. Second, it glorifies the warrior who kills her. Third, it has the warrior commit the ultimate sacrilege of defiling the womb that previous mythologies named as the Source of Life. Finally, this "epic" is regularly reenacted, in this case as part of the Babylonian New Year celebration, to reinforce the long-lasting moods and motivations it is designed to engender.

In Greece, there are a number of versions of the myth of the slaying of the Goddess. One of them is the story of Apollo's conquest of Delphi, told in the *Homeric Hymn* "To Pythian Apollo" (c. 700–600 B.C.E.). Aeschylus says that the first to be worshiped at Delphi was the Earth (Gaia), followed by Phoebe (the Moon) and Themis (the Goddess of Social Order).[56] Delphi, which is etymologically related to the word for womb, was understood to be the birthplace of the universe.[57] Archaeological evidence confirms that Apollo's shrine replaced an earlier one to Gaia, the Earth.[58] To justify Apollo's acquisition of the site, the hymnist states that when Apollo came to Delphi, he

> *Slew with his mighty bow a female dragon,*
> *A well-fed, powerful monster, savage and bloody,*
> *Who worked many evils on men who lived in that land.*[59]

Like Tiamat, the female "dragon" who guards the shrine of Mother Earth is portrayed as the source of evil. The dragon's demise is every bit as bloody and sadistically portrayed as Tiamat's. She was

Gasping for breath and rolling about on the ground.
Then a hideous scream, past words to describe, split the air
As she thrashed back and forth in the wood, and she gave up her life,
Gushing out red blood.[60]

Not content with that act, Apollo also desecrates the sacred river Telphusa. The female dragon, or large snake, and the sacred river are part of the language of the Goddess, and it is clear that the Goddess is the intended victim of the story. Like the *Enuma Elish,* the story of Apollo's slaying of the dragon was regularly performed at Delphi in a liturgical drama called the *Septerion.*[61]

In another well-known version of the patriarchal takeover myth, Zeus kills the Goddess Metis (whose name means "Wisdom") by "swallowing" her. From his head is born the Goddess Athena fully armed and prepared for battle. But lest any mortal woman understand from this story that she can resist her oppression, the story of the defeat of the Amazons by the Greek army is depicted on Athena's temple, the Parthenon.[62]

The slaying of the Mother is justified in the stories of Clytemnestra, Agememnon, and their children. As the trilogy the *Oresteia* by Aeschylus makes clear, men can kill their daughters and their mothers and lead their sons to death in war and still be called heroic. But a woman who kills her husband, even to avenge the death of her daughter, will be rejected by her own children, both son *and* daughter. And when the Furies, those avatars of ancient female rage, come forth to protest her death, they will be pacified by the unnatural Goddess Athena, who betrays her sex and tells the world that

No mother ever gave me birth:
I am unreservedly for male in everything
save marrying one—
enthusiastically on my father's side.
I cannot find it in me to prefer
the fate of a wife who slew her man:
the master of the house.[63]

Athena fails to mention that the man who was slain by his wife (Agememnon) first sacrificed his own daughter (Iphegenia) to the winds of war. Bragging that she was not born of a mother, Athena also confirms the pseudobiology proposed by the God Apollo a few minutes previously.

The mother is not parent of her so-called child
but only nurse of the new-sown seed.
The man who puts it there is parent;

she merely cultivates the shoot—
host for a guest—if no god blights.

I shall give you proof of what I say.
There can be fatherhood without a mother.
The living truth stands there:
the daughter of Olympian Zeus—
never nurtured in the darkness of a womb,
a shoot no goddess struck.[64]

The patriarchal lie that the mother is but the soil for the seed man plants was repeated by Aristotle and influenced western "scientific" views for centuries.[65] The *Oresteia*, which blatantly justifies male dominance, forms part of the classical canon that stands as the foundation of European-based educational systems and thus continues to be taught in high schools and universities around the world, as well as performed on the stage.

In the classical mythology of Greece, each of the Goddesses is deprived of the power that once was hers. In Homer, Hera, once the autonomous Goddess of the Argive plain and of Samos, becomes the frustrated and unhappy wife of Zeus.[66] In Hesiod, Pandora, the Goddess whose name means "Giver of All," is portrayed as a woman who opens a jar (often incorrectly translated as "box") and releases evil into the world. Aphrodite is born from the severed genitals of Ouranos: Once again, the Goddess comes out of the God; emerging from his genitals, the Giver of Life is portrayed as a projection or stimulator of male desire.[67] The many stories of Zeus raping Goddesses, nymphs, and mortal women are yet another version of the myth of the slaying of the Goddess.

In the Hebrew Bible, there is no fully told myth of the slaying of the Goddess, though the Hebrew God's victory over sea monsters is mentioned in passing.[68] In the mysterious verse of Genesis 1:2, scholars have seen echoes of Tiamat: "The earth was without form and void, and darkness was on the face of the deep; and the spirit [or wind] of God was moving over the face of the waters."[69] The words *tohu wabohu*, "the formless and the void," and *tehom*, "the [great] deep," suggest the abode of Tiamat, and some have argued that *tehom* is etymologically related to the name Tiamat.[70] The wind of God blowing on the waters recalls the wind that entered Tiamat and destroyed her. But by the time this biblical story was written, the Goddess could be subdued without even being named.

If we read the story of Adam and Eve from the perspective created by the myths of the slaying of the Goddess, we can see that it performs a similar function, as Merlin Stone has argued.[71] In the familiar story of Genesis 2–3, Eve, whose name may mean "Life," is also called "The Mother of All the Living."[72] These are names or titles of the Goddess, who does not appear in the story, and the images of the snake, the tree, and the naked woman are easily recognized as part of the language of the Goddess. On the symbolic level, the Genesis story tells us that the Mother of All the Living, the Sacred Snake, and the Sacred Tree are the source of suffering. Stone argues, and I agree with her, that the authors of the Genesis story, like the authors of the other myths and epics discussed in this section, wrote with the deliberate intention of discrediting the worship of the Goddess.

In Jewish tradition, the story of Adam and Eve has been interpreted as showing woman's propensity to act foolishly and immorally.[73] In Christianity, the Genesis story becomes foundational when it is used to set the scene for the salvation brought by Christ. The letters of Saint Paul first make this connection. "For as in Adam all die, so also in Christ shall all be made alive" (I Corinthians 15:22). In the first letter of Paul to Timothy, the Genesis story is interpreted to blame Eve for the first sin. "For Adam was formed first, then Eve; and Adam was not deceived, but the woman was deceived and became a transgressor" (I Timothy 2:13–14). Although the letter to Timothy is now believed by many scholars to have been written by someone other than Paul,[74] it nonetheless became the foundation for traditional theological interpretations that blame Eve for original sin and the fall of "man."

In Christian theological tradition, the Genesis story is interpreted through the classical dualisms that identify rational control with men and sensuality with women. According to theologians, woman was deceived because of her lesser rational capacity or because her sensual nature made it impossible for her to control her bodily passions.[75] Christian tradition thus identifies woman with sexuality and death and views her as the origin of sin and evil. In Christian myth, woman is the chaos monster who is not slain and therefore leads all humanity into sin and death. According to Tertullian, woman is "the Devil's gateway."[76] Her sin causes the death of the savior.

Theological tradition posits Mary as the New Eve, who through her faithfulness overcomes the sin of the first woman. The theologian Justin Martyr wrote that "for Eve, being a virgin and uncorrupt, conceived the word spoken of the serpent, and brought forth disobedience and death. But Mary the Virgin, receiving faith and grace [gave birth to him] by whom God destroys the serpent."[77] But the Mary of theological tradition does not restore to woman the power she had before the Goddess was slain. As Ever-Virgin, Mary's uncorrupt womb sets her apart from all other women who give physical birth through "corrupt" wombs. Mary, as author Marina Warner tells us, is "Alone of All Her Sex."[78] A well-known Christmas carol makes this clear when in its third verse it tells us that there is "Only one unabhorrent womb."[79] In the "abhorrent wombs" of all other women, the patriarchal denigration of Tiamat, the Source of Life, is reenacted.

The myth of the slaying of the Goddess is echoed in Roman Catholic and Christian Orthodox depictions of Saint George slaying the dragon. This dragon, which is often portrayed with a snakelike body and tail, as we now can see, was once the guardian of the shrines of Mother Earth. And like Marduk before him, Saint George brutally thrusts his sword into the mouth or swollen belly of the dragon. The repeated slaying of the snake/dragon confirms the overthrow of the Goddess. In an odd inversion, Mary as the New Eve is sometimes pictured trampling the snake under her feet. This image both confirms and disconfirms the slaying of the Goddess.

The Patriarchal Lie

Psychologist of religion Naomi Goldenberg has argued that a simple, basic, and fundamental lie must be maintained for patriarchy to function. This lie is the denial of the womb that gives us birth. The lie of patriarchy tells us that the Father is the only true parent. Its corollary is that whatever the Father does is justified because he is the Father. Goldenberg argues that the lie of patriarchy is contrary to fact and experience. Everyone knows that it is the Mother who gives birth. There can be very little doubt about who the mother is, while the identity of the father can always be questioned. But if the lie of patriarchy is so obvious, why is it believed? Why doesn't the audience laugh and go home when Apollo and Athena speak nonsense? Why have whole cultures believed that powerful women are monsters and dragons who must be slain because they are the source of sin and evil in the world? Goldenberg's answer is simple. We believe the patriarchal lie because it is "performed," repeated, reenacted, read, told, sung, and taught again and again in so many contexts that we finally accept it as true.[80]

Survivals of the Ancient Goddesses

Once we recognize the myths of patriarchy for what they are, we can begin to look again at the familiar images of the Goddesses that come to us through later patriarchally influenced cultures. As Gimbutas has taught us to see, there are many survivals of Old European religion in classical mythology, in folk tradition, and even within Christianity.[81] Though Athena is in some respects a very patriarchalized Goddess and a traitor to her sex, we can also glimpse the Old European Goddess through her. We can understand that she, rather than a male God, was the guardian of patriarchal and warlike Athens because she was the ancient Goddess of the Rock that was later named the Acropolis. The olive tree she produced in her contest with Poseidon connects her with the agricultural Goddesses. Her companion animals, the owl and the snakes that protect her shield, are symbols of the Old European Goddess.

Aphrodite is trivialized in Homer and Hesiod, but we can recognize her as Mother of All the Living in the invocation to her in one of the *Homeric Hymns*:

> *Aphrodite the golden, who stirs up sweet longing*
> *In gods and subdues the tribes of mortal mankind*
> *And the birds that fly in the air and all the wild beasts*
> *Of the many kinds the dry land supports and the sea.*[82]

And we can imagine a woman's relation to Aphrodite as we read the surviving fragments of the poems of Sappho (c. 600 B.C.E.), in which the patriarchal myth of her birth is never mentioned. In one poem, Sappho asks a beloved young woman to "think of our gifts to Aphrodite and all the loveliness that we shared."[83] In another, she calls Aphrodite to come to her:

> *You know the place: then*
>
> *Leave Crete and come to us*
> *waiting where the grove is*
> *pleasantest, by precincts*
>
> *sacred to you; incense*
> *smokes on the altar . . .*[84]

Sappho's Aphrodite is an object of prayer and ritual, a Goddess who is invoked in an intimate and personal way. In one poem, Sappho asks Aphrodite to

> *Fill our gold cups with love*
> *stirred into clear nectar.*[85]

And in another, she entreats

> *snare-knitter! Don't, I beg you,*
> *cow my heart with grief!* [86]

The Goddess of Old Europe can also be glimpsed in devotion to Mary the Mother of God and the female saints. Theologically, Mary is not a Goddess, and the Church's insistence that she is the only woman whose womb is pure reaffirms the myth of the slaying of the Goddess. Yet in the minds of many worshipers, the Mother of God and the female saints do not differ greatly from the Goddess. Indeed, many of the places dedicated to Mary and the female saints were originally sacred to the Goddesses.

In Crete, there is a cave with a huge stalactite formation that looks like an enormous shaggy bear drinking from a pool. This bear is worshiped as the "Panagia Arkoudiotissa," Mary the Bear. Archaeologists tell us that this cave was once sacred to Artemis the Bear.[87] In Mexico, the shrine of the Virgin of Guadalupe is built on a hill sacred to the pre-Aztec Goddess known as Tonantsi.[88] In Ireland, the sacred fire of the Goddess Briget was maintained by the nuns of the monastery at Kildare, said to have been founded by the legendary Saint Brigid.[89] Such survivals demonstrate that those who attempted to slay the Goddess were never fully successful.

Whose Goddesses?

The Goddesses of patriarchal mythology dimly reflect the power of women and Goddesses in prepatriarchal societies. They are the ones who gave rise to the scholarly myth that Goddesses are the creations of men and that their images everywhere support male power. But more ancient images of the Goddesses and echoes of their power in later myths and customs challenge the widely held belief that "in the beginning God created the heavens and the earth." They provide alternatives to the conventional view that men have always been dominant in religion and society. Knowledge is power. As we learn about ancient Goddess religions and cultures, we begin to understand that we do not have to live as we do today: in cultures that worship one male God, where the domination and the control of women, the earth, and other people are taken for granted, and warfare is perpetual.

4

Resistance
to Goddess History

The story of women and Goddesses presented in the previous chapter is by no means widely accepted among scholars. The well-known and respected classicist Moses Finley expressed a common view when he dismissed the notion of a Mother Goddess as nothing more than "a remarkable fable."[1] Resistance to Goddess history can be traced back to the myths of the slaying of the Goddess that rewrote history, defining man and his Gods as superior to woman and nature. Contemporary scholars often uncritically accept the views presented in these biased accounts as a true picture of religious origins. Many scholars are uncomfortable with an interpretation of the history of religion and culture that challenges long-held beliefs about who we are and what has come before us. But the desire to secure and preserve male dominance is not named as a motivation for distortions and denials the history of the Goddess in either ancient or modern works. Because those who study the Goddesses are often intimidated (as I have been) by academic authorities, I devote this chapter to considering the reasons the history of the Goddess is so frequently dismissed or ignored. Anyone who has already encountered the attitudes discussed in this chapter will know why it is necessary to learn how to counter them; those who have not will be forewarned of what to expect when they begin to talk about the Goddess history they have learned from the previous chapter.

A Remarkable Fable?

In his definitive book on Greek religion, Walter Burkert spends only a few pages on the Neolithic period. Without devoting any serious attention to the evidence, he comments on the female "figurines":

> An earlier, widely accepted interpretation saw them as representations of a Mother Goddess, the embodiment of fertility in man [sic], animal, and earth. It is tempting to proceed to draw numerous connections with the predominance of female deities in the historical Greek cult and with the Mycenean Mistress. This goes far beyond the evidence. . . . the Mother Goddess interpretation has come to be regarded with increasing skepticism.[2]

A number of female scholars agree.[3] The vehemence with which this debate is being carried on (especially among women) proves that classicist Sarah B. Pomeroy was correct when she wrote that "the roles of females both divine and human in prehistory has become an *emotional issue with political implications* as well as a topic of scholarly debate [italics added]."[4] Those arguing that attention be paid to Goddess history are often contemptuously dismissed by both male and female scholars as emotionally biased, politically motivated, naive, idealistic, unscientific, wishful thinkers. One female archaeologist characterized the work of women interested in the Goddess with the words "fads and fictions," "simply hopeful," "idealistic creations," and a "search for a social utopia."[5] The high ground of "objective" scholarship is generally reserved for those whose work celebrates and helps to preserve male power.

Is History True?

Elisabeth Schüssler Fiorenza, a feminist historian of early Christianity, radically questions the truthfulness of the history we have been taught. Her clear delineation of the biases at work in traditional scholarship on Christian history can help us become critical of conventional views about Goddess history.[6]

We must recognize, Schüssler Fiorenza argues, that historians whose theories and conclusions support the (male) power elite are more likely to be given the resources to write (academic appointments, time off, fellowships) and are more likely to have their books published, preserved, and quoted. Male-centered models and paradigms serve long-established interests and therefore must be questioned. Similarly, the truthfulness of the primary and secondary texts that have been handed down through male tradition must be challenged. Schüssler Fiorenza argues that a feminist critical approach to religion must be historical, viewing religious ideas as rooted in time and space and as affected by power relations. The history of women's religious and social roles and the history of resistance to women's power are ignored in traditional scholarship, but they must become central in feminist analysis. Schüssler Fiorenza cautions that feminist scholars cannot be content with the concession of certain facts and hypotheses, but must insist on the construction of critical paradigms, or frameworks of interpretation, in which the new facts and hypotheses hold together, make sense, and affect our understanding of other facts and hypotheses. This is not a simple agenda. It requires careful and subtle analysis to become aware of the various ways interpretive frameworks influence the presentation of data.

As applied to the origins of religion, a feminist critical approach questions the alleged universality of patriarchy and asks whether prepatriarchal societies existed. It considers the roles of women and female symbolism in religious history to be important issues. It seeks to understand the language of the Goddess and asks whether Goddesses at any time correlated with women's social power or religious leadership. Arguing that women once held power in religion, it raises the question: What happened? And finally, it asks why we have not been taught the truth about our history.

Many traditional scholars concede that Goddesses were worshiped or that women may have invented agriculture, weaving, and pottery. But these facts are passed over as unimportant in the overall historical story that is told. A feminist critical approach requires that a framework of interpretation be constructed in which women are recognized as important historical and religious actors. In the preceding chapter, I proposed a critical framework in which the conceded facts of women's invention of agriculture, pottery, and weaving; anthropological and other theories about women's roles in gathering and hunting and early agricultural societies; and hypotheses about the meaning of female or Goddess symbolism hold together and affect the interpretation of a variety of other facts and hypotheses. I have called this critical paradigm "the Goddess hypothesis."

Not surprisingly, the Goddess hypothesis challenges many well-established theories about the nature and origin of religion. Because it holds together disparate facts and theories, the Goddess hypothesis as a whole has greater persuasive power than any of its parts considered separately. It is important that a critical framework be addressed in its entirety when it is being evaluated or criticized. Far too often, scholars who remain situated within old paradigms take swipes at isolated facts (a wrong date here, an overgeneralization there) without ever addressing the challenge a new critical framework presents to their own unexamined presuppositions.

"Pre"-history

One of the assumptions the Goddess hypothesis challenges is the notion that so-called pre-history is unintelligible. As we have seen, feminist research has begun to uncover an untold history of female power in Paleolithic and Neolithic religions and cultures. Because Goddess symbolism originated in eras that are called *prehistoric* due to the absence of written records, feminists have begun to insist that greater attention be paid to these periods.

But the feminist reading of Goddess history is often attacked on the general grounds that nothing can be known about the Paleolithic and Neolithic periods due to the absence of written records. Walter Burkert, for example, writes, "Ancient religion is tradition, as old, perhaps, as mankind [sic]; but its tracks are lost in prehistory."[7] Many respected scholars state that there is no "conclusive" evidence that the female images from these periods are Goddesses. They argue that they may be dolls, fertility fetishes, or sex objects, or that because we cannot know for certain what they are, no conclusions can be drawn from them. Here is Burkert again: "Are they representations of a Great Goddess, the mother of life and death, or are they goddesses, or nymphs, or gifts to the dead man intended to serve him in another world? . . . all attempts at interpretation must remain conjecture."[8] Scholars like Burkert also insist that there is no evidence that proves that prehistorical societies were not patriarchal. They brand those who argue otherwise as indulging in fantasy.

Most historians will acknowledge that *all* history writing is the product of selective reading of data. History is not so much a matter of fact as it is a matter of interpretation, affected not only by time and space, but also by power relations. Many historians will even admit that the existing written records for most historical periods are themselves limited and biased in favor of the powerful, given that most people were not literate and that only a few had the skills and the time to write. Moreover, they will agree that both chance and power politics have dictated that only a small number of the written records from the past have survived. That is to say, many, if not most, historians will concede that our views of the past are neither complete nor unbiased.

Yet when asked about the history of periods for which no written records exist, most historians draw a sharp distinction between so-called *history* and so-called *prehistory*, which they define by the absence of written records. They state that nothing can really be known about "pre"-history, while a great deal can be known about history. They argue that interpretation of physical data is largely subjective, whereas interpretation of text is, by contrast, relatively objective. Such scholars insist that in the absence of written records, vast periods of human history must remain unintelligible. Responding to this view, Marija Gimbutas wrote, "I do not believe, as many archaeologists of this generation seem to, that we shall never know the meaning of prehistoric art and religion."[9] Naomi Goldenberg points out that scholars are more likely to say that we cannot know anything with certainty about prehistory when the conclusions drawn from the interpretation of the archaeological record challenge the status quo.[10]

The terms *history* and *prehistory* themselves, rather than being descriptive, reflect bias in favor of the written word. Where there is no text, we have no history, it is said, but only a prelude to history. This naming serves to diminish the importance of prehistory, almost to render it nondata. I suggest that we abandon the term *prehistory* and speak rather of early or ancient history or use the descriptive terms *Paleolithic* and *Neolithic*.

Can Written Records Lie?

The questions raised by historian of Christianity Margaret Miles about the reliability of texts can help us become critical of traditional historians' dismissal of prehistory. According to Miles, images can sometimes tell us more about a culture than written records. For example, the texts available to the historian of premodern Christianity, which are mostly theological, create a distorted picture of Christian spirituality. Written by elite males, they would have been inaccessible to the average Christian, who was illiterate. A clearer understanding of what Christianity meant to the common person, female as well as male, can be gained through a careful study of images. The architecture, sculptures, and wall paintings in churches would have been the "text" the common person "read" to learn about the Christian faith. Not surprisingly, Miles found that the intellectual disputes that are the subject of theological tomes were not always reflected on the walls of churches, and thus, presumably, also not in the faith of the people.[11]

Nearly a century earlier, classicist Jane Harrison questioned the reliance on texts in the study of Greek religion. Harrison wrote that Hesiod, whose *Theogony* and *Works and Days* (c. 700 B.C.E.) are among the major surviving written sources for our knowledge of Greek religion, was motivated by "the ugly malice of theological animus. Zeus the Father will have no great Earth-goddess, Mother and Maid in one, in his man-fashioned Olympus, but her figure *is* from the beginning, so [Hesiod] re-makes [the myth]."[12] Not surprisingly, Harrison's critique of Hesiod and her reconstruction of earlier myths of the Goddesses from the artistic record are not allowed to dislodge Hesiod from his position as "the" authority on "the beginnings" of Greek religion. Few scholars have followed Harrison's method, checking the accuracy of the literary record against artistic evidence. Burkert, for example, tells us that "the most important evidence for Greek religion remains the literary evidence."[13]

Hesiod is the one who wrote that Pandora was the first woman and that she was responsible for unleashing sorrow and evil into the world by opening her jar.[14] Yet Harrison argues convincingly, on the basis of artistic evidence, that Pandora, whose name means "All Gifts," was worshiped as the Earth Goddess in Hesiod's time and afterward.[15] Hesiod also tells the improbable story that the Goddess Aphrodite was born from the severed genitals of Ouranos. Neither the surviving *Homeric Hymn* "To Aphrodite" nor the fragments of Sappho make any mention of this story. Could it be that the people who worshiped Pandora and Aphrodite knew nothing of these "myths" devised by Hesiod or that they ignored them, just as people who worship the Mother of God pay little attention to theologians' views of the proper limits of their devotion?

Most of Sappho's words did not survive, and even her views of Aphrodite, for which we do have several surviving poems, are not necessarily quoted to challenge Hesiod because they do not confirm patriarchal and heterosexual assumptions about Aphrodite. The words of Hesiod continue to shape scholarly assumptions about Greek religion because they are readily accessible, systematic, and clearly assert the primacy of men and Gods.

When scholars quote Hesiod and other androcentric texts uncritically, even though their own theories acknowledge that they should question their reliability, and after Hesiod's views of Greek religion have been questioned by other scholars, we must ask why. We have already noted that the desire to preserve patriarchal power underlies established theories, but there are other and more subtle reasons that make it difficult to dislodge them.

Time, Text, and God

Traditional views of the origin and history of religion are reinforced by deeply held presuppositions about time, text, and God found in biblical religion. These views affect the writing of the history of religion, even in the work of scholars who claim no religious bias.

For those studying western religion from within the framework provided by biblical religion (still the vast majority of scholars in religious studies), *time* is often said to begin with the Hebrew patriarchs, with Abraham (c. 1800 B.C.E.) or with Moses (c. 1300–1200 B.C.E.). Time proceeds through the Davidic kingship (c. 1000 B.C.E.), to the time of the prophets of Israel (c. 800–500 B.C.E.), to the time of the classical Greeks (c. 500–300 B.C.E.), to the time of the origins of Christianity and rabbinic Judaism in the first century C.E.

When time before Abraham is mentioned, it is usually discussed within the framework provided by Samuel Noah Kramer's book *History Begins at Sumer.*[16] The Babylonian creation epic, the *Enuma Elish*, which depicts the slaying of the primordial Mother Tiamat, and the *Epic of Gilgamesh*, in which the hero curses the Goddess Ishtar and refuses her gifts,[17] may be mentioned as providing evidence about the origins of religion in the Near East. Frequently, even this material is presented primarily as backdrop to the "distinctive and superior" contributions of Hebrew religion. It is clear that if history begins at Sumer, then all history is patriarchal history. We may discover the roles of women within patriarchal history—and these may be substantial—but we will not have the history of a time when women's roles in religion were central and unquestioned.

In contrast, the Goddess hypothesis challenges us radically to expand our conception of time. The time of the Neolithic revolution is some eight thousand years before the times of Moses and David, more than five thousand years before history was said to have begun at Sumer. Evidence of religion in the Paleolithic period occurs tens of thousands of years before the Neolithic revolution. Yet the time from Moses to the present is only about three thousand years. Still many historians of religion continue to ignore the time before history supposedly began at Sumer.

Those who study non-Christian religions, including Judaism, rapidly become aware that the Christian naming of time as "before" and "after Christ" makes it difficult to conceptualize the scope of history and to grasp the relationships of historical periods. There was in fact no major break in history at the time of the birth of Jesus of Nazareth. Christianity did not become the dominant religion of the Roman Empire until the time of Constantine and Theodosius "the Great" in the fourth century C.E.

The naming we give to time is not a trivial matter, as Christian rulers recognized when they took control of the calendar. It will be difficult for us to grasp fully the most ancient history as long as we are rooted in the Christian naming of time. Anthropologists have recognized this problem and devised their own counting of time as "before the present," or "B.P." From this point of view, the suggestion made by Merlin Stone that we rename time from a feminist perspective—she proposed that we begin from the time when women invented agriculture—is by no means trivial.[18]

The Goddess hypothesis also challenges scholarly commitment to *text*. To pay attention to time before Sumer, scholars must develop methods for dealing with the nontextual artifacts of history. Because resistance to this is so great, we also must ask whether the commitment of historians of religion to the written word might also be rooted in unquestioned assumptions derived from biblical religion.

And God spoke, and said, 'Let there be light.' (Genesis 1:1)

In the beginning was the Word, and the Word was with God, and the Word was God. (John 1:1)

Scholars are aware of the complex meanings embedded in the notions of speech and word in these texts, and they recognize them as being historically and culturally situated. But they implicitly accept the deep meaning of these texts, which is their reverence for Word, for words, for text itself. Though they know that nonliterary religions exist, most scholars in the history of religion focus on the interpretation of texts—whether these be Hebrew or Christian or other scriptures and myths or the writings of Jewish or Christian or other theologians, philosophers, mythologists, or interpreters of texts.

The texts about the Goddesses come from times when patriarchy was already established; thus if we rely on texts alone, we might be forced to concede that Goddesses do not reflect female power. But when we expand our notion of history to include records that are not written, we can begin to allow physical data to transform not only our understanding of Goddesses and women in religion, but also notions about religious origins and theories about the nature of religion.

Ritual studies, which by some accounts of the nature of religion ought to form the core of religious studies, are usually relegated to the periphery. Ritual embodies, in a fuller way than text, the nonrational, the physical side of religion, putting us in the presence of body and blood, milk and honey and wine, song and dance, sexuality and ecstasy. Underlying scholars' preference for the study of text lies a fear of the nonrational and the physical, a fear of chaos, a fear that, as we have seen, undergirds the ethos of objectivity in scholarship.

The Goddess hypothesis challenges historians of religion to abandon their almost exclusive commitment to text, requiring them to accept physical evidence—paintings, sculptures, bones, pots, weavings, etc.—as reliable evidence upon which to build theory. Once the commitment to text as the only valid form of evidence is broken, historians will not only be able to come to a clearer understanding of the role of the Paleolithic and Neolithic periods in the shaping of religious history, but they will also be forced to pay more attention to nonliterary expressions of religion wherever they are found—in tribal and folk religions as well as *within* so-called higher religions.

The Goddess hypothesis also challenges biblical and traditional ideas about the nature of *God*. The Goddesses are presented in the Bible as "abomination," and it is hard for scholars to shake the mind-set that has encouraged all of us to think of Goddesses in relation to terms such as *idolatry, fertility fetish, nature religion, orgiastic cult, bloodthirsty,* and *ritual prostitution.* These terms and others like them are used to depict Goddess religion in scholarly volumes.[19]

All of these prejudices can be countered. An idol is someone else's religious symbol. The Goddesses represent fertility and sexuality as the cosmic power of transformation. There is little evidence of blood sacrifice in Neolithic religion, but it becomes a widespread practice in later patriarchal Bronze and Iron Age societies. Sexuality in Goddess religion is transformative power. Prostitution is not the oldest profession. Rather, it is the product of patriarchal and class-stratified societies. When sexuality is mutual and women are equal, there is no question of buying and selling.[20] Yet these labels stick in the mind.

Scholars' inability to understand the Goddesses is reinforced by a deep and unquestioned assumption that divinity represents rationality, order, and transcendence, as opposed to the alleged irrationality and chaos of the finite, changeable world of nature and body. The contrast between rationality and irrationality, order and chaos, transcendence and immanence, is genderized as a contrast between male and female. The origin of this idea can be found in the myths of the slaying of the Goddess, but it comes to full bloom in philosophy.

Scholars have been unable to see naked female images as Goddesses because they have been taught to view the body and sexuality, especially the female body and female sexuality, as being "lower" than the rationality that is associated with divinity and "man's" "higher" nature. Naked female images must therefore be "fertility fetishes" or "sexual objects," or if they are called Goddesses, they must be understood to reflect a "lower" and more physical stage in the "evolution" of religious consciousness.

In the worldview defined by the prepatriarchal Goddesses, the divine power is present within nature and within the processes of birth, growth, death, and regeneration symbolized by the female body. Sexuality and birth are sacred, and death and disintegration are not negations of life because they are followed by regeneration. Clearly, the prehistoric Goddesses can only be understood if we question the assumptions that divinity is transcendent of the body, nature, and change and that it is man's spiritual destiny to rise above, conquer, or tame nature, the body, and the female.

Ignoring Women and Goddesses

Given that the questions raised in this chapter are nonquestions for most traditional historians of religion, it is not surprising that the scholarly establishment continues to resist the feminist reading of Goddess history. One strategy is briefly to dismiss or simply to ignore evidence that challenges traditional views.

Women and Goddesses were not even mentioned in an exhibit called "Neolithic Culture in Greece" at the Nicholas P. Goulandris museum in Athens. This exhibit could have provided an opportunity to speak of the contributions of women to human history and to document the important role of Goddesses in early religious symbolism. The exhibit and the lavishly illustrated book accompanying it were a joint production of scores of scholars, including many women.[21] They might have told us that the Neolithic revolution was quite likely created by women. But though the invention of agriculture, pottery, and weaving in the Neolithic period is mentioned, women are not. Both the book and the descriptions for the exhibit use the male generic (o ánthropos in Greek, man in English) and simply ignore the theories that women played important roles in Neolithic culture.[22]

That women are disregarded is all the more surprising given that the significant roles of women in Neolithic culture are hinted at in the black-and-white photographs of traditional Greek agricultural life that were used to illustrate both the exhibit and the book about it. These show women actively participating in all the agricultural tasks depicted. Two women winnow wheat with wooden pitchforks; two women pound pulses (beans) with weights attached to long poles; a man and a woman herd a large flock of sheep; a woman furrows with a wooden plow drawn by two oxen while a man hoes; a woman grinds with a stone hand mill; two women and two men shear sheep; a young woman and two girls spin wool.[23] Needless to say, no implications are drawn from these photographs.

Though the exhibit included more than forty "female figurines" (some of them excavated by Marija Gimbutas herself), the theory that these might be Goddesses is not even mentioned. The English version of the essay "Figurines and Models" (written by a woman) states that "Neolithic figurines and models represent man's [sic] animate and inanimate world, and of course, man [sic] himself."[24] Since Marija Gimbutas's work is frequently cited in the bibliographies in the book, the failure to discuss her interpretation of the language of the Goddess in Neolithic religion (even if only to refute it) is shocking.

Women and Goddesses Don't Fit the Theory

Another strategy for denying Goddess history is to admit some of the evidence but to present it within the framework of androcentric theories. This occurs in the work of the influential historian of religion Mircea Eliade.[25] Eliade admits that women and Goddesses exist (especially in the Neolithic), but he does not develop a critical framework that makes sense of this evidence. The result is that women and Goddesses do not appear to have contributed anything essential to the history of religion. Study of Eliade's work confirms Elisabeth Schüssler Fiorenza's contention that new critical frameworks, or paradigms, must be developed if the roles of women in religion are to be understood.

A giant in his field, Mircea Eliade is the most prolific, widely read, and influential historian of religion of the twentieth century. Author of many books and articles and teacher of several generations of scholars, he was also the editor-in-chief of the sixteen-volume *Encyclopedia of Religion*, which was produced toward the end of his life. Though Eliade's theories and methods have been challenged within the field of religion, his work remains foundational. Scholars in other fields often cite Eliade without apparent awareness that religion scholars do not use his work uncritically.

I have chosen to examine Eliade's work in detail because only thus can we see exactly how and why scholarship governed by patriarchal assumptions cannot come to terms with the Goddess. I was astonished at how blatant some of Eliade's prejudices were once I started looking for them. Yet I had overlooked them in earlier readings of his work. I focus on Eliade's definition of the sacred and his interpretations of Paleolithic, Neolithic, and Greek religion because his ideas on these topics can easily be compared to the Goddess hypothesis proposed in the previous chapter. (Those who do not need further convincing about the biases of androcentric scholarship can skip this section.)

In *A History of Religious Ideas*,[26] the culminating work of his career, Eliade concedes many elements of the Goddess hypothesis. He acknowledges the "extensive" distribution of "feminine representations" in the Paleolithic[27] and writes that with the discovery of agriculture in the Neolithic, "woman and feminine sacrality are raised to the first rank."[28] Eliade states that Neolithic societies were violently overthrown: "The irruption of the Indo-Europeans into history is marked by terrible destruction."[29] He asserts that new social structures were introduced by the invaders, noting that "pastoral nomadism, the patriarchal structure of the family, a proclivity for raids, and a military organization designed for conquest are characteristic features of Indo-European societies."[30] Eliade recognizes that new religious symbols and conceptions accompanied the Indo-Europeans, for whom "the (god of the) sky is supremely father."[31] In his discussion of Greek religion, Eliade mentions that Zeus's dominance is achieved by "appropriating the pre-Hellenic local goddesses, venerated from time immemorial."[32] Despite these points of agreement with the Goddess hypothesis, Eliade's interpretive framework precludes women and Goddesses from playing significant roles in the history of religion.

Eliade defines religion as an apprehension of "the sacred":

> *Through experience of the sacred, the human mind has perceived the difference between what reveals itself as being real, powerful, rich, and meaningful and what lacks these qualities, that is the chaotic and dangerous flux of things, their fortuitous and senseless appearances and disappearances.*[33]

Using this definition, the Goddesses who are associated with the body and changing life, which Eliade calls "the chaotic and dangerous flux of things," cannot be understood as representations of the sacred. In addition, Eliade states that his history of religion will focus on "crises in depth and above all, the creative moments" in which religion is transformed and renewed. Eliade therefore finds the religions of relatively peaceful and stable societies (like the Neolithic) uninteresting. Eliade makes what he calls "later valorizations" of religious ideas and symbolisms one of his criteria of inclusion: Thus religious symbols and ideas that turn up in later patriarchal religions are given more weight than ideas that do not.[34] "Man the hunter" and his creation, "the projectile weapon," provide the archetypal patterns of a male Supreme Being, sacrifice, and blood communion that Eliade finds repeated again and again in the history of religion. This framework shapes the questions Eliade asks, the data he chooses to look at, and the interpretations he makes; in it there is no real place for women and Goddesses.

In his consideration of Paleolithic religion, Eliade focuses on man the hunter, endowing humans' "decision to kill in order to live" with the highest significance:

> *In short, the hominians succeeded in outstripping their ancestors by becoming flesh-eaters. For some two million years, the Paleoanthropians lived by hunting; fruits, roots, mollusks, and so on, gathered by the women and children, did not suffice to*

insure the survival of the species. Hunting determined the division of labor in ac-cordance with sex, thus reinforcing "hominization", for among the carnivora, and in the entire animal world, no such difference exists.[35]

By alleging that meat eating is decisive to human survival and by emphasiz-ing the "creative invention" of the projectile weapon, Eliade values the con-tributions of man the hunter, while ignoring the contributions of woman the gatherer. Moreover, Eliade asserts that a hierarchal ordering of gender roles is typical of the earliest human societies and of human nature itself.

According to Eliade, the "projectile weapon" is an archetypal religious symbol because "it is, above all, mastery over distance, gained by the projec-tile weapon, which gave rise to countless beliefs, myths, and legends."[36] Eli-ade's framework prevents him from seeing that tools for the preparation and preservation of food and clothing may have been equally important in human evolution and endowed with equally significant sacrality, as later religious symbols such as the ritual dressing of statues, the weaving of fate, the com-munal or communion meal, and the magic cauldron suggest.

Considering the rituals of the hunters, Eliade hypothesizes on the basis of very little concrete evidence that "divinities of the type Supreme Being—Lord of the Wild Beasts" as well as animal spirits were probably worshiped in the Paleolithic era. But when discussing what he calls "feminine representations in the last Ice Age," he does not use the words *Supreme Being, Lady of the Wild Beasts,* or *Goddess.* Instead he tells us:

It is impossible to determine the religious function of these figurines. Pre-sumably they in some sort represent feminine sacrality and hence the magico-religious powers of the goddesses [note lower case]. The "mystery" constituted by woman's particular mode of existence has played an important part in numer-ous religions both primitive and historical. [emphasis added].[37]

Eliade leaves the reader with the impression that aside from a few indeci-pherable "figurines," Paleolithic religion was a male affair, an interaction be-tween (male) hunters and a (male) Lord of the Wild Beasts. Since Eliade is not at all tentative in discussing the religious symbolism associated with hunting, we must ask why he suddenly becomes circumspect when confronted with images that suggest a female Supreme Being.

Since images associated with the female body symbolize the "dangerous and chaotic flux of things" that Eliade defines as antithetical to the sacred, it is not surprising that he cannot imagine that women or female symbolism were central in Paleolithic religion, at the time of origins. In contrast, Eliade finds the alleged symbols of hunting religion, including a male Supreme Being, sacrificial death, and blood communion, validated in later patriarchal religions, most especially in Christianity.[38]

Despite his statement that in the Neolithic, "women and feminine sacrality are raised to the first rank," Eliade pays relatively little attention to women's religious roles and to female images in his discussion of Neolithic religion. At one point, he notes that in the Neolithic, "feminine sexuality becomes inseparable from the miraculous enigma of creation," but even there he does not speak of a female Supreme Being or Creatress.[39]

Eliade ignores women and Goddesses in his depiction of Neolithic religion as "cosmic religion." He speaks of the World Tree as a central symbol of cosmic religion, without speculating on its relation to Goddess imagery, and of the sacralization of space and dwellings, without mentioning that in matrilocal societies, dwellings would have been passed through the motherline and that some of the earliest religious structures seem to be modeled on the body of the Goddess.[40] When he mentions the "feminine statuettes" of the Neolithic period, he designates them as part of a "fertility cult," not as central images of cosmic religion.[41]

Eliade concludes that the "archaeological documents" of "Neolithic religion run the risk of appearing simplistic and monotonous,"[42] perhaps because they do not validate his assumptions about the nature of religion. If he had looked more closely at Neolithic religion and its images, he would have been forced to revise the interpretive framework that tells him that religion is about transcending the "dangerous flux of things."

Eliade finds the religion of the Iron Age more interesting. He notes that with the rise of the miner and the smith, "the artisan takes the place of Mother Earth in order to hasten and perfect the 'growth' of the ores. The furnaces are in some sort a new, artificial womb, in which the ore completes its gestation."[43] Given his stated aversion to the "chaotic and dangerous flux of things," it is not surprising that Eliade would prefer an artificial to a physical womb, and the religious symbol of the smith who improves on nature over the Goddess who is identified with nature.

In his discussion of the transformation of hunters into warriors, Eliade depicts brutal conquest without a hint of irony or criticism:

The invasions of the Indo-Europeans and the Turko-Mongols will be undertaken under the sign of the supreme hunter, the carnivore. The members of the Indo-European confraternities (Männerbünde) and the nomadic horseman of Central Asia behaved toward the sedentary populations that they attacked like carnivores

*hunting, strangling, and devouring the herbivores of the steppe or the farmers'
cattle. . . .*

*The pursuit and killing of the wild animal becomes the mythical mode for the
conquest of a territory (Landnáma) or the founding of a state.*[44]

Eliade appears to admire the killing that produces male bonding, no matter
what form it takes.

Eliade's treatment of Greek religion begins with a consideration of the "irruption of the Indo-Europeans into history" in a chapter on the Vedic Gods.
His survey assumes the conquest of the inhabitants of the land and islands
now called Greece by the Indo-Europeans. He recognizes that the patriarchal
mythologies and symbolisms of Greek religion were the product of violence.
For example, he states that Delphi was a "venerable oracular site, where from
ancient times the sacrality and the powers of Mother Earth were mani-
fested."[45] And he comments that the stories of Apollo's conquest of Delphi
are an "aggressive mythology" that "is the history of his replacing, more or
less brutally, many pre-Hellenic local divinities, a process that is characteristic of Greek religion as a whole."[46]

Despite his recognition of its more ancient sources, Eliade treats Greek religion as a finished product, relying almost exclusively on androcentric texts,
such as Homer, Hesiod, and the tragedians, written hundreds of years after
the entrance of the Indo-Europeans into Greece. He pays relatively little attention to archaeological records, such as wall and vase paintings, sculptures,
temples, votive offerings, and inscriptions. Jane Harrison showed that the
artistic record demonstrates the lingering presence of the power of the Goddesses,[47] but Eliade ignores her work. If he had taken a historical approach to
Greek religion, Eliade might have begun, as art historian Vincent Scully does,
with a discussion of the pre-Indo-European origins of the Greek Goddesses.[48]
Instead, Eliade inserts brief discussions of four of the Greek Goddesses in between the Gods and the heroes, while two others are the subject of his final
chapter.

Eliade opens his discussion of Greek religion with a lengthy summary of
Hesiod's version of creation that uncritically accepts Hesiod's account of the
"triumph and sovereignty of Zeus."[49] He restates Hesiod's myth that the first
humans in the so-called age of gold were exclusively men. He comments that
the myth of the "'perfection of beginnings' and of primordial bliss, both lost
as the result of an accident or 'sin,' is comparatively widespread."[50] Eliade does
not find the absence of women from this primordial scene scandalous, nor
does he comment on Hesiod's misogyny.

When discussing Zeus's "appropriation of the pre-Hellenic local God-desses," Eliade speaks of "a series of marriages," "numerous liaisons," "hi-erogamies," and "erotic adventures." He does not mention that many of Zeus's "sacred" "marriages" were rapes.[51] Later Eliade states that in Greek religion,

> man [sic] ended by realizing the perfection and, consequently the sacrality of the human condition. In other words, he rediscovered and brought to full the religious sense of the "joy of life," the sacramental value of erotic experience and the beauty of the human body.[52]

Here Eliade's genderized language conveys an unintended irony. From the perspective of the conquering and ruling males, Eliade's statement may have seemed valid. But it could not have been true for those who were conquered, enslaved, and raped.

Eliade's interpretations of the Greek Gods focuses on their "valorizations" of themes brought out in his discussions of Paleolithic and Iron Age religion. Discussing Apollo and the "symbolism of the bow," Eliade elaborates his conception of the symbolism of the projectile weapon:

> Thanks to Apollo, the symbolism of the bow and of archery reveals other spiritual situations: mastery over distance (and hence detachment from the "immediate," from the viscosity of the concrete), the calm and serenity implied by every effort of intellectual concentration.[53]

Here we see the connection between Eliade's "valorization" of the symbolism of the projectile weapon "above all" and his conception of religion as providing release from the "chaotic and dangerous flux of things." We can also see in Apollo's bow the "valorization" of the calm and serene "intellectual concentration" of the twentieth-century scholar, who while writing about his conceptions of religion attempts to detach himself from the "'immediate,' from the viscosity of the concrete," presenting the history of religion as if it were a question of the progression of ideas, rather than as (at least in part) an aspect of the struggles of certain groups for dominance over others.

Careful and systematic analysis of Eliade's work has revealed that it is shaped throughout by androcentric assumptions and passions. Eliade's framework of interpretation is rooted in his theory that religion is about transcendence and shaped by his conviction that religions repeat the symbolic patterns associated with man the hunter, his projectile weapon, and a male Supreme Being. Given these presuppositions, it is no wonder that women and Goddesses are relegated to the background. Once these biases are unmasked, we can never again read Eliade's work, or others like it, as a complete, comprehensive, or "objective" telling of the history of religion.

Recognizing that the work of a man whose works are so widely recognized as great could be so thoroughly biased when it comes to understanding Goddess history should incline us to be suspicious of the work of other major figures as well. Critiques of other seminal thinkers in the fields of religion, archaeology, classics, and ancient history are likely to reveal similar biases at work in their theories, interpretive frameworks, and conclusions.

The Unconscious Goddess

Because traditional scholarship in classics and religion provides so little guidance in uncovering the history of the Goddess, many have turned to the archetypal theories of Jungians Erich Neumann and Joseph Campbell and poet and mythographer Robert Graves, who at least devote considerable attention to the Goddesses. Unfortunately, the work of each of these men is also deeply flawed, and the cause of historical accuracy is not served when their work is quoted uncritically.

Following his teacher, the archetypal psychologist Carl Jung,[54] Erich Neumann believed that human life is best served by a conjunction of "masculine" and "feminine" principles. For Neumann, as for Jung, the so-called masculine represents consciousness, rationality, and the "light" of the ego, while the so-called feminine represents the unconscious, the irrational, a "dark" and primitive stage of (pre)consciousness where the ego has not yet emerged from the group.[55] Jung believed that the healthy individual must integrate "masculine" and "feminine" aspects. The ego is sterile unless animated by the unconscious; the unconscious is a fertile source, but it remains irrational and dangerous unless it is brought under the control of the conscious mind or ego. Neumann agreed with Jung that modern western society had veered too far in the direction of the so-called masculine and needed an infusion of the so-called feminine for balance. This intuition gave rise to his classic work, *The Great Mother*.[56] The many pictures in this book were an important source for the emerging Goddess movement.

Like Jung, Neumann identified the feminine and thus the images of the Goddesses with the unconscious mind and with a stage of consciousness where the ego had not yet emerged. Since the powers of the Goddess rise up from the uncontrolled and uncontrollable unconscious, the Goddess is a dangerous figure whose nurturing power may at any time erupt into destruction. Viewing the Goddesses through the lens of dualistic thinking, Neumann distorts the cyclic image of the Goddess as Birth, Death, and Regeneration by polarizing it into the archetype of the Great and Terrible Mother. Neumann argues in *The Origin and History of Consciousness* that it was necessary for the age of the Goddess to come to an end so that the ego and the light of rationality could emerge from the chaos and darkness of the unconscious.[57] In his and other work influenced by Jung, the destruction of Neolithic cultures by Indo-European warriors is viewed as necessary for "civilization" to "advance."

Jungian mythologist Joseph Campbell's *The Hero with a Thousand Faces*, his three-volume history of myth and religion *The Masks of God*, and his posthumous testament *The Hero's Journey* are shaped by similar Jungian theories that provide a limited and ultimately disparaging view of the history of the Goddesses.[58] Here is a characteristic statement:

> *Woman in the picture language of mythology, represents the totality of what can be known. The hero is the one who comes to know. As he progresses in the slow initiation which is life, the form of the goddess undergoes for him a series of transformations.*[59]

For Campbell, the Goddess (and woman) are the unconscious material background for the spiritual quest of the male hero, who gradually comes to know what will always remain unknown (unconscious) for her. Toward the end of his life, Campbell proudly recalled his answer to a female student who found his theories limiting: "The woman's the mother of the hero; she's the goal of the hero's achieving. . . . What more do you want?"[60] It is unlikely that Campbell's appreciation of the work of Marija Gimbutas, expressed shortly before his death, would have led to a reformulation of his basic ideas.[61]

Robert Graves was also influenced by Jungian theories. In his classic work, *The White Goddess*, he wrote that he viewed the Goddess as the inspiration of poetry.[62] Not surprisingly, he understood the poet as the masculine ego fertilized by the mysterious feminine. Graves provides his own version of the Goddess as Terrible Mother when he depicts Goddess religion as inevitably involving the sacrifice of the Son to the Mother Goddess. Since this practice does not seem to be widespread in Goddess religion, one wonders about the source of Graves's theory. Could it be that the poet believed he suffered for his dedication to his craft and fancied himself as sacrificed on the altar of his muse? Graves's predilections for masochistic submission to dominant females shed further light on this question.[63]

The work of Jung, Neumann, Campbell, and Graves on the Goddesses must be approached with great caution. They have uncovered important information and brought it to a wide audience. But they have each distorted the history of the Goddess through the imposition of theories that see the Goddess as symbolic of the unconscious feminine. In this view, there could never have been a "civilization" of the Goddess because civilization is considered a product of the emergence of "man" into the "light" of "rationality" and "consciousness." Nor could there ever have been a "conscious" Goddess because consciousness is identified as the realm of the masculine ego. Women, as representatives of the unconscious feminine, cannot be expected to play anything but supportive and animating roles in the male project of culture. Unfortunately, such views have been unintentionally repeated in various ways in some recent work by women on the Goddesses. This in turn has led critics to view the Goddess movement as restricting women to stereotyped roles.

Shifting Focus

Because theories that make it difficult to understand the history of the Goddesses are so widely and deeply held, it should not surprise us that the scholarly establishment has not rushed to embrace the Goddess hypothesis. To do so would require more than the concession of a few (trivial and unimportant) facts and hypotheses that leave overall theories and frameworks of interpretation intact. To recognize the roles of women and the importance of the symbol of the Goddess at the time of religious origins requires the development of new frameworks of interpretation: new theories of the nature and origins of religion, and new methodologies for studying them. Such theories and methods are being developed by scholars like Marija Gimbutas and others. But we should not expect that new theories and methods will be readily accepted. We are talking about a revolution in consciousness, a paradigm shift, the giving up of powerful, pervasive, and long-lasting moods and motivations. We can only hope that this shift will occur. Until then, we can expect that feminist work on women and religion and the Goddess will continue to be characterized as nothing more than "a remarkable fable."

❦ 5 ❦

The Meaning
of the Goddess

Once we have a sense of who the Goddess was in the past, we can begin to think about what she means today. It is becoming clear that the Goddess calls us to transform powerful, pervasive, and long-lasting images and ideas about God. We have been taught that God is male, that he transcends the earth and the body, and that he is the light shining in the chaotic darkness of the natural world. Yet the Goddess is female; the earth, the body, and nature are her image; and the darkness as well as the light are metaphors of her power. We cannot understand the Goddesses unless we question dualistic and hierarchical assumptions about God's relation to the changing world that arose in the wake of the slaying of the Goddesses of earth. Reflecting on the limitations of the God we have known, we can begin to envision more holistic ways of thinking about the Goddess, the earth, and our place in it.

Earth as the Body of Goddess

Images of the earth as body of the Goddess challenge the traditional view that God transcends the earth, the body, and nature. The image of the Goddess as earth also calls into question traditional images of the female: We have been taught that the female body is soft, delicate, and vulnerable. But solidity and strength are portrayed in the earliest images of the Goddesses. (See Figures 1 to 5.) The *Homeric Hymn* "To Earth" reflects this ancient understanding:

The mother of us all
the oldest of all,
hard,
splendid as rock.[1]

The Goddess as earth is the firm foundation of changing life.[2] She is "the stone foundation / rockshelf further forming underneath everything that grows."[3] A contemporary Goddess chant expresses this sense of vital power: "You can't kill the spirit, She is like a mountain. Old and strong, She goes on and on."[4]

When we speak of the earth as the body of the Goddess, particular images are called to mind: The earth is not an abstraction, but the place where we live. In California, the Goddess is the tallest redwood and the tiniest hummingbird. In New England, she is intrepid crocuses and exuberant forsythia, sweetly scented lilacs and lacy dogwoods. In the American midwest, she is wide open spaces and amber waves of grain. In Hawaii, she is Pele, the volcano. In Denmark and Ireland, she is holy wells. Hera is the Goddess of the Argive plain, while Aphrodite came ashore in Cyprus or in Kythera. So, too, the Virgin Mary and the saints are worshiped at the tops of nearby hills and mountains, in the shelter of safe harbors, in places where water bubbles up from beneath the earth.

But while we know the earth in particular places, the image of the whole earth as the body of the Goddess must keep us from identifying the Goddess primarily or exclusively with any particular part of the earth or with ethnic, cultural, racial, or national interests. It is important for Germans to learn about Goddess traditions in Germany, English about Goddess traditions in England, while at the same time remembering that the Goddess is equally present in places far away as in those close to home.[5]

The image of the earth as the body of Goddess provides support for an ecological theology. "What if we dared," Christian theologian Sallie McFague writes, "to think of our planet and indeed the entire universe as the body of God?"[6] Such a metaphor would inspire us to "love and honor the body, our own bodies, and the bodies of all other life-forms on the planet."[7] Such an image would would challenge the traditional view that God is in heaven and we are going there when we die, and thus we do not have to worry too much about destroying the earth body. However, McFague limits the iconoclastic power of the image of earth as the body of God when she interprets it through the Christian doctrine of the incarnation and the image of the body of Christ.[8] Not insisting that the earth is (also) the body of Goddess, she leaves us free to assume (as our culture has taught us to do) that "the body of God" is somehow superior to female bodies.

When the earth is the body of Goddess, the radical implications of the image are more fully realized. The female body and the earth, which have been devalued and dominated together, are resacralized. Our understanding of divine power is transformed as it is clearly recognized as present within the finite and changing world. The image of earth as the body of the Goddess can inspire us to repair the damage that has been done to the earth, to women, and to other beings in dominator cultures.

Though McFague asked if we could think "of our planet and indeed the entire universe as the body of God," it is far more common to imagine the earth rather than the universe as the body of Goddess. But if the earth is the body of Goddess, then does every planet have its own deity? Is there another deity whose body is the universe as a whole? If not, then why don't we refer to the universe rather than the earth as the body of Goddess?[9]

It seems logical to *acknowledge* that the whole universe is the body of Goddess. Many ancient and contemporary worshipers of the Goddess have viewed the starry heavens, the sun, the moon, and the planets as well as the earth as the body of the Goddess. And surely this is true. But in contemplating the universe as a whole, there is a danger of abstracting ourselves from the concrete immediacy of our lives on this earth. Thus it seems practical to continue to *speak* most frequently of the earth (or the world) as the body of Goddess to keep our focus on the ground beneath our feet and the beings with whom we share this planet.

The Female Body and the Nurturing of Life

In the language of the Goddess, the female body is an important metaphor for the creative powers of the earth body. But though the Goddess is popularly viewed as Mother Earth or Mother Nature, the Goddess as pregnant or holding a human child is not the only or even the most common image in ancient traditions. Marija Gimbutas insisted that the Goddess of Old Europe was not primarily the Earth Mother.[10] Of the three aspects of the Goddess as Giver, Taker, and Renewer of Life, only the first refers to the Goddess as Mother. Moreover, the Goddess as Giver of Life is more accurately called Creatress, since she gives birth to plants and animals as well as human children. The connection of creation with mothering is "not so much the power to give birth . . . but the power to make, to create, to transform."[11]

Still, there is no denying that in the language of the Goddess, the power of women and female animals and earth itself to give birth is celebrated. And if Goddesses are not always portrayed as pregnant or holding children, their nakedness and the emphasis on their breasts, buttocks, and female triangles calls attention to the life-giving powers of the female body. For many women and men, celebration of the female body and the nurturing of life in the language of the Goddess is attractive because it reverses thousands of years of devaluation.

But some feminist thinkers argue that if our theories or our symbols acknowledge any "essential" differences between women and men (universal differences or differences rooted in biology), this will inevitably be used (as in the past) to define women as subordinate to men. "Anti-essentialist" thinkers label theories that admit meaningful biological differences between women and men "essentialist." While not denying that women give birth and men do not, they state that this biological fact plays a minor role compared to the social construction of gender and parenting roles. They fear that the emphasis on women's biology in Goddess symbolism will inevitably be turned against women.[12]

Goddess priestess Zsuzsanna Budapest frequently encounters this argument. Her response is concise:

People come to me and say, "Z., how can you allow biology to become destiny again. You know what they did with that before." "I'm sorry," I reply, "we do give birth, we do issue forth people, just as the Goddess issues forth the universe. . . . It is not something I am going to keep quiet about. It is what women do, we make people."[13]

While I do not want to confine women to traditional roles, I agree with Budapest that it will not help women to pretend that giving birth and nurturing children are not important in our lives.

I suspect that the anti-essentialist view is not fully embodied, that it implicitly accepts the dominant western view that the self is located in the mind, rather than in the body-mind continuum. Of course women's minds are as good as men's. But if our bodies are ourselves,[14] then women's location in female bodies must shape the way we experience the world. To keep quiet about the fact that women give birth and nurture children is to deny the physical realities of most women's lives in every existing culture in the world.

At the very least, women who bear children (the vast majority of women) share their bodies with the growing child for nine months. If they nurse, women develop a special relationship with their infants and with their own bodies that cannot fully be shared by the father or other adults. In addition (whether we like it or not), women around the world care for children. According to anthropologist Judith Brown, "nowhere in the world is the rearing of children primarily the responsibility of men."[15] Many feminists have argued that women's equality depends on men taking half the responsibility for the rearing of children. I believe that this is a desirable goal, not only because it would free women to participate more fully in other aspects of life, but also because deep involvement in caring for children on a daily basis would teach men (as it has taught women) the value of nurturing life. Yet feminist efforts of the last quarter of the twentieth century have not succeeded in taking child care out of the hands of women. Women who work outside the home and have children face what is called the "double day of work": a full day on the job, and another in the home. Women like myself, who have not given birth to children, have usually taken major responsibility for the care of siblings, nieces and nephews, stepchildren, or the children of friends at some point in their lives. Even if feminists were to succeed in getting men to take more responsibility for nurturing children, women would still devote a great deal of their time to pregnancy and child care. Wouldn't we be better off if our symbols and theories acknowledged the creative powers inherent in the female body and in the nurturing of life?

So-called anti-essentialists rightly point out that male theorists have used so-called biological "facts," many of them now proved to be false, to deny women's full humanity and equality with men. But in limiting their critique to theories they label essentialist, they fail to recognize that all theories can be used against women. In modern societies, for example, the (anti-essentialist) theory that all workers are the same has caused those workers who are also primarily responsible for children (usually women) to suffer disadvantages in the workplace.

Women must participate equally in the creation of symbols and theories. If theories are defined exclusively by dominant men, they will probably be used to women's disadvantage. But if the power of naming is shared by women and men, then biological or other differences between women and men do not have to be interpreted to define one sex as subordinate to the other. Indeed, anthropologists are coming to the conclusion that in many traditional cultures, sex roles are distinguished without giving one sex control over the other.[16] The conjunction of the rebirth of the Goddess with the rebirth of the women's movement means that both the Goddess and motherhood take on different meanings than those presented in male theories.

The celebration of the female body, female sexuality, giving birth, and nurturing in a Goddess religion created by women (or created equally by women and men) will not magically bring equality to women as mothers in modern societies. But if mothers were truly valued, it is unlikely that women and our dependent children would be the poorest of the poor the world around.

The Male Body

Does identification of the images of the Goddesses with the female body imply that men are not holy or that they cannot participate as fully as women in the mysteries of life? Is Goddess religion as unfair to men as God religion has been to women? In thinking about these questions, it is important to bear in mind that all images of the Goddess are metaphor. As Starhawk says, "the Goddess is not 'she' or 'he'—or she is both—but we call her 'she' because to name is not to limit or describe but to invoke."[17] But this is a familiar argument, employed by religious traditionalists to justify male images of God. Knowing the harm male images of God have done, why insist on female metaphors? We must remember that the Goddess is emerging at a time when women, women's bodies, and nature have been devalued and violated for centuries. In this context, the metaphor of the Goddess has the power to shatter long-standing cultural attitudes and prejudices about women and nature. The Goddess as metaphor brings healing to our historical situation.

It is true that the reemerging Goddess has been a more powerful symbol for women than for men. But increasing numbers of men are recognizing her power to bring healing in their lives. Many men have never felt comfortable with our culture's image of male heroes as warriors, conquerors of women and nature. Though some religions and philosophies have attempted to deny man's connection to woman and nature, this relationship can never be fully forgotten. The male body, too, has its mysteries of generation and regeneration that have been explicitly celebrated in many religions. The Goddess can help bring men back in touch with their physicality, reminding them of their participation in the rhythms of life, death, and rebirth within nature. The images of the Goddess can help men learn to value their own nurturing power.

As the Goddess continues to emerge in our times, I believe that her images will become more varied and will be supplemented by new images of God as male. Men are experimenting with reclaiming images that connect men to nature, such as St. Francis of Assisi,[18] the Green Man,[19] the Horned God,[20] the Navajo Twins, several of the Greek Gods and heroes,[21] and Iron John.[22] Some of these images are genuinely healing, while others seem to reiterate patriarchy's antipathy to the female.

Womanist midwife and healer Arisika Razak proposes that the new images of masculinity we need will be created not by wild men who separate from women, but by men who participate in childbirth and affirm themselves as nurturers of life:

Nurturing is not a genetically feminine attribute. Tears and laughter are not the province of women only. The last time I looked, men had tear ducts. They had arms

for holding babies. They cared about their children. And they cried at births. . . .
Let the shared experience of childbirth reclaim the human soul.[23]

As men become more involved in childbirth and child care, new images of sacred nurturing fathers can emerge to complement images of birth-giving Goddesses.

Creating or discovering new images of male sacrality is more difficult than might first be imagined because most of the male images we know are of dominant and dominating male power. It is logical to assume that new imagery of the earth as the body of the deity would celebrate phalluses as well as wombs and fatherhood as well as motherhood. It is harder to imagine this in practice. In our world, too many have experienced fathers as dominating others and the phallus as an instrument of rape. It seems reasonable to expect that the process of the creation of new images of the male body and men's experience as nurturers will take time. New images can only emerge as men and culture change.

Light and Darkness

The images of the Goddesses also call us to transform deeply held cultural understandings of light and darkness. When the black woman in Ntozake Shange's play sang, "i found god in myself / and i loved her / i love her fiercely," she was not only saying that God is female, but also that she is black. When a white woman hears Shange's words, she may not hear them fully. She may find "god in herself" as a white woman, not understanding that for a black woman, the whiteness of God can be every bit as offensive as his maleness. As many black women have said, the image of a "white" Goddess sculpted of white marble in classical Greek statues is not necessarily liberating for black women.

According to womanist theologian Delores Williams, one of the manifestations of racism is a devaluation of blackness:

In North America, popular culture, religion, science, and politics have worked together to assign permanent negative value to the color black. . . . In this kind of consciousness, nothing black can be violated, because illegality and disaster are associated with blackness.[24]

Among the examples Williams cites are blackmail, black market, Black Monday (the day the New York stock market fell in 1929), the association of white light with heaven, blackness with hell, and naming the devil as the Black One.

To this list we might add the depiction of Africa as the dark continent, the psychological understanding that negative qualities represent our dark side, the notion that evil monsters come out in the night, and the images of salvation as light shining in the darkness, or en-light-enment.

In this context, the work of thealogians of color like Luisah Teish and Gloria Anzaldua who recover and reclaim images of the Goddess as black and brown is crucial.[25] Carol Lee Sanchez urges Goddess feminists to pay more attention to "the many women-centered, equalitarian Native American cultures that are presently 'alive and well' in the continental United States."[26] The work of theorists of culture who document Near Eastern and African influences on many traditions called European is also important.[27]

The negative valuation of blackness and darkness is intensified in modern racist societies, but its origins go back to the Indo-Europeans and their shining Gods of the sky—in other words, to the time of the slaying of the Earth Mother Goddesses. In Old Europe and other traditional cultures, white, the color of bone, was the color of death, whereas black, the color of earth and the womb, signified transformation and rebirth.[28] This symbolism was reversed by the Indo-Europeans. It is likely that the Indo-Europeans used the symbolism of light to justify their conquest of "darker" peoples. And, as we have seen, one of the foundations of dualistic thinking is the notion that the "light" of reason enables "men" to transcend the "dark" earth.

The contrast between Old European thinking and modern western thinking is sharply drawn when we understand the positive valuation of blackness as one of the primary symbols of the Goddess.[29] In attempting to understand the origins of the black Madonnas of France, Emile Saillens stated that a valuing of blackness and night is one of the characteristics of Goddess religion. "The worship of Mother Earth has been universal. She is the night from which arise all living things and into which they vanish. Hence the innumerable black goddesses."[30]

The positive understanding of blackness in Goddess religion is also expressed in the understanding of caves as the womb of the earth. In our culture, caves evoke fear. Thus entering into the darkness of a cave can evoke a profound metaphoric shift. This happened to me when I went alone into the cave at Skoteinó in Crete.[31] As I descended into the darkness, I was afraid, but I remembered that caves have been understood to be the womb of the Goddess. My desire to find her compelled me to continue. After descending three levels into the earth, I eased myself through a narrow passageway, and there was no more light. I extinguished my candle and sat in the silent blackness. Later, I learned to call the Goddess "Skoteiní," which means "Darkness" or the "Dark One." In my prayers I often invoke Skoteiní and Photeiní, "Light" or the "Light One" together. I begin to understand that like night and day, darkness and light are intertwined.

Since that time, my view of the relation of light and dark has changed in ways that I can only begin to articulate. I find myself drawn to the darkness, viewing it as a place of transformation. Going into the dark has become a metaphor for going into the unknown, the unshaped, the unformed. I understand that just as a seed must stay in a dark cool place to sprout, so must I embrace the darkness at the center of myself if I am to find healing, transformation, new life. A few months after my journey into the Skoteinó cave, I was finally able to name and transform the source of what I now see as a lifelong despair. I have begun to let go of the need to know, to be in control. I am learning to trust that I will find the path of my life and that I do not need to know what lies ahead at every turn. This is a profound liberation from ways of thinking deeply ingrained in me by my culture. This new understanding is expressed in a song we sing in the caves on Goddess pilgrimages to Crete. Its words are simply, "Light and darkness, light and darkness, light and darkness." Singing these words again and again has a profound effect on the deep mind.

Transforming the connotations we associate with darkness and blackness is important for all women. In patriarchal cultures, the darkness of the womb is viewed as symbolic of women's irrationality, ignorance, and deceitfulness and is associated more with death than with regeneration.[32] To reclaim the darkness is thus to reclaim the female body.

The Warrior Goddess

In Jungian "archetypal" psychology, in the "history" of religion, and in some feminist thealogies, the warrior Goddess is identified as an aspect of the "Dark" Goddess.[33] Warrior Goddesses such as the Mesopotamian Inanna and Ishtar, the Egyptian Sekhmet, and the Hindu Durga and Kali are invoked as images of the "Dark" Goddess. It is said that these Goddesses allow women to express the full range of our anger at patriarchy,[34] enable us to accept our own death,[35] and may even help us to accept the death of the human species.[36]

But the warrior Goddess is not an eternally occurring image. The Goddess of Old Europe as vulture and owl is Taker of Life, but she is not armed. Images of armed Goddesses reflect the transformation of earlier Goddesses by patriarchal warrior societies. In ancient Mesopotamia, which was ruled by warrior kings, the Goddess was pictured on a seal with her foot on the back of a lion and weapons emerging from her shoulders.[37] This is a very different image from that of the Goddess at Çatal Hüyük, who rested her hands on two leopards as she gave birth. In one case, the Goddess is part of nature; in the other, she "conquers" it.

In a hymn called the "Exaltation of Inanna," the Goddess is portrayed as delighting in the brutalities of warfare:

In the vanguard of the battle,
  everything is beset by you.
My Lady [flying about] on your own wings,
  you feed on [the carnage].
. . .
That you destroy the rebellious land,
  let it be known! . . .
that you devour corpses like a beast,
  let it be known!

. . .
that you achieve victory,
  let it be known![38]

Similarly, the Egyptian Goddess Sekhmet proclaims, "when I slay men, my heart rejoices";[39] the Hindu Durga exults in the slaying of demons; Kali holds a sword, wears a necklace of severed human heads and a skirt of severed human arms, and holds a skull filled with human blood.[40]

The death aspect of the Goddess must be affirmed and is integral to our understanding of the Goddess as Giver, Taker, and Renewer of Life. But I find it contradictory to criticize the warrior aspects of the God we have known as a dominating other and then to affirm the warrior Goddesses. The images of the warrior Goddesses, like the images of the warrior Gods, convey the understanding that the unrestrained taking of life in battle is a fundamental or essential aspect of reality. The bloodthirsty warrior Goddesses legitimate warfare and violence, large-scale blood sacrifice, and a dualistic understanding of good and evil. In the long term, they will not help us transform dominator societies. Moreover, I find it racist to identify the "Dark" Goddess primarily with death and destruction. As we have seen, the Old European understanding is that black is the color of earth, womb, and night, darkness a place of transformation.

Transforming Hierarchical Dualisms

As new images and metaphors of divinity begin to emerge, it becomes clear that we must also reformulate the philosophical and theological understandings of God that are found in the western traditions. The most fundamental of these is the notion that God transcends the changing world. If the earth is the body of the Goddess, then the Goddess is not transcendent of change, for change is the nature of life on earth.

When Mircea Eliade defined the sacred as standing in opposition to what he called "the chaotic and dangerous flux of things," he was not expressing a private or idiosyncratic prejudice. He was restating a widely accepted and largely unquestioned idea about the nature of the divine. This view has been alluded to in previous chapters, but it is useful to examine its source. In the *Symposium*, Plato wrote that the highest good is unchanging:

> *This beauty is first of all eternal; it neither comes into being nor passes away, neither waxes nor wanes. . . . It [is] absolute, existing alone with itself, unique, eternal, and all other beautiful things partaking of it, yet in such a manner that, while they come into being and pass away, it neither undergoes any increase or diminution nor suffers any change.*[41]

In Plato's view, that which is unchanging is far superior to that which changes. Thus for Plato, the physical world is inferior to the nonmaterial world of divine beauty:

> *What may we suppose to be the felicity of the man who sees absolute beauty in its essence, pure and unalloyed, who, instead of beauty tainted by human flesh and colour and a mass of perishable rubbish, is able to apprehend divine beauty where it exists apart and alone?*[42]

The dualistic understanding of perfection expressed by Plato became the model for philosophical and Christian theological understandings of God as a disembodied mind or spirit, totally transcendent of the world, of nature, of change. Woman's body and its changeable nature became the image of all that was imperfect, corrupt, and physical. These conceptions became fixed as the polar opposites of dualistic and hierarchical thinking: the unchanging is valued over the changing; soul or mind over body; spirit over nature; rational over irrational; spiritual over sexual; male over female.

The notion that the Goddess is involved in changing life is reflected in the ancient understanding of the Goddess as Giver, Taker, and Renewer of Life. Thealogian Hallie Iglehart Austen articulates this conception:

> *The unity of birth, growth, death and rebirth . . . are the basis of the Goddess' teachings. They are reflected daily to us in cycles of night and day, waking and sleeping, creating and letting go. Thus the Goddess is she who gives life and, when*

the form is no longer viable, transforms it through death. And then, through the exquisite pleasures of creativity and sexuality, she brings forth new life.[43]

The conception of the Goddess as the source of change in the cycles of birth, death, and regeneration forces us to rethink our notions of divine power.

The images of the Goddesses call us to reject the all-too-familiar hierarchical dualisms that shape our understanding not only of God, but of ourselves and our world. Because dualistic habits of thinking are so deeply ingrained, it is tempting simply to turn them upside down: to affirm nature, body, sexuality, the nonrational, and the female and to deny or devalue spirit, mind, rationality, and the male. While it can be radicalizing to think this way for a period of time, dualistic habits of thought are not thereby transcended.

To transform the way we think, we must find alternatives to dualistic and hierarchical habits of thought. Philosopher and thealogian Mara Keller proposes three foundations on which a nondualistic or holistic philosophy can be built. The first is the intuition of the unity of being and the interdependence of life; the second is recognition of the tendency of the human mind to think in pairs or dualities that are "interactive and interdependent" and "together are part of a larger whole"; and the third is appreciation of "endless plurality [or] infinite diversity, . . . [which is itself] part of a larger whole."[44] I would add that thinking in dualities is a simplification of an ultimately unified and plural reality. Simplified thinking can be useful in some contexts but deceptive and dangerous in others.

In holistic and embodied thinking, spirit and nature, mind and body, rationality and nonrationality, are not distinct entities or absolute categories that stand in hierarchical opposition to each other. They are not even poles within a horizontal continuum because this would imply that the poles—e.g., "pure mind," "pure spirit," "pure rationality," and their antitheses—exist. Spirit and nature, mind and body, rationality and irrationality, are artificial distinctions we have created: It is more accurate to say that these are different ways of looking at the same reality.

When nature is defined as antithetical to spirit, the hidden assumption is that there can be no meaning in a life that involves change and ends in death. But in holistic thinking, spirit and meaning are found within nature. Traditional scientists operating within a dualistic framework have argued that because our mental and psychological processes have physical correlates, human beings are nothing more than a series of chemical reactions. But if we think holistically, we can accept the traditional scientific view as evidence of our embodiment, while recognizing that it does not account for our sense that we really do think and make decisions. Neuroscientist Candace Pert expresses a more holistic view of the relation of mind and body when she writes, "The mind is some kind of enlivening energy . . . throughout the brain and body that enables the cells to talk to each other, and the outside world to talk to the whole organism."[45] Similarly, it is only from the standpoint of a narrowly defined rationality that other modes of thinking and feeling appear irrational. The insights that come from what poet Audre Lorde calls our "deepest non-rational knowledge" are not irrational if by this is meant chaotic, confused, or meaningless. Once we become familiar with our deep feelings, we learn that they have their own kinds of patterns and logic, and they enter into the larger meaning systems we construct.

As we attempt to rename the world, we must be careful about the language we choose. Dualistic and hierarchical assumptions have shaped the conclusions of traditional theologies as well as the ways questions are posed. As we begin to articulate a thealogy of the Goddess, we must find new ways of thinking. The binary oppositions of traditional theology, including transcendence-immanence, theism-pantheism, and monotheism-polytheism, do not accurately describe the meaning of the Goddess.

Transcendence-Immanence and Theism-Pantheism

In the western traditions, thinking about God is very much bound up with the dualistic categories of transcendence and immanence. In philosophical terms, *transcendent* means "beyond," "surpassing," or "supreme," whereas *immanent* means "existing within." In traditional theologies, God's transcendence means that God is beyond, surpassing, or dominant over nature and human nature. This viewpoint has been called *theism*. God's immanence means that what has been called "God" is found (entirely or exclusively) within nature and human nature. This understanding has been called *pantheism*, meaning all is God, or *humanism*, meaning "man" is the measure of all things.[46]

In theistic theological traditions, God's transcendence is reflected in the notion that God as Creator and Lord of nature is not in any way subject to or dependent upon nature's laws, and this in turn is said to guarantee that God is free. In their most radical forms, theologies of God's transcendence state that God is "Wholly Other," not in any way "like" nature or "like" human nature. The root of this idea is, of course, Plato's notion that absolute beauty exists "apart and alone," untainted by "a mass of perishable rubbish."

In the traditional theistic understanding, God's qualities of being all-powerful, all-knowing, all-good, and all-just are said to define the mode of his transcendence that distinguishes him absolutely from nature and humanity, from all that is finite and limited. Traditional theism defines God's power as an omnipotence that stands totally outside the laws of nature and morality and above or beyond history. It is asserted that God can do whatever he wants, but that since God is all-good and all-just, he never chooses to do evil. Further, it is said that God is all-knowing, or omniscient, that he knows everything that will happen before it happens, and that he knows the consequences of everything he permits to happen. If he permits earthquakes, volcanoes, hurricanes, cancer, AIDS, war, and genocide, it is because somehow these things are part of his larger will and purpose. Philosophical conceptions of God's power as absolute hierarchical transcendence justify and are justified by biblical images of God as a masculine dominant other: King, Lord, Ruler, Warrior, and even Creator, Father, and Husband when understood as patriarchal lawgivers and authority figures.

Both Christian and Jewish traditions also affirm God's immanence, though usually subordinating it to God's transcendence. Theories of God's immanence state that because God is the Creator of nature, God's purposes are reflected in natural processes. Roman Catholic natural law theology rests on the premise that careful study of nature, including human nature, reveals the Creator's purposes and intentions. Theologian Matthew Fox elevates this school of thought in his reformulation of Christian tradition as Creation Spirituality.[47] Process theology also emphasizes God's immanence and connection with the world.[48] In Jewish tradition God's relation to nature is eloquently expressed in the theology of Martin Buber.[49] Feminist theologian Rosemary Radford Ruether argues that traditional theologies stressing God's transcendence have been harmful to both women and nature. Her ecofeminist Christian theology attempts to redress this balance, as does Lynn Gottlieb's feminist vision of Jewish renewal.[50]

However, Christian natural law theology traditionally asserts that because of sin, both nature and human nature have become corrupted, so that knowledge gained through observation of nature must be "completed" and "corrected" by revelation. And Jewish tradition states that the law was given to create "a fence" around nature, so that we can be taught to control our natural "impulses." Jewish and Christian theologies that emphasize God's relation to nature have been questioned by traditional authorities.[51]

Goddess thealogians, not surprisingly, have rejected traditional notions of divine transcendence along with the masculine dominator imagery that helps to define it. Nelle Morton, for example, states,

When I speak of Goddess as metaphoric image I am in no way referring to an entity "out there" who appears miraculously as a fairy godmother and turns the pumpkin into a carriage. . . . In the sense that I am woman I see the Goddess in my-

self, but I need something tangible, a concrete image or a concrete event to capture my full attention and draw me into the metaphoric process.[52]

The entity "out there" that Morton rejects is defined in terms of the traditional polarity between immanence and transcendence. For Morton, the Goddess seems to be a transitional figure who ushers in immanence: "Since the Goddess works herself out of the picture, we are better able to come into our full and whole inheritance that would make us one in our bodies, minds, and spirits."[53] The image of the Goddess is the catalyst that enables women to clear away the false consciousness of self-hatred, dependence, and dualistic thinking created by patriarchal religion. Once this is accomplished, the image of the Goddess is no longer necessary.

Starhawk explicitly names the Goddess's power as immanence:

Earth-based spirituality is rooted in three basic concepts that I call immanence, interconnectedness, and community. The first—immanence—names our primary understanding that the Earth, Goddess, God—whatever you call it—is not found outside the world somewhere—it's in the world: it is the world, and it is us.[54]

In another place she writes, "The Goddess, the Gods are our [human] potential."[55] Understanding of the Goddess as immanent is appealing because it sharply distinguishes the Goddess from traditional theism's notions of God as transcendent. In answer to the question, "Is the Goddess simply another name for the God we have known?" Starhawk responds with a resounding "No!"

But when the Goddess's power is defined as immanence, other questions arise. If the Goddess is found in nature, is she simply an image for the sum total of natural processes? If the Goddess is found in the deepest self, is She simply an image for the deepest self? Is our understanding of the Goddess thus pantheistic, affirming that all is Goddess? Or humanistic, affirming that all is in us? Is it being denied that the Goddess is in some sense a personality who cares about the world? The language of immanence would seem to suggest that the answer to these questions is yes.

If this is the case, Morton may be right that the Goddess will "work herself out of the picture" once the metaphoric work of shattering false understandings is completed. Alternatively, it might be asserted that symbolic or mythic personal language about divinity fulfills a function in human consciousness that we will not outgrow. Even though there really isn't a Goddess who will listen to our prayers and hymns, it is important for us to speak as if there were. This may be Starhawk's position, though she never fully clarifies this point.[56]

While I find the philosophical notions of immanence and pantheism attractive, in the end they fail to do justice to my experience of the Goddess. Like Starhawk and Morton, I find the Goddess "in" nature and "in" myself. I experience the Goddess by fully entering into relationship with a particular tree, a mountain, or another person, not by attempting to separate myself from other people or other beings.

Yet, for me, the Goddess is also a personal presence, a power that I invoke in prayer and ritual. When I speak the name of the Goddess, I believe I come into a relationship with a power who cares about my life and the fate of the world. The more I sing to the Goddess, pray to her, and invoke her name in my daily life, the more certain this conviction becomes. I could attribute this feeling to suggestion and interpret the voice that speaks in me and the power that acts in synchronous events that happen to me simply as projections of my own experience and deepest self. But it makes more sense to me to understand the Goddess as a kind of a person, fully embodied in the world, with whom I am in relation. For me, the Goddess has not by any means "worked herself out of the picture." Quite the contrary, she has become a more and more living presence in my life.

Pan-en-theism and the Power of the Goddess

If the Goddess is more than immanent, then is she like the transcendent God of theism after all? Does this make her a fairy Godmother with the power to turn pumpkins into carriages? Or in a more serious vein, able to end the threat of nuclear war if she wishes? The answer to these questions is no. The terms immanence-transcendence and theism-pantheism have been given meaning within dualistic and hierarchical philosophical and theological frameworks. Thus it is not surprising to find that neither term in the polar opposition is adequate for defining the nature of divine power in Goddess spirituality.

Process theology provides a way out of the impasse created by understandings rooted in classical dualism.[57] Process theology's notion of "pan-en-theism" (all is *in* God) provides a way of understanding God that moves beyond the polarities of immanence and transcendence, pan-theism (all is God) and theism (God is above or beyond all). Process theology finds the notions of God's transcendence expressed in traditional theism morally and spiritually reprehensible, as Goddess feminists do. Process theology's God is not omniscient or omnipotent and, most important, not immutable and impassive, not removed from the world. In process theology, God is fully immanent within the world and within us. For process theology, God as the ground of all being and the earth as the body of God are appropriate metaphors.

But for process theology, God is transcendent as well as immanent because God is "more" than the sum total of all the discrete beings in the world. Just as an organism is more than a collection of cells, just as the mind is more than a collection of chemical reactions, "God" is, so to speak, the "organism" that unites the body of the world or, in more traditional terms, the "mind" or "soul" of the world body. But these metaphors of cell and organism, mind or soul and body, are understood nondualistically. Just as our minds are not separable from our bodies, so, too, God's mind or soul is not separable from the body of the world. Rather "God's body" and "God's mind or soul" are two different ways of looking at a single unified reality. Modifiying the words of Candace Pert quoted earlier, we might say that the mind of the Goddess is an enlivening energy throughout the world body that enables everything from cells to plants to animals to communicate with each other, and individuals to talk to the whole.

Process theology says that God is internally related to everything in the world. This means that God is affected in the depth of God's being by everything that exists and everything that happens in the world. God suffers with our suffering and rejoices in our joy. As fully embodied in and related to the world, God's power is limited both by the laws of nature and the weight of history. God cannot end death because the processes of birth, death, and transformation are the way nature works. God is also affected both positively and negatively by the events that occur in the world. When the world is suffering, God is diminished. When the world is joyous, God is enhanced.

Process theologians speak of God's power to affect the world as a power of persuasion, rather than coercion. In process theology's understanding, God is "in" every being in the world. As the ground of being and life, God attempts to "persuade" or inspire all beings to respect being and life and to seek the greatest harmony of the whole. God as the ground of being is also "in" those who violate the web of life. But God does not inspire their actions or condone them. Those who violate the web of life do so by ignoring or denying the "persuasion" that God is offering them. When this happens, God's body is diminished. God suffers.

Using the analogy of the difference between a collection of cells and a unified organism, scientists Lynn Margulis and James Lovelock proposed the Gaia theory, named after the Greek Goddess Gaia, whose name means "earth." They hypothesized that the earth itself functions as a unified, self-regulating organism. The major changes in the earth's ecosystem, such as ice ages, global warming, and the coming and going of species may reflect the earth's internal self-regulating system. Margulis and Lovelock have been careful to state that they are not talking about Gaia as a Goddess, but simply as a unified system.[58] Yet their theory is compatible with and provides a partial scientific grounding for process theology's view of God.

I find process theology helpful for understanding the nature and power of the Goddess. As fully immanent, the Goddess is embodied in the finite, changing world. She is known in rock and flower and in the human heart, just as in thealogies of immanence. As the organism uniting the cells of the earth body, the Goddess is the firm foundation of changing life. As the mind, soul, or enlivening power of the world body, the Goddess is intelligent, aware, alive, a kind of "person" with whom we can enter into relation.[59] Thus the Goddess can "speak" to us through the natural world, through human relationships, through communities, through dreams and visions, expressing her desire to manifest life ever more fully in the world. And we can "speak" to her in song, meditation, prayer, and ritual, manifesting our desire to attune ourselves with her rhythms, to experience our union with the body of the earth and all beings who live upon it.

The Goddess seeks the greatest good for the greatest number of beings, but her power is limited. The Goddess cannot change the natural cycles of birth, death, and renewal that form the context of all life because the Goddess does not stand outside the "laws of nature." The cycles of nature are her cycles. Death is not the enemy. It is part of the cycle of life.

The relation of the Goddess to the history of species and to human history is more complex. Here, her power is persuasive, but not coercive. The Goddess is "in" everything that happens in the world as its ground of being. And everything that happens in the world becomes a part of the body of the Goddess. In this sense, the Goddess does not stand outside history. She cannot wipe out the weight of the past with a wave of a magic wand.

Yet everything that has happened in the history of the world is not "the will of the Goddess." The Goddess is always attempting to persuade us to love intelligently, concretely, and inclusively. When we do so, the "will of the Goddess" is achieved, and she rejoices. But the Goddess can influence and inspire us only if we open ourselves to her power. She must work in and through finite and limited individuals who may resist her power and within communities with histories. When we violate the web of life, we fail to recognize, ignore, or deny the persuasions of the Goddess. The body of the Goddess is desecrated. She suffers.

The power of the Goddess is thus neither omnipotence nor omniscience, qualities attributed to the God of theism by virtue of his alleged transcendence of nature and history. The power of the Goddess is a limited power that operates within a finite and changeable world. She cannot transform the crises that the world faces—historical injustice, environmental destruction and pollution, the threat of nuclear catastrophe—without the cooperation of all of those who affect and are affected by them. Because her power is not co-ercive, the Goddess depends on us, as we depend on her. But her power is real, and our power becomes greater when we work in conjunction with her.

Intelligent Embodied Love as the Ground of All Being

The power of the Goddess is the intelligent embodied love that is the ground of all being.[60] This intelligent embodied love undergirds every individual being, including plants, animals, and humans, as we participate in the physical and spiritual processes of birth, death, and renewal. If intelligent embodied love is the ground of all being, then intelligence, love, embodiment, relationship, and interdependence are the "stuff of life" and are "in the nature of things."

That the power of the Goddess is intelligent embodied love is consistent with the understanding of the Goddess as internally related to every being in the world. Yet for a long time I hesitated to define the power of the Goddess as "love" because the notion that "God is love" had been repeated so often in Christian theology that is seemed to me to have lost its metaphoric power. In an earlier draft of this manuscript, I used the word *eros*, which I defined as the feeling of deep connection to other people and all beings in the web of life. Now I believe that *love* is a more accurate and inclusive word for the power that is the ground of all being. But why use words like *eros* and *love* at all? Why not use more neutral words, such as *relation*, *connection*, and *interdependence*?

My answer is that this is my experience, an experience shared by others, and, I believe, available to everyone. As my mother died, I was given a mystical insight: a revelation of the ground of being as love. I began to understand that I am surrounded by a great matrix of love and always have been.[61] The mystical experience of the ground of being as a great matrix of love was also experienced by the character Shug in Alice Walker's *The Color Purple*. Shug's insight begins with a sensing of deep connection of all beings in the web of life:

> My first step from the old white man was trees. Then air. Then birds. Then other people. But one day when I was sitting quiet and feeling like a motherless child which I was, it come to me: that feeling of being part of everything, not separate at all. I knew that if I cut a tree, my arm would bleed. And I laughed and I cried and I run all around the house. I knew just what it was. When it happen, you can't miss it.[62]

In conversation with her friend Celie, Shug names the bond of deep connection between all beings as the power of "love":

—God love everything you love—and a mess of stuff you don't. But more than anything else, God love admiration.
—You saying God vain? [Celie] ast.
—Naw, she say. Not vain, just wanting to share a good thing. I think it pisses God off if you walk by the color purple in a field somewhere and don't notice it.
—What it do when it pissed off? [Celie] ast.
—Oh, it make something else. People think pleasing God is all God care about. But any fool living in the world can see it always trying to please us back.

. . .

Yes, Celie, she say. Everything want to be loved. Us sing and dance, make faces and give flower bouquets, trying to be loved. You ever notice that trees do everything to git attention we do, except walk?[63]

Everything wants to be loved: Love is the ground of being, the power that sustains and motivates people, the flowers and the trees, and even God. Like Martin Buber, Shug commits what has been called the "pathetic fallacy" of attributing feelings to trees and flowers. From a traditional point of view, she also errs in imagining that God needs anything. Yet I believe Shug's vision reveals the mystery of life.

The great matrix of love that supports life is "embodied," "intelligent," and "the power of all being." To say that the love of Goddess is "embodied" means that concrete relation is the ground of all being. Embodied love is grounded in senses, in seeing, hearing, tasting, touching, and smelling, and in the emotions and passions that arise from the senses. Embodied love is not the dispassionate moralistic concern sometimes identified as Christian love or the love of God. Embodied love is rooted in deep feeling: In this sense, it is erotic.

But as "intelligent," love is not "blind" emotion. Our relationship to other beings, our interdependence, is not an ephemeral, passing, irrational feeling. The "deep feeling of connection to all beings in the web of life" is reflected in the nature of reality. In philosophical terms, it is an ontological insight, a revelation of being. To say that the love that is the ground of all being is "intelligent" is also to recognize intelligence in all beings.

When we understand intelligent embodied love as the "ground of all being," we know that we are interdependent with all beings in the web of life. Specific loves, for one's own child, for the flowers in the field behind one's house, occur within the context of the whole of life. Thus we must strive ever to widen the scope of our love. When we love concretely, intelligently, in our bodies, and in concern for the whole web of life, we are listening to the persuasion offered to us by the Goddess whose intelligent embodied love is the ground of all being.

Monotheism or Polytheism?

The most familiar Goddesses come from traditions that are usually called polytheistic. But like many others, I have spoken both of "the Goddess" and "Goddesses" in this book. This raises the question of whether the Goddess is to be understood within a monotheistic or a polytheistic framework. In theory, monotheism means the worship of one God, while polytheism means the worship of many Gods and Goddesses. The three monotheistic faiths are Judaism, Christianity, and Islam; some define all other religions as polytheistic, but an intuition of the unity of being is found in most if not all religions.

Though the word *monotheism* is not found in the Hebrew Bible, the roots of monotheism are often traced to the commandment given to Moses to make no image of God and to worship no other Gods before him. Yet the monotheism reflected in the Hebrew Bible could more accurately be called tribal monotheism because it asserts that the Hebrew tribe should worship the God who brought them up out of Egypt, the God whose name is Yahweh. Scholars have noted that the first commandment neither denies the existence of other Goddesses or Gods nor the right of other peoples to worship them. And it appears that the Hebrew people often worshiped other Gods and Goddesses, including Baal, El, Asherah, and Astarte. Still, the Hebrew Bible is filled with assertions that other deities lack the power of Yahweh. Over time, Hebrew tribal monotheism expressed more universalistic claims. The prophets ridiculed other deities as mere pieces of wood, while in Isaiah 60:2–3, it is predicted that "all nations" shall see the glory of Yahweh.

Biblical monotheism prohibited the making of images of God, but this prohibition was not consistently practiced in Hebrew religion, as the rantings of the prophets testify.[64] Nor has it been strictly adhered to in Christian tradition. Feminists argue that it has not been practiced at all, since the verbal image of God in both Judaism and Christianity is consistently male.[65] According to feminists, Hebrew, Jewish, and Christian monotheism might more appropriately be called male monotheism.

When Hebrew-based traditions came into contact with Greek philosophy, monotheism was defined as "the religious experience and philosophical perception that emphasize God as one, perfect, immutable, creator of the world from nothing, distinct from the world, personal, and worthy of being worshipped by all creatures."[66] This definition incorporates many of the ideas of divinity associated with the dualistic understandings of divine transcendence; it should not be confused with the intuition of the unity of being.

Proponents of monotheism argue that it is the source of a superior ethical system, based upon the one law revealed by the one God. In recent years, it has been asserted that the God of monotheism calls humanity to recognize the relativity of familial, ethnic, and national loyalties.[67] Monotheists often state that polytheism, because it incorporates many deities and thus many competing principles of value, is incapable of sustaining a unified ethical vision. Others respond that in practice monotheistic societies have not been more successful than any others in eradicating injustice. They note that monotheism, because it claims to know the "one right way" easily becomes the source of religious discrimination, religious persecution, and religious wars.

Polytheists have also been known to claim religious or ethical superiority. Still, the polytheistic frame of mind is generally more conducive to tolerance than the monotheistic. When confronted with a new God or Goddess, polytheists ask, "What can she do?" And if she fulfills a need in people's lives, they adopt her into their pantheon. Polytheists are less concerned with the name given to a deity than monotheists. It is monotheists who assert, "There is one God, and his name is Yahweh . . . Christ . . . or Allah" (excluding female names and images). Polytheists are likely to respond, "Your God is like the one we call the Great Father, but why insist that he is the only one?" As Karen McCarthy Brown remarked in recognition of this phenomenon, "It is only the monotheists who seem to have the need to count."[68]

Many of those attracted to the emerging Goddesses have experienced monotheistic traditions as coercive. Those who have been taught that they must believe a revealed dogma or practice a revealed law, no matter what their own conscience tells them, are rightly suspicious of monotheism. Thealogian and archetypal psychologist Christine Downing argues strongly against understanding the Goddesses within a monotheistic framework.[69] She correlates monotheism with a monolithic understanding of the self and overly rigid conceptions of morality. She feels that there is a danger in coalescing the many images of the Goddess into the single image of the Great Goddess. To do so might suggest that there is only one way to live "in her image," for example, by giving birth to children as the Goddess gave birth to the world. The many images of the Goddesses, Downing proposes, correspond to the many facets of the self. The different images of the Goddesses and the different myths associated with each of them, provide a fuller and richer picture of the self than the singular image of the Great Goddess can do. To have particular images and stories of particular Goddesses enables us to appreciate the different life choices and ethical styles among women, and even more important, to appreciate that each of us is not one, but many.

Writing from a Jewish feminist perspective, Marcia Falk criticizes exclusivistic male monotheism but argues in favor of an expanded notion of monotheism that embraces a plurality of images. Falk notes that Jewish feminists who have made the relatively modest change of using the feminine pronoun *She* to refer to God have been accused of the "heresy" of "paganism," of undermining the monotheism of the Jewish tradition.[70] Rejecting the argument that monotheism means that we can have only one male image of God, Falk asked herself what monotheism means. She concluded,

> *Monotheism means that,* with all our differences, *I am more like you than I am unlike you. It means that we all share the same source, and that one principle of justice must govern us equally. . . . It would seem, then, that the authentic expression of an authentic monotheism is not a singularity of image but an embracing* unity *of a multiplicity of images, as many as are needed to express the diversity of our individual lives.*[71]

Here, Falk asserts an intuition of unity underlying diversity while agreeing with Downing and others on the need for a multiplicity of images.

Contemporary Goddess spirituality seems to fit Falk's model. Though the Goddesses are invoked under many names and with a variety of images, the use of the phrase *the Goddess* in liturgy and prayer as well as reflection suggests that multiplicity is not the final word. An intuition of unity is expressed in one of the Goddess movement's most popular chants: "We all come from the Goddess and to her we shall return like a drop of rain flowing to the ocean."[72] The intuition of the unity of being is given philosophical form in the notion that the Goddess is the ground of all being.

Does this mean we should define Goddess religion as monotheistic? I would argue against this because the monotheistic traditions carry too much negative baggage. I do not believe monotheism can be abstracted from its history of separating itself from and opposing other faiths, and in particular from opposing Goddess worship. This became intuitively clear to me several years ago in Turkey. There I saw three ancient copies of the many-breasted image of Artemis of Ephesus for the first time. (See Figure 12.) Spontaneously, I raised my arms to one of them, opening my palms. Power flooded my body. Hours later in the bazaar in Ismir, I stepped inside a mosque. There were no images there. A few men were prostrating themselves before empty niches in the wall. Suddenly I understood: The prohibition of images is a prohibition of the Goddess. If images are permitted, there is no way to stop the human mind and the human hand from creating images of female power.

It has been noted that "monotheism often arises in antagonism to other views of divine reality."[73] Monotheistic faiths not only separate their God from other Gods and the Goddesses, but also from that which the Goddesses are said to represent, namely woman, the body, nature, sexuality, the so-called dangerous flux of things. This is why cries of idolatry, paganism, and heresy are repeated by Christians and Jews whenever female imagery is used for God. Because of its origins, I doubt that monotheism can ever be as inclusive as Marcia Falk hopes.

Contemporary Goddess religion is polytheistic in practice, admitting a multiplicity of names and images of the Goddesses and even of the Gods. But this is not to say that contemporary Goddess worship should be understood through the philosophical definition of polytheism, which states that "central to polytheism is the notion of *theoi*, personal divine beings within nature and society. . . . The functioning of nature is seen as the operation of a plurality of wills, and this plurality and conflict are extended to human life and society."[74] In other words, polytheism denies the intuition of unity underlying a plurality of images. By this definition, polytheists would deny that "with all our differences we all share the same source." But let us remember that the term *polytheism* is not part of the self-definition of any religion. Many religions defined as polytheistic incorporate the intuition of unity behind a multiplicity of images.

It seems, then, that neither monotheism nor polytheism is an adequate description of contemporary Goddess religion. This is not surprising, given that both terms are a product of monotheistic debates. At the conclusion of her spirited defense of Goddess polytheism, Christine Downing writes that "we need the goddess and the goddesses."[75] I agree. We need "the Goddess" as an affirmation of an intuition of the unity of being underlying the multiplicity of life. And we need a multiplicity of "Goddesses" (and Gods) to fully reflect our differences and to remind us of the limitations of any single image.

❦ 6 ❦

The Web of Life

To know ourselves as of this earth is to know our deep connection to all people and all beings. All beings are interdependent in the web of life. This is the distinctive conception of nature and our place in it found in Goddess religion. Images of Goddesses that combine human female and animal forms convey a mystical sense of the connection of all life on earth. Though some have argued that rational thought has enabled humanity to evolve beyond this ancient sensibility, I agree with Marija Gimbutas that the vision of ancient Goddess religion was never completely lost. We feel deeply within ourselves that we are part of all that is, but we must learn to speak of what we know. We know, too, that we participate fully in the earth's cycles of birth, death, and regeneration, though some have attempted to deny that this is true.

A Mystical Sense of Connection

The fundamental insight of connection to all beings in the web of life is experienced by children, poets, mystics, and indeed, I suspect, by all of us, though we may lack the language to express what we feel. When I began to study theology, I wanted to speak about my sense of mystical connection to the natural world. But I was told that I had not yet learned to think clearly and that those whose words I quoted (even Martin Buber and Paul Tillich!) were "confused." Buber and Tillich and I didn't understand "fundamental distinctions" between God, man, and nature.

I know how difficult it can be to articulate a sense of deep connection to all beings in the web of life in the face of criticism rooted in dualistic thinking. Thus, I feel it is important to acknowledge those who have taught me. Though they do not all use the name of the Goddess, the ideas and images of the thinkers I discuss below provide a lens through which I understand nature and our place in it. Savor their words as I have. Let them sink into your bones.

Jewish theologian Martin Buber wrote eloquently of his I-Thou relation to a tree:

> I contemplate a tree.
>
> I can accept it as a picture: as rigid pillar in a flood of light, or splashes of green traversed by the gentleness of the blue silver ground.
>
> I can feel it as movement: the flowing veins around the sturdy, striving core, the sucking of the roots, the breathing of the leaves, the infinite commerce with earth and air—and the growing itself in its darkness. . . .
>
> But it can also happen, if will and grace are joined, that as I contemplate the tree I am drawn into a relation, and the tree ceases to be an It. The power of exclusiveness has seized me.[1]

For Buber, moments of pure relation with a piece of mica, a tree, a horse, and other people are "the cradle of actual life,"[2] an unfolding of the mystery of being.

Buber was asked by those whose presuppositions about the difference between humanity and nature made it impossible for them to comprehend a mutual relation with a "less than human" partner: "Does the tree then have consciousness, similar to our own?" To this question Buber replied, "I have no experience of that."[3] With this simple response, Buber asserted that we do not need to have a complete rational explanation of the nature of a tree's relation with us to know that it exists. The tree may have a consciousness "like" our own, or it may have a different mode of relating to us.

American Indian writer and mystic Paula Gunn Allen speaks movingly of our connection to earth, arguing that awareness of this connection is the basic insight of the spirituality of Native Americans:

> We are the land. To the best of my understanding, that is the fundamental idea that permeates American Indian life; the land (Mother) and the people (mothers) are the same. As Luther Standing Bear has said of his Lakota people, "We are of the soil and the soil is of us." The earth is the source and being of the people and we are equally the being of the earth. The land is not really a place separate from ourselves, where we act out the drama of our isolate destinies. . . . The earth is not mere source of survival, distant from the creatures it nurtures and from the spirit that breathes in us, nor is it to be considered an inert resource on which we draw in order

to keep our ideological self functioning. . . . Rather for the American Indians . . . the earth is being, as all creatures are also being: aware, palpable, intelligent, alive.[4]

It is difficult for Allen to express her understanding that "we are the land" because the notion that the land is only a "place" where we happen to live, only a "material resource" that we "exploit" to survive, is deeply embedded not only in dualistic thinking, but also in western languages. For Allen, human beings are so fundamentally part of the earth that the earth is as intimate to us as our own bodies. We could not live, we would not be, without our grounding in the earth.

In her classic book, *Woman and Nature*, poet and philosopher Susan Griffin names our deep feelings of connection to earth while at the same time challenging the assumptions of dualistic philosophy:

I know I am made from this earth, as my mother's hands were made from this earth, as her dreams were made from this earth and all I know, I know in this earth, the body of the bird, this pen, this paper, these hands, this tongue speaking, all that I know speaks to me through this earth and I long to tell you, you who are earth too, and listen as we speak to each other of what we know: the light is in us.[5]

In prose that becomes poetry, Griffin evokes the sensuality of material life. In explicit allusion and contrast to traditional philosophers and theologians, Griffin affirms that human beings are of the earth. Even our "thoughts," she argues, come through the body and are expressed in matter. Matter is not a "mass of perishable rubbish," as in Plato. The "light," symbol of transcendence in Plato's allegory of the cave,[6] does not shine from a source outside the earth, but is "in us" "who are earth."

Many writers express their sense of a mystical connection to the earth and other beings through language that is sensual and erotic. I believe this is because the experience of connection can be intensely physical—breathing may quicken or slow, the skin may tingle, a sense of excitement or deep peace may come into the body. All of these feelings are reminiscent of sexual experience. Indeed, sexuality can be a way of experiencing deeply our connection to another being and to the life force.

In a passage addressed to "This Earth," Susan Griffin writes simultaneously of her love for the earth and for a woman, evoking the mystery of a passage into a sea cave and a woman's body:

As I go into her, she pierces my heart. As I penetrate further, she unveils me. When I have reached her center, I am weeping openly. I have known her all my life, yet she reveals stories to me, and these stories are revelations and I am transformed. Each time I go to her I am born like this. Her renewal washes over me endlessly, her wounds caress me.[7]

The body of the earth and the body of the lover become metaphors that reflect and interpret each other. As Griffin learns to appreciate the one, her appreciation of the other is deepened. Both the earth and the lover are sacred, healing, transforming. Each teaches us how deeply we are connected to life that flows on within us and without us.

In a somewhat different vein, memoirist Alix Kates Shulman describes an awareness of connection that occurred in a New York subway:

I was sitting alone on the downtown IRT on my way to pick up the children at their after-school music classes. . . . Then suddenly the dull light in the car began to shine with exceptional lucidity until everything around me was glowing with an indescribable aura, and I saw in the row of motley passengers opposite the miraculous connection of all living beings. Not felt; saw. What began as a desultory thought grew into a vision, large and unifying, in which all the people in the car hurtling downtown together, including myself, like all the people on the planet hurtling together around the sun—our entire living cohort—formed one united family, indissolubly connected by the rare and mysterious accident of life.[8]

Though not occurring in wild nature, this too is an experience of the deep connection and interdependence in the web of life.

A perception of great beauty is an important aspect of the experience of connection. Shulman sees everything "glowing with an indescribable aura." Alice Walker's Shug tells Celie that God wants us to admire a field flowering in the color purple. At the end of her prose poem to "This Earth," Susan Griffin writes,

This earth is my sister; I love her daily grace, her silent daring, and how loved I am how we admire this strength in each other, all that we have lost, all that we have suffered, all that we know: we are stunned by this beauty, and I do not forget: what she is to me, what I am to her.[9]

To be "stunned" by the beauty of the earth is more than an "aesthetic" appreciation. It can be described as an ontological insight, a sense of wonder caused by a revelation of the miracle of life. But this is not to deny that the experience we have of the earth and its beings is of great *beauty*.

The Navajos of the American southwest express their sense of the beauty of the world in their ritual chants. There are several songs in the Goddess movement based on Navajo chants. One of them is

With beauty behind me,
with beauty before me,
with beauty around me,
in beauty I walk.
With beauty below me,
with beauty above me,
with beauty inside me,
in beauty I walk.[10]

Repeated again and again in a ritual context until it takes root in the unconscious and conscious mind, this chant defines an attitude of great respect, attention, and appreciation directed to all beings in the web of life.

When I first began to articulate the mystical sense of connection to earth and life I am describing here, I searched for theories that would express my understanding. To my surprise, I found that most of the literature on mysticism sharply distinguished between "higher" and "lower" forms. In so-called higher forms of mysticism, the earth and the body were transcended. According to dualistic thinking, my experiences and those described in this chapter fall into the "lower" category. I was thus forced to create new theory to name experiences that I felt had not been properly understood. In *Diving Deep and Surfacing*, I called the kind of mystical experience depicted in this chapter "nature mysticism," "sexual mysticism," and "social mysticism."[11]

When I lectured about my understanding of mysticism, others often came up to me and said something like, "Do you mean that feeling I had two years ago while hiking in the woods was a mystical experience? It seemed important at the time, but since then, I'd kind of forgotten about it." I think most of us have had "that feeling" not once, but many times in our lives, but we have not had the words to name it as spiritual. And thus "it" has not shaped our understanding of ourselves and our place in the universe.

The Earth as Intelligent, Aware, Alive

When she writes that "we are the land," Paula Gunn Allen speaks of the earth and all creatures as "aware, palpable, intelligent, alive." Recognizing that this is not the traditional western (dualistic) view, she explains that

many non-Indians believe that human beings possess the only form of intelligence in phenomenal existence (often in any form of existence). The more abstractionist and less intellectually vain Indian sees human intelligence as rising out of the very nature of being, which is of necessity intelligent in and of itself.[12]

According to Allen, only the hierarchical consciousness characteristic of western thought could imagine that human beings have the only form of intelligence in the universe. When Allen says that all beings have "intelligence," she means that all beings have a particular wisdom and ways of communicating it. Human beings will not endure as long as the mountains, fly with the grace of birds, nor penetrate the earth's deepest recesses with the ease of snakes. We can learn from plants and animals, sea and stones, not only by observation, but also through sensing our connection to them.

Susan Griffin also recognizes that the earth is "intelligent" and "aware" and "alive" when she writes of "This Earth":

> I taste, I know, and I know why she goes on, under great weight, with this great thirst, in drought, in starvation, with intelligence in every act does she survive disaster.[13]

For Griffin, the earth, like a lover, like herself, is a "sister" who has suffered, yet with great intelligence, has survived.

For ecofeminist philosopher of science Elisabet Sahtouris, the intelligence of the earth body can be seen in the process of evolution. Building on the Gaia hypothesis of scientists Lynn Margulis and James Lovelock, Sahtouris imagines that the intelligence that guides evolution is not outside nature, but embodied in it as the "body wisdom" of the earth. The "great Gaia being knew itself in the same sense as our bodies know themselves, having the body wisdom to take care of itself and keep on evolving."[14] Sahtouris argues that a similar inherent principle of intelligence or wisdom can be seen in the self-organization of all beings. She criticizes the neo-Darwinian view that "random accident and natural selection are the sole 'mechanisms' of evolution," arguing that "much evidence is accumulating that well-organized, healthy creatures and their ecosystems are produced by self-organization."[15] Sahtouris describes the self-organization of all beings from the smallest microscopic organism to humans to ecosystems as essentially cooperative rather than competitive.

> In every Gaian ecosystem, we can regard each creature as something like a cell in our bodies, each species as something like an organ. Each ecosystem is an ecologically balanced body evolving as a whole. We really should talk about co-evolution, rather than evolution, to remind ourselves that no species can or does evolve by itself.[16]

According to Sahtouris, life is interdependent. Each form of life requires others, not only for food, but to carry on the cycles of growth, death, and regeneration in the larger ecosystem in which it lives. Sahtouris believes that we can learn to see cooperation and intelligence rather than brutal, blind competition in the way some flowers cling to the side of bare rocks, drawing bees, forming topsoil, allowing other plants to take root, holding water in what had once been a dry and barren place, creating the conditions for other life-forms to flourish.

Sahtouris points out that the Darwinian view of nature as competitive, brutal, blind, and operating by "mechanical" laws arose in tandem with society's change to "competitive and exploitative industrial production."[17] This was also the time of the final (brutal and blind) European expansion into the Americas, Africa, Asia, and Australia, when Europeans justified their conquest as "survival of the fittest." It can now be seen that this view is a threat to the survival of the human and other species, as we are destroying each other and the ecosystem with which we are interdependent. Sahtouris hopes that the image of the Gaia being as inherently wise and the model of cooperative co-evolution can help us find ways of solving the ecological and social crises we have created by our disregard of our essential connection to each other and to nature.

Difference and Diversity within Nature

To live in awareness of the deep connection of all beings in the web of life does not mean that all is absorbed in a oneness or unity where difference is denied. Difference and diversity are the great principles of nature. The sense of our connection to all beings in the web of life is at the same time a perception of difference, an awareness of the uniqueness of other beings. Susan Griffin recognizes this when she writes,

> The red-winged blackbird flies in us, in our inner sight. We see the arc of her flight. We measure the ellipse. We predict its climax. We are amazed. We are moved. We fly. We watch her wings negotiate the wind, the substance of the air, its elements and the elements of those elements, and count those elements found in other beings, the sea urchin's sting, ink, this paper, our bones, the flesh of our tongues with which we make the sound "blackbird," the ears with which we hear, the eye which travels the arc of her flight. And yet the blackbird does not fly in us but somewhere else free of our minds, and now even free of our sight, flying in the path of her own will.[18]

We sense our connection to the blackbird and delight in her powers of flight, at the same time recognizing that we will never fly as she flies, that the flight she takes in our minds is not the flight she takes in her own black-feathered body, circling as we will never circle over a pond or a field. We may call her "blackbird," but that does not make her the same as other beings we call "birds": she is not the hawk or the owl, the swallow or the hummingbird. She is uniquely herself. We feel connected to her grace, her beauty, her power, her energy, at the same time recognizing that we are each, uniquely, ourselves. If we open ourselves to life, we can experience similar joy in the power of each being in the universe, in the birds singing outside our windows in the city, in trees coming into bud, in flowers bursting into bloom, in a child's laughter, in a lover's embrace.

Martin Buber also affirms that to stand in relation means to acknowledge difference, not to become lost in a mystical oneness. Of his relation to a tree, Buber writes,

> Whatever belongs to the tree is included: its form and its mechanics, its colors and its chemistry, its conversation with the elements and its conversation with the stars —all this in its entirety.
>
> The tree is no impression, no play of my imagination, no aspect of a mood; it confronts me bodily and has to deal with me as I must deal with it—only differently.
>
> One should not try to dilute the meaning of relation: relation is reciprocity.[19]

Buber's thinking is holistic: The scientific view of the tree is not lost when relation is established. Buber's thinking is fully relational: The tree is not an aspect of his own subjectivity, a creation of his own artistic soul. As an earlier translation of Buber's work put it in more literal translation of the German, the tree is "bodied forth over against me."[20] Buber's point is not that the self and other are eternally "opposed." He is asserting the reality of relationship with an other who is different from the self.

Elisabet Sahtouris approaches the question of difference and diversity within nature from a scientific perspective. She writes,

> No place on earth today, not even the barest-looking mountaintop or the deepest part of the sea, has fewer than a thousand different species from various kingdoms [sic]—monera, protists, fungi, plants, and animals. Yet what we humans see as living things are only the largest of the plants and animals—beings the size of bugs and bushes and beluga whales, creatures on our own size scale. The vast majority of the earth creatures, however, continue to be microscopic monera and protists.[21]

The variety of beings within nature is far greater than most of us can imagine. Each being plays a vital role within the Gaia body. From a scientific point of view, each is necessary to the survival of the earth as we know it.

A thealogy that envisions the earth as the body of the Goddess will recognize, appreciate, and celebrate the great diversity of life within the earth
body. We may not love all the things the Goddess loves. But if we cannot love
all beings in the web of life, perhaps we can at least begin to recognize that
each plays a role in creating the things we do love.

A Sense of Place

Though we reflect on the infinite variety within the earth body, we experience the concrete perception that the ground on which we stand is holy.[22]
American Indian philosopher, poet, and mystic Carol Lee Sanchez stated that
connection to place is a fundamental element in her people's formal rituals
and daily life.[23] A sense of place is celebrated in my adopted home, Greece.
Everyone who can travels to the part of Greece where their ancestors were
born to celebrate the spring rituals of death and rebirth. The focus of the
Greek Easter celebration is the roasting and eating of the paschal lamb, outside, in nature. The other major festival of the year, the Dormition or "Falling
Asleep" of the Mother of God on August 15, occurring at the time of the summer harvest, is also celebrated, if possible, at the place of origin. Other major
festivals celebrated communally in nature are Clean Monday, the beginning
of Lent, when children fly kites, and May Day, when everyone goes to the
countryside to pick wildflowers and make wreaths. On hearing of the Greek
May Day custom, an American friend wrote, "Thank you for telling me about
the national holiday for picking wild flowers and making wreaths. Just knowing that there is such a place on earth makes me very happy!"[24]

Sanchez asks whether "Euro-Americans waste the resources and destroy
the environment in the Americas, because they have no mythos or legendary
origins rooted to this land."[25] Greeks who have such a mythos are also wast-
ing resources and destroying the land as capitalist greed supercedes the traditional sensibilities that have sustained life for centuries. Still, myths and rituals can create a climate in which certain patterns of action become more
likely. Sanchez urges Euro-Americans to create stories, mythologies, and rituals that celebrate a spiritual connection to the American land. Needless to
say, such stories would not be about conquest or possession (as in the notion
that America is the land promised by God to specific groups of white Europeans), but rather about the gift of interdependent life in a particular place.
The ritual of celebrating the spring equinox by creating a flower wreath for
the earth body described by Charlene Spretnak is one of many examples of
such a beginning.[26]

Yet there is so much in modern life that alienates us from nature in the places where we live. I write these words on a gray and rainy day, closed into an apartment alone, in a city where most of the ground has been covered by concrete and the air is polluted by leaded gas, heating oil, and factory emissions. I think a walk in the country might do me good. But there is no country near me. I could walk to a place in the city where pine trees still cling to the side of a hill, but it seems too far. And still, I would be alone. Though there is little violence against women on the streets where I live, I am afraid to walk on a shaded hillside by myself. Clearly, if we are to celebrate our connection to this earth in our daily lives, one of the things we must do is change the ways we live in alienation from nature and from each other.

Though some have proposed that we must all move out of cities, Carol Lee Sanchez envisions living in cities in conscious awareness of our connection to nature:

> Imagine an entire city of people waking and rising together at 5:00 or 6:00 a.m. and the first thing they do is sing themselves—body, mind, and spirit—into the day. . . . They send out . . . loving goodwill while visualizing all the creatures, all the plants, all the elements, and especially all the microorganisms (bacteria, viruses, molecules, and atoms) that plants, creatures, and humans depend on to keep the balancing machinery working. . . . Picture, if you will, this city of people singing to the water Spirits of bubbling brooks and streams, of laughing happy rivers filled with water life, of saltwater seas and oceans filled with saltwater life.[27]

Singing to nature every morning might encourage us to plant trees and flowers on our balconies in the city and to take more care in conserving the water and electricity we use every day. As a community that shared this ritual, we might work together to reforest the surrounding hills, to create more parks and walkways in the city, to plan for the needs of urban life with a consciousness that we not destroy the ecosystem. And if the earth really is a living organism, our rituals might have the power to activate the earth's self-healing wisdom.

Denying Our Connection to Earth

While many have celebrated our connection to the earth, this connection continues to be denied in dualistic philosophies and theologies. According to Protestant theologian Gordon Kaufman, the severing of divinity and humanity from nature was one of the decisive characteristics of monotheism.[28] In the philosophies and theologies that follow the victory of monotheism, "Nature is not conceived primarily as our proper home and the very source and sustenance of our being."[29] The severing of divinity and humanity from nature led in turn to philosophies in which "God," "man," and "nature" are seen as separate and distinct categories.

But if Goddess is an intelligent power that is fully embodied in the world, then the notion that divinity, nature, and humanity are three totally distinct categories collapses. If Goddess as fully embodied intelligent love is the ground of all being, then it makes sense to speak of intelligence and love as rising out of the very nature of being and of all beings as intelligent and infused with love. Human intelligence and our capacity to love do not separate us from nature. Instead, everything we are arises from the nature of being, from our grounding in the earth. If Goddess is fully embodied in the earth and is influenced by all that exists and all that happens, then the Goddess is accurately described as wounded, as suffering, and yet with enormous strength, surviving. If the world is the body of the Goddess and we are part of the world, then of course we experience her love in our bodies, including our sexuality. And if all this is true, then the mystical experiences discussed in this chapter reflect ontological insight or revelation of the nature of being.

Finitude and Death

Then why have so many western philosophers and theologians denied that we are part of nature? Perhaps it is because to know ourselves as of the earth is to experience not only a sense of connection to all of nature, but also a profound dependence and limitation. We are born from the body of a mother, and we require love and nurture from other people and from the earth itself to survive. We are drawn to others, yet in our experience, all relationships end in death.

Some psychoanalysts argue that human beings innately fear dependence, limitation, and death.[30] Yet the vision of Goddess religion (both ancient and modern) suggests that this need not be the case. A historical point of view argues that the achievement of a degree of technological control over nature combined with success in controlling others through force gave rise to the idea that "man" (or some men) could exert control over all that made him limited and dependent.

The notion that we can control the conditions of our lives is reflected in the modern idea that humans are defined by our individual moral will. This view is encoded in the American dream, which tells us that if we work hard enough, we will succeed. The success that is promised in return for hard work is not only financial, but also physical, moral, and spiritual. The idea of control has worked itself into our consciousness in many insidious and often unrecognized ways. Even those who have rejected the grosser material aspects of the American dream often still believe that through an effort of will they can find physical, spiritual, and social health and well-being.

Recently, I received a copy of a New Age Goddess publication that included an "Affirmation [of the basic principles] of Women's Spirituality." This statement envisioned the Goddess as immanent in the body and the earth body:

- *That the Goddess or life force energy is within me;*
- *That I shall grow to understand the cyclic, life affirming rhythms of the earth, and always act with love toward all her plants and creatures.*

It affirmed nonrationalistic ways of knowing:

- *That my instincts and intuition can be used to guide me;*
- *That I shall grow in wisdom, strength, and understanding.*

Diversity within the human community was treated positively:

- *To accept and understand those whose ethnic or racial background, social or economic class, appearance, or sexual preference are different from my own.*

Though the authors of these affirmations no doubt believed that they were rejecting dualistic traditions of rational control and domination, they stated that we can control the conditions of our life through the right spiritual practice:

- *That I can create my own reality and that sending out a positive expectation will bring a positive result;*
- *That I shall transform all [that is] negative in my environment;*
- *To take responsibility for myself and my actions and to know that consciously or unconsciously, I have drawn situations to me.*[31]

In New Age philosophies, the view that "we create our own reality" is common.

I believe that the idea that we create our own reality is a dangerous and misleading partial truth. It is true that sending out a positive expectation *may* bring a positive result. It is true that we can transform *some* of the negative energies in our environment. It is true that consciously or unconsciously we *may* draw situations to ourselves. But to believe that we can completely control our environment and all the positive and negative things that happen in us, to us, and around us is to deny the embodied and social nature of reality. The power of our minds to control physical reality is limited by our bodies and by our immersion in a finite and changing world. Our individual wills are embedded within a web of relationships in which we are not the only significant actors. I may be able to cause myself to think positively (though this has not always been possible in my experience), but I cannot cause everyone else in the world to do the same. Other people are affected not only by me, but by their own bodies and experience. The social world composed of symbol systems, institutions, and historical memories in which we live affects each one of us deeply. The power of any one individual to change all of these systems is limited.

All the goodwill that I have within me will not stop the poisoning of the water I drink unless my society makes very different decisions about what is an "acceptable level of pollution." If I decide to eat healthy food, to exercise, and to relax more, I may keep my immune system strong enough to ward off some forms of cancer. But if I have a genetic weakness or there are many cancer-producing agents in the larger environment where I live and work, I may still get cancer. If I feel tired and helpless when I walk down a dark street, I may draw a rapist or mugger to me (but only if I live in a society ruled by violence). Yet if society is in a state of breakdown and violence is everywhere, I may be a victim of violence even when I take reasonable precautions, send out good vibrations, and walk through the city in broad daylight. The idea that we create our own reality becomes ludicrous and obscene when applied to starving mothers and children in Africa or even to children growing up in the inner cities of America. To believe that we fully control our lives is still not to have divorced ourselves from our culture's attempt to escape the conditions of finitude. Until we give up the illusion of control, we have not fully integrated the meaning of finite and interdependent life.

If I am critical of certain trends within New Age and feminist spirituality, it is because I have discovered within myself the tendency to believe I can control my life. I was born to a father who had a limited capacity to love. I spent many years trying to make myself acceptable to him to gain his approval. I believed that influencing his behavior and his feelings about me was within my control. My mother told me that if only I did this, or didn't do that, I would receive my father's love and admiration. Yet no matter what I did, my father always found fault with me. Finally, I realized that he probably would not change no matter what I did. I had not consciously or unconsciously drawn myself to the situation of being born to a father with a limited capacity to love. Nor had I as a little child done anything to cause him to reject me. And probably nothing that I could do would ever cause him to love me uncritically. I was born dependent and helpless to a limited human being. I had suffered enormously. And nothing could change that fact. For me, the acceptance of limitation was freeing, while the constant struggle to change a situation that was beyond my control was not.

Death

Traditional Christian theology denies that death is part of the cycle of life. A classic interpretation of the story of Adam and Eve is that death entered into the world because of sin. The wages of sin is death. Christ entered into the world to conquer sin and vanquish death. Saved by Christ, we will gain eternal life.

In Goddess religion, death is not punishment for sin. The great mystery is that life and death are intertwined. The fundamental rule of nature is that everything is born, everything will surely die, everything will be transformed. The life that has been given to us is not absolute, but conditional on the lives of other beings and finite. Not all seeds fall on fertile ground. Some sprout but do not receive water. Some blossom and then die. Other seeds become trees that live longer than we do. Many human eggs are not fertilized in the womb. Many fertilized eggs are spontaneously aborted. Some humans who are born die in infancy, some in childhood, some in young adulthood, some in maturity, some in old age.

One of my brothers died soon after birth. One of my grandmothers consciously chose to die in her seventy-eighth year, while the other died at sixty, her body and mind ravaged by cancer. One of my grandfathers had a stroke that left him helpless and bedridden for several years. From the perspective of Goddess religion, none of these deaths was wrong or unjust.[32]

My brother's death was almost unbearably sad. I still do not understand why my brother died after living only five days. But I now know that if I choose to love finite, embodied life, I must accept his and other deaths. My brother's death is one of the reasons I studied theology, but even if I write an important book, this will not justify his death or make up for my mother's suffering or my own. Like other things in life that we cannot control, my brother's death simply is.

My experiences of death have brought me to the understanding that life is a gift that is renewed every day. Neither our own lives nor those of our children nor those of our friends nor those of our lovers nor those of our parents are guaranteed to last for a specific amount of time. We cannot possess another human being. We can only love others for as long as they are with us.

We have been taught to think that human life is eternal, or if not eternal, at the very least subject to our control. But this is not true. To worship the Goddess as embodied in the earth means accepting that we and those we love may die at any time. There is no promise that the proper course of a human life is a certain number of years or that it should be lived without suffering.

Foster parents who care for dying children can perhaps teach us all something about loving less possessively. They nurture sick children for as long as they are alive—simply because they need love—knowing that they will lose these children to death.

To recognize death as part of life does not mean that death is not sad or that we should not grieve. Grieving, too, is part of the cycle of life. Tears release pain and open the way for a renewal of life. When my mother died, I felt sad for about a year. I cried nearly every day while washing dishes, talking to friends, or watching movies on television. After about a year, my intense grieving came to an end, though I still think about my mother often. My adopted Greek culture has death rituals that I think would have helped structure my time of mourning. Besides the funeral, there are other rituals after three days, after nine days, after forty days, and after a year that aid the process of remembering and letting go. Women wear black clothing and men wear black arm bands for a period of time, depending on the degree of relationship to the deceased.[33] When my mother died, I felt separate from other people who were not experiencing the same loss. It would have felt comforting to wear black for a period of time, so that others would have understood immediately that I was passing through a ritual of transformation.

We live in a time when death is not simply a matter of personal loss. Large numbers of people are starving or being killed in war, species are becoming extinct every day, and humanity itself stands on the brink of annihilation. It is a source of tremendous sadness to realize that we belong to a species that preys on its own kind and whose expansion across the planet is depriving many other species of the possibility of life. While I remain hopeful that somehow humanity will wake up in time to save itself and some other species, I know that this outcome is not assured. Even if we do manage to save ourselves, the world will be less rich and diverse than it was on the day each of us was born. When facing the overwhelming despair this thought engenders, I find it necessary to acknowledge sadness, grief, and anger. Joanna Macy has created rituals to deal with despair about the destruction of life. These rituals release denied feelings and empower participants to work for change.[34]

I also find it helpful to take a long view. For millions of years, species have come and gone on the face of the earth, yet the earth itself has survived. If the time of the human species and that of many other species comes to an end, the Gaia body will be diminished. But some species, however small and however few, will be left. The Gaia body will survive. The processes of birth, death, and renewal will continue. New species will develop. And many of them, too, will come to an end. This is the way of the Gaia body.[35]

Life Feeds on Life

One of the ways in which life and death are intertwined is that we must kill to live. Whether we eat plants or animals or both, we take the lives of other beings. If we do not do so, we will die. Animals may or may not be aware that they kill other beings to live. But we are. And when not denied, this knowledge is both a source of discomfort and cause for gratitude.

Much of ancient ritual, it is thought, revolved around this fact and knowledge of it. Ancient peoples approached the taking of life with great restraint. They thanked the spirits of the plants and animals who gave their lives to them. They prayed that the individuals they killed would be replaced so that their species would survive. They thanked the earth for supporting their lives and all lives.

According to anthropologist Ruth M. Underhill, a Papago Indian woman felt a sense of reverence even when taking clay from the earth to make a pot. "She told the clay, 'I take only what I need. It is to cook for my children.' In exchange, she left a gift."[36] In agricultural societies, the offering of first fruits and the pouring of libations of water, wine, and oil are a way of acknowledging the gift of life. The much maligned yet deeply meaningful custom of saying grace before meals is a remnant of these traditional rituals.

In pastoral societies, some of the lambs (usually the males because they cannot produce milk) are killed so that the mother may be milked. If these lambs remained with their mothers, there would be no extra milk, no yogurt, no cheese. If they were simply set free on the hillsides, the lambs would starve or eventually eat all the grass and deplete the ecosystem. Shepherds developed the ritual of a communal feast to thank the lamb for providing them life. The custom of fasting before the lamb is slain (still a part of Greek Easter customs) reflects the understanding that the taking of life is a serious matter. (The idea that Christ gave his life so that those who eat his body and blood might live is a symbolic interpretation of the literal sacrifice of the spring lamb.)

The masses of bloody sacrifices offered in patriarchal religion originated in the notion of returning a gift to the earth in exchange for all that has been given to us. But patriarchal sacrifice violates the notion of taking and giving only what is needed. Instead, the number of sacrifices build up the reputations of those who offer them and by analogy the prestige of the God or Goddess to whom they are offered.

It is deeply true that we all live because others have given their lives for us and that we will all die so that others may live. This is neither altruism nor sacrifice, but simply the way things are. It is believed that in Neolithic Çatal Hüyük, the bodies of the dead were set out to be eaten by vultures, a graphic reminder that death to one brings life to another. One day our bodies, too, will be returned to the earth, providing food for other beings.[37] I hope that Goddess religion will develop new rituals to help us acknowledge the connection of life and death, death and life.

Disaster and Disease

Finitude is also denied in dualistic philosophies that call natural phenomena such as hurricanes, floods, fires, earthquakes, volcanic eruptions, and disease "natural evil." From a dualistic point of view, "natural evil" is one of the reasons humanity must seek to rise above "nature." But from the point of view of the Gaia body, hurricanes, floods, fires, earthquakes, volcanic eruptions, and even disease are part of the cycle of birth, death, and renewal. In ancient Egypt, the annual flooding of the Nile was celebrated in myth and ritual because it was understood that through this process, croplands were regenerated. Natural phenomena are perceived as evil only because human beings have been taught to believe that we should be able to control all the conditions of life.

During an earthquake in San Francisco, one of my friends was in her office when a floor-to-ceiling metal bookcase fell to the floor. My friend was not hurt, but it took her many months to recover from the experience. An earthquake is scary. And a certain degree of trauma is understandable and healthy. But I believe my friend suffered for such a long time because the earthquake shattered her illusion that she was in control of her life and she was struggling to regain that sense of control. In fact, like all of us, she never had been in control of her life. She lived, as we all do, in interconnection and interdependence with other human beings and all beings in the web of life.

Once we realize, as our ancestors did, that life does not exist only for us, we can begin to see that hurricanes, floods, fires, earthquakes, and volcanic eruptions are not evil. They are one of the ways the earth body renews herself.

Disease, too, is part of life. It is the mode of survival of other beings in the web of life and an aspect of regeneration and renewal. When the human body is healthy and functioning optimally, it has great capacities to resist and endure disease. In addition, from time immemorial wise women and healers have discovered remedies within nature (the antecedents of many modern medicines) that aid the body in maintaining health and warding off disease. To recognize that disease is part of life is not to accept that the human body must succumb to it in every instance. But we should not believe, as we have been taught by modern medicine, that all disease (and perhaps even death itself) can or should be "conquered."

When one of my friends was diagnosed with the early stages of breast cancer, she went into shock. Her prognosis for recovery was excellent, but she experienced her cancer as threatening to her belief that she was in control of her life. When she was considering various treatments, she kept saying, "I don't have time for this. I want to get on with my life." She did not recognize that her disease was a part of her life.

Irretrievable Loss and Tragedy

Accepting our finitude means understanding irretrievable loss as one of the conditions of life.[38] To accept finitude does not mean to deny, to attempt to rationalize, or to rise above suffering. To carry a baby for nine months only to lose it at birth is sad. The baby is not better off for having died, and we are not necessarily better because we have suffered. A person who loses a home in a flood or an earthquake is not necessarily made stronger. Nor is a person who endures a long and protracted death from disease. The appropriate response to irretrievable loss is grief. We mourn our losses, and then we go on, knowing that death is not the final word. Rebirth and renewal will follow, in time.

Suffering that has a human cause also produces irretrievable loss. A child who is sexually abused continually for years does not necessarily learn a lesson from her experience. And no matter what she learns, nothing can make up for the loss of her childhood. Those who suffer the violence of war or the institutionalized violence of poverty also suffer in ways that cannot be rationalized away. The appropriate response to such suffering is a combination of grieving and taking action to prevent the same things from happening again.

In talking about irretrievable loss, it is important to distinguish preventable from inevitable suffering. Warfare, pollution, and patterns of domination are not part of the conditions of finitude. Yet even if we healed the environment, shared the earth's resources, learned to treat each other with embodied intelligent love, and ended war, finite life would still involve irretrievable suffering and loss. If there is a life after death, it does not explain away our suffering in this life.

Accepting that life involves irretrievable loss does not mean that life is essentially tragic. The view that life is tragic asserts that loss and suffering define the nature of existence, finally outweighing life and love. For much of my life, I believed this to be true. Growing up feeling unloved, experiencing the deaths of five close family members in my teenage years, watching my mother suffer a grief that seemed not to heal, and then learning about the horrors of the twentieth century in college, I was quite prepared to believe that life is tragic. But when my mother died and I experienced a great matrix of love, my perspective changed. I now believe that if love did not outweigh loss and suffering, the human species would not have survived. This has prompted me to take another (and more historical) look at the tragic worldview I embraced in my college years.

The tragic worldview derives from the perception of the limitations of the heroic ideal. It is a product of patriarchal warrior society in ancient Greece. The tragic writers asserted that the cosmos was unfeeling and uncaring, unconcerned with the heroic struggles of man. "All is impermanent. Even the mighty shall fall," the tragic chorus was fond of repeating.[39] In my opinion, the writers of tragedy in classical Athens were correct in pointing out the limitations of the heroic quest. The status achieved by the ancient hero who believed he could dominate woman and nature and other men with his will, intelligence, and weapons was indeed impermanent. Because he had violated the bonds of interdependence that are the basis of life, the earth body shook the ground on which he stood. Looked at from the point of view of the hero, "nature" was unfeeling and uncaring because it did not support his attempts to control reality. Looked at from the point of view of all beings in the web of life, the fall of the hero was just.

The dominated groups in classical Athens—wives of citizens, foreign slaves and prostitutes, both female and male, citizen boys required to perform sexual services for older men, and soldiers—may have experienced their lives as tragic. They may have understood the fall of the hero as revenge for what dominant males had caused them to suffer. But the tragic worldview provided them no opening to resist their suffering. It told them that suffering was inevitable.

The writers of the classical tragedies were able to present nature only as a boundary, a limit to the pretensions of the hero. Looked at from the point of view of birth, death, and renewal, the tragedies stop the action at the point of death. Perhaps the comedies and satyr plays that followed them completed the cycle. But the tragedies alone are incomplete.

Tragic writers could not or did not present the satisfactions of a life lived in interdependence with nature and other humans as an alternative to conquest and domination. In *The Iliad*, the hero, Achilles, is asked to choose between the simple life of a farmer or certain death on the battlefield that will lead to his being celebrated as a hero. Though Homer questions the wisdom of Achilles's choice and laments the horrors of war, he cannot imagine a compelling alternative to the rule of force.[40] Unless we accept the warrior's view that the structures of domination are an inevitable part of life, classical tragedy should not be taken as providing the essential insight into the human condition.

European-based educational systems grounded in "the classics" have stated that the Greeks of classical Athens are the first "rational men" who provide the foundation for modern western culture. Uncritical of the values of warrior cultures, western "civilization" courses present the "tragic hero" as an eternal model of human nature. We are taught (subtly and often without recognizing what we are learning) that the suffering caused by warfare and the structures of domination is one of the conditions of finitude. And we are given no tools to understand the difference between inevitable and human-caused suffering.

Life After Death

Goddess religion counsels us to accept death as part of the cycle of life. Death is understood as a return to earth, to the womb that gave us birth. This means that death does not separate us from the web of life or from the power of the Goddess. Our bodies will be transformed, providing nourishment for the earth and for other creatures. Our spirits will live on in the lives of those who remember us. Our spirits and our bodies (like those of all beings) will live on in the memory of the Gaia body.[41] This is as much as I know.

Is there, in addition, a personal survival after death? Communications from ancestors in dreams and visions and near-death experiences suggest that there might be. A few hours before my mother died, I felt that her mother and father, her baby sister who died, and her own baby who died were waiting for her.[42] Several years later, I had a vivid dream in which my mother asked me to forgive her for not telling me the truth about my father's feelings about me. Does this mean that my mother and her relatives survived death?

Experiences like these have been interpreted as verifying the Christian notion of eternal life, but, in fact, they tell us nothing about eternity. If they are more than projections, experiences of life after death tell us about the moment of death and about communication with those who have died. They do not tell us how long or in what form we survive death. I suggest that experiences of life after death might be interpreted as hinting at a conditional and finite survival after death.[43] Survival after death would be dependent on continuing connection with the living. We would survive after death and have the capacity to influence the present and future as long as the living remember us. When we are no longer remembered by the living, our personal presence in the world will fade away. For those who have developed strong connections with others during life, the transition to final death would not be abrupt, but gradual.

This understanding is congruent with the notion of life as interdependent. It resonates with the views of many traditional peoples who believe that the ancestors survive as long as their graves are tended. It also explains the continuing influence of the saints who are said to care for those who visit their shrines. The idea that we survive death as long as the living remember us is consistent with my experience and understanding, but I view it as a possibility, not a certainty. I am willing to live with uncertainty about things I cannot know.

A number of adherents of present-day Goddess religion believe in reincarnation. In my opinion, reincarnation is a plausible interpretation of the meaning of the symbol of the Goddess as Giver, Taker, and Renewer of Life. Surely our bodies are re-in-carnated (re-in-fleshed) when they become food for other beings in the web of life. Our spirits live on for better or worse in the memories and in the lives of those who remember us. There is also a sense in which we share collective or communal memories of times, events, and people in the past. Reincarnation, in this sense, is fully consistent with the understanding of life as connected, interdependent, and embodied.

Theories of reincarnation often go a step farther, asserting that our unique individuality, personality, or soul is reborn in another body. I have no experience to suggest that this is true. I have not had a "past-life" experience, nor have I sought one. I find that there is enough buried in my childhood to keep me busy excavating for a lifetime. I am inclined to view the stories of past lives told to me by others as metaphoric retellings of feelings or experiences in this life. And while I do not totally reject the idea of some kind of personal reincarnation, I find it a less compelling interpretation of my experience than the notion of conditional survival of death.

I am suspicious of theories of reincarnation when they are presented as rationalizations of human suffering. From my perspective, New Age understandings of reincarnation often seem to be an attempt to assert that we really are in control of every aspect of our lives. Popular understandings of reincarnation state that our position in this life is reward or punishment (or, in milder form, opportunity for education), determined by our actions in other lives. Followers of New Age philosophies often claim that we "choose" to be born into particular human situations. They insist that if we suffer incest or abuse as children or if we are born to starvation or if the country into which we are born is ravaged by war, we "chose" that situation because it offered us a "lesson" we needed to learn. When such theories are used to provide an explanation for our own suffering, they seem to me to be an attempt to deny that we really are finite, interdependent, and not fully in control of the conditions of our own lives. When they are used to provide justification for the suffering of others, I believe they become pernicious.

Goddess religion, as I understand it, enjoins humility. There are many things in life that we cannot control or change. There also are many things we cannot understand or know. As long as we delight in the life that has been given to us, approach the taking of life with great restraint, and accept death as the inevitable ending of life in our bodies, I do not believe we need to know the exact form our renewal and regeneration after death will take.

7

Humanity
in the Web of Life

And we are nature. We are nature seeing nature. We are nature with a concept of nature. Nature weeping. Nature speaking of nature to nature.[1]

The first truth about human beings is that we are part of nature. Like other beings, human beings are relational, interdependent, and embodied. Like many other animals, we are communal and social. Powers of reflection and action, once said to set us apart from nature, must now be used to shape a new place for humanity within the web of life.

We Are Nature

Qualities and capacities once viewed as distinctively human do not absolutely separate humans from other beings in the web of life, nor do they set us "above" or "outside of" nature. Our intelligence does not set us apart from nature, but rather is an expression of the intelligence that exists within nature.[2] Stones and trees, rivers and mountains, can communicate their wisdom to us if we are willing to listen. Humans are not the only animals that can express feelings. Dogs whimper, cats purr, horses whinny. Nor are we the only animals that create technologies: Spiders spin webs, birds make nests, beavers construct dams, and other primates use "tools" such as sticks and stones to gather food and prepare it for eating. We are not the only animals to engage in symbolic behavior. Peacocks spread their tails to gain attention; dogs roll over and expose their bellies to indicate they don't want to fight; monkeys bare their teeth when threatened. Humans are not even the only animals that can learn to use human language, because chimpanzees and gorillas have been taught to communicate with us in sign and other languages. It has been argued that animals have a moral sense.[3] A group of Australian and New Zealand scientists have proposed a revision of the genus *Homo* to include gorillas and chimpanzees because of the closeness of their DNA to that of humans.[4]

Yet, though our intelligence arises from within nature, as far as we know, human beings are the only creatures within nature with the ability to develop a concept of nature, the only species to attempt to control nature, the only species to think about our relation to other beings within nature, and the only species to reflect on the consequences of our actions. Indeed, we can contemplate not only the consequences of our actions, but also the consequences of our ways of thinking. This is our uniqueness as human beings, just as the power of flight is the uniqueness of winged creatures. Though we are not "better" or "higher" than other creatures, we are different to some degree.

Understanding human nature as part of nature inspires greater respect for the diversity of human experience than defining human nature primarily through our rational capacities. If the essentially human is said to be (as it is in much of the western tradition) rational consciousness, rational self-reflection, or the ability to make rational moral decisions based on universal principles, it is hard to avoid the conclusion that some humans, especially educated white males, are more human than others. This view has often led to the naming of "the other"—women, children, and ethnic, cultural, and racial groups—as closer to nature, as "barbarians" and "savages." But if the essentially human is intelligently to love other people and all beings in the web of life and to rejoice in the finite, embodied life that has been given to us, then (white male) intellectuals are by no means self-evidently superior. Indeed, quite the opposite might be the case.

Human Being as Relational and Interdependent

Human beings are essentially relational and interdependent. We are tied to others from the moment of birth to the moment of death. Our lives are dependent in more ways than we can begin to imagine on support and nurture from the web of life, from the earth body. The first gift that we are given as human beings is our birth, and the second is nurture, both food and love. Without these gifts, we would not be here, and we would not survive. Embodied intelligent love *really is* the ground of our being.

We are so fundamentally interdependent that, as Martin Buber says, there is no "I" without a "Thou," no self that is not created in relationship with another:

The basic word I-You can be spoken only with one's whole being. The concentration and fusion into a whole being can never be accomplished by me, can never be accomplished without me. I require a You to become; becoming I, I say You. All actual life is encounter.[5]

I become an "I," a "whole being," a self, only when I say "You," only in relationship. Buber states further that it is wrong to say that first we "are" and then we "enter into" relationships:

Rather, the longing for relation is primary, the cupped hand into which the being that confronts us nestles. . . . In the beginning is the relation—as the category of being, as readiness, as a form that reaches out to be filled.[6]

Because there is no self apart from relationship, parents have the power to create their children as intelligent and loving by treating them with intelligent love. Psychotherapist J. Konrad Stettbacher recognizes this when he writes:

How you were born is how you will live. If you were really wanted by your mother and father, you will be able to love. You will want to live and take pleasure in living. If you were really respected by your mother and father, you will respect life.[7]

This sounds simple, but it is also true. We learn to love because we are loved. We learn to respect life because life is respected in us. The self is created in relation.

From this perspective, the independent self of traditional philosophies and theologies can be seen to be a fiction. Many philosophers have portrayed "man" as an isolated rational and moral individual who must "give up" a portion of his "independence" to enter into relationship. Some philosophers even speak of an intrinsic "opposition" between "the self" and "others" who are perceived to "impinge upon" the "freedom of the self." But if our lives are fundamentally interdependent and our sense of self is created in relation with others, then this understanding is false.

In contrast, feminist anthropologist of religion Karen McCarthy Brown finds that in many traditional cultures, "developing a strong sense of self does not lead to self-sufficiency but to stronger and more sustaining social bonds." If we took this view as normative, we might conclude that "it is precisely in responsive and responsible relation to others that one has the clearest and most steady sense of self."[8]

Rupturing the Bonds of Life

Understanding that relationships create, nurture, and sustain the self also means recognizing that relationships can damage and destroy it. When embodied intelligent love is withheld or denied, the web of life is ruptured. A child who is not loved becomes desperate and wishes she or he could die. Stettbacher writes, "*'I can't live if you don't want me and cannot love me'* is the inevitable refrain of every unwanted, and therefore unloved child."[9] Because it is too painful, children attempt to suppress the primal experience of rejection. Rather than facing their past, unloved children come to believe that the world is an unloving place and that they are unworthy of love.

I believe Stettbacher's theory is valid because I know it to be true in my own experience. Throughout my twenties, thirties, and early forties, I suffered periodic bouts of serious depression, usually brought on by perceived rejection by lovers, friends, family, or colleagues. At those times, I repeated endlessly within myself, "No one loves me, no one will ever love me, I would rather die." When I slipped into depression, I felt vulnerable, I knew no way out of my despair, and I did not understand the cause of my suffering.[10]

Though it may sound a bit melodramatic, Stettbacher's description of a traumatized child accurately describes the undertones of my life, particularly as applied to the drama that inevitably surrounded my most intimate love relationships. "We will not love life. We will endure it, unable to come to terms with ourselves or the world. Everything we do will be agony. Our world will be overshadowed by anxiety, our lives tyrannized by fear."[11] Even though I was not always consciously suffering, I lived under a continual cloud of fear that my deep feelings of worthlessness would be activated by the very relationships I felt I needed most.

Recently, I was able to recognize that my father was unable to love his children fully and wholeheartedly without attempting to control them. His failure to affirm my unique individuality was the cause of my suffering. And true to Stettbacher's theory (though I read his book after I had made the essential breakthrough), the way to make sense of my suffering was to understand it. Once I understood that my suffering had a cause and that its cause was neither my own essential worthlessness nor the absence of love in the universe, I breathed an enormous sigh of relief. And as I breathed, the emptiness I had always felt began to fill up with life and love. Since then, I have been able to understand that I am and always have been deserving of love. I survived my father's rejection because I was loved by my mother and grandmothers. I can now more easily accept the love that is given to me because I do not need to magnify it to fill up a hole inside me. Rejection by others is no longer threatening because it does not have the power to make me feel that perhaps, after all, I am undeserving of love.

To entertain the thought that we were not loved and not wanted might seem inordinately painful. But for those of us who were not loved, the pain we are already suffering is worse. Many of us are suffering, many of us feel an emptiness inside, many of us find little joy in our lives, and we wonder why. I believe that the most basic reason for this is that we were not fully loved, wanted, and accepted as children.

Psychotherapist and theorist Alice Miller alleges that child abuse is embedded in traditional child-rearing methods considered normal in our cultures. The notions that children are to be seen and not heard, must do as they are told, and must conform to their parents' will, deprive children of spontaneity, individuality, and life itself. The idea that to spare the rod is to spoil the child legitimates violence as a way of achieving parental control. Even parents who do not hit their children often try to control them in more subtle ways. Children brought up with this poisonous pedagogy learn that they have no right to their own lives. They suppress their feelings and sensations, the power of the life force within them, in their desperate attempts to please their parents. The price they pay is that they can no longer feel joy in their own lives. And unless they are given an opportunity to understand and heal their own suffering, they will probably inflict it on others.[12]

To focus on the healing and harm that can be done to small children in the family does not mean that we are not deeply affected by other relationships in our lives. That there can be healing from childhood trauma underscores the importance of all our relationships. All have the power to create us as loving, responsive, and responsible. All have the power to rupture our bonds with one another and the web of life.

Relational Independence

While it is true that there is no self apart from relation, feminism has called attention to the danger of "losing ourselves" in relationships. Many women have been defined or defined themselves so exclusively through their husbands, families, or lovers that they have no sense of individuality and value. In addition, many women have suffered violence and abuse, both mental and physical, including incest and battering, in relationships. Recognizing the problematic dimensions of relationship, feminists have rightly argued that women, like all human beings, need to develop a sense of self strong enough to resist abuse. Furthermore, feminists have insisted that relationships are richer when we bring a clear sense of self to them.

But in seeking to affirm women's individuality and value, many feminist thinkers err in uncritically adopting the model of the "independent self" from western literary and philosophical traditions. The dominant western view that relationships are essentially limiting to the freedom of the self is found in Henrik Ibsen's classic play *The Doll's House*. Its protagonist, Nora, asserts her independence by closing the door and walking out on her husband and children. Her dramatic act tells us that a woman must choose between her "self" and her family. Nora became a model for the feminist heroine. In her influential book *Sexual Politics*, feminist theorist Kate Millett wrote, "Ibsen's Nora Helmer is the true insurrectionary of the sexual revolution."[13] In the early days of the late-twentieth-century women's movement, many feminists believed that marriage and children were incompatible with women's freedom. One of the reasons that I did not have children was that I accepted this view.

Womanist theologian Delores Williams criticized white feminists for urging women to seek "freedom" at the expense of relationships and responsibilities to family and community. According to Williams, black American women, as a group, have never had the economic or psychological freedom to abandon their family ties. Only within family and community can black people find the resources to combat the racism of the larger society. Williams coined the term *relational independence* to name her understanding that for black women, personal freedom must be found within the context of ties and obligations to others.[14]

Though rooted in her particular struggle as a black woman in a racist and sexist society, Williams's model of relational independence is appropriate for all of us whether we are black or white, yellow or brown, female or male. The joining together of the terms *relational* and *independence* expresses the insight that relationships are necessary in human life and that life-sustaining relationships promote the independence of both partners. In this model, selfhood is not gained by becoming independent of relationships, but by learning to live independently and interdependently within them. Relationships that promote independence need not always be based on a notion of equality. Many relationships, such as that of a parent to a small child or a teacher to a student, are not mutual in that sense. But in such relationships, the goal should be the achieving of relational independence, a strong sense of self, by both partners.

Yet it must not be denied that relational independence can be difficult for women to achieve in modern societies. My female friends who have children speak of years during which they, like Nora, felt they had lost the independence of self within relationships. This may be especially true in the mobile middle class, where ties to neighborhood, family support, and friends have been severed and where one or both parents work at jobs that are not designed to allow them time to participate fully in the rearing of their children. Because of society's expectation that a woman is primarily responsible for the care of "her" children, a woman often feels that she must cope alone with overwhelming demands and responsibilities. Clearly, mutual independence could be more easily achieved by mothers and children if jobs were structured to allow all of us (male and female, parents and others) to spend time with children and if mothers and fathers had networks of family, friends, and community support on which they could depend.

The model of relational independence also applies to those who live alone for longer or shorter periods of time. Relational independence does not mean that we are whole only if we are married or live in "a" committed relationship to a partner or children. Like many others who are single or have been divorced, I have felt tortured by society's expectation that a person can find fulfillment only within "a" relationship. In relationships based on the assumption that women must give more than men, it is difficult for women to achieve relational independence. In this time of changing sex-role expectations, it has not been possible for all of us to find a partner who will support our independence within a relationship. But just as surely as those who live with partners or in families, those who live on their own are created, shaped, and nurtured in relationships.

Whether living with others or alone, we need to learn to recognize and value all our relationships, not only those that are sanctioned by the legal systems or expectations of our societies. During a period of time when I wanted to have a child, a woman I scarcely knew told me that she didn't know whether I would have any physical children, but that I already had many spiritual daughters.[15] Recently, I have also begun to name and value the seven years I spent "as a second mother" to my younger brother Kirk, from the time when he was born when I was ten years old until I left for college.

To celebrate bonds not usually recognized, lesbians and gay men have created commitment ceremonies. For the past twenty or so years, there has been an underground thread of conversation among women who are married, single, and in lesbian relationships that acknowledges the importance of our friendships and imagines that we will live near one another and care for one another in our old age. Perhaps we can develop many kinds of new rituals to acknowledge, celebrate, and deepen the sustaining bonds that are beginning to function for us as new models of family, extended family, and community.

Two of my closest female friends and I have shared rituals in which we adopted one another as sisters.[16] When conflict subsequently developed in one of those relationships, we both knew that our commitment to each other was, as one of us said in a letter to the other, "to my sister through thick and thin."

Nurturing Life

Giving birth and nurturing children are important expressions of relational, interdependent, embodied life. Goddess imagery celebrates the female body and its powers, inspiring a sense of respect for mothers and mothering that has been lost in patriarchal societies, and especially in modern cultures. Goddess religion provides an important antidote to the widespread view (all too often promulgated by "educational" institutions, including the university) that "success" is to be found in individual achievement and independence of relationship.

On the other hand, becoming a physical parent is not the only way to embody the Goddess's power as nurturer of life. Sisters and aunts, stepparents, teachers, and others are often as involved in the nurturing of children as parents and grandparents. Animals and plants are also children of the Goddess. Everyone who has cared for a garden, lived with a pet, or worked for the preservation of rivers and streams is engaged in the nurturing of life and growth.

In this time when human beings represent a great threat to the survival of plants, animals, and the earth body, the decision to give birth to children (for those of us who have a choice) is not always the wisest decision. Birth control and abortion are consistent with a concern for the nurturing of life. Contrary to some contemporary understandings, birth control and abortion are not modern technological inventions. Wise women in many traditional cultures knew of herbs to prevent conception or cause early abortions. One of the main charges against the women accused of witchcraft in the *Malleus Maleficarum* [The Hammer of Witches] was their ability to cause or prevent birth.[17] This charge probably was based in fact.[18] Several years ago, I told some of my students that I had read in a radical feminist newspaper that certain herbs cause abortion. "Ah yes," a young Mexican-American Catholic woman replied, "*Rosamaria*, tea made from rosemary. My grandmother says it brings on a very late period."

The responsible use of birth control can protect us from sexually transmitted diseases and may prevent the conception of children we are not prepared for or unable to nurture. When birth control fails, when we have not had access to it, or when we have not understood its importance, abortion can be the best choice. Archetypal psychologist Ginette Paris made the radical claim that *"it is a sin against life*, the child, and the collectivity not to abort when necessary. Since the failure of contraception leads to abortion, and since the error is human, it is inhuman not to accept abortion." In contradistinction to the opponents of abortion, she argued that in most cases abortion is not selfish but unselfish, not egotistical but responsible. In recognition that life is interdependent and relational, Paris alleged that it is a great wrong both to the woman *and* to the unborn child if a woman is forced to bear a child she does not want:

> *Because the bond between mother and child is the most intimate of all, forcing a woman to bear and raise a child against her will is an act of violence. It binds up and degrades the mother-child bond, sowing hatred where there should only be love, receptivity, and welcome.*[19]

Abortion, as I understand it, is the taking of a potential life. All taking of life should be approached with great restraint. We should take only what we need from the body of the earth, and abortion should not be undertaken thoughtlessly. In Goddess religion, abortion, like the taking of life to eat, should be marked by a ritual acknowledging that we take only what we need, honoring the life that is taken, thanking the web of life for all that has been given to us, and, if possible, leaving a gift.[20]

Conflict and Suffering in Relationships

To say that intelligent embodied love is the ground of being and that the self is formed in relationship does not mean that conflict and suffering can be avoided. Just as we cannot live without taking the lives of other beings as our sustenance, so too conflict inevitably arises in all human relationships. We are born helpless and dependent on others for food, comfort, and nurture. And yet the other or others on whom we are dependent have their own needs, some of which have nothing to do with ours. There will be times when a baby's crying will interrupt a mother or father's legitimate need for sleep, nurture, conversation with friends, time alone, or work.

As we grow, we become less dependent, but we never outgrow our need for love and connection. Yet in human relationships, one person often needs what the other cannot give or can give only at what seems like great cost to the self. Because we are different, both limited and enriched by our particular backgrounds and perspectives, we will not always see things the way others do. Thus, conflicts in vision and judgment will arise.

Karen McCarthy Brown found a recognition of the inevitability of conflict in the sensibility of the Haitian communities she studied. She states that "the moral sense that emerges . . . is one that, if it does not always delight in life's conflicts, at least accepts them as somehow deeply and inevitably true."[21] Such realism is an important corrective to Christian and New Age ideals of selfless or unconditional love that lead us to imagine that we can live in perfect harmony with one another. When conflict is suppressed because it does not fit into an ideal of loving behavior, it can poison relationships.

In my childhood, the only anger I experienced had been withheld until it became judgmental and punitive. In contrast, in the culture of modern Greece, anger is easily expressed. The longer I live in Greece, the more I learn to appreciate the simple and direct expression of anger. It sends a signal that conflict has occurred in a relationship. This can lead both parties to seek a resolution. Reconciliation can occur much more easily if anger and conflict are seen as part of the natural rhythm of relationship. But while simple and direct expression of anger can bring healing, anger that is stored up or used to punish or to destroy the other is abusive. The difference is that clear anger says, "Stop, this hurts me," while abusive anger says, "How could you do that, you worthless good for nothing."

Because we are limited, it is also inevitable that we will unconsciously cause suffering to others. This often happens in relationships when unresolved suffering leads us to become so self-involved that we do not see how our behavior is affecting others. The appropriate response when we recognize that we have caused another to suffer is to take responsibility and apologize. When we apologize, the other's suffering is not compounded by wondering what she or he did to cause our behavior. Taking responsibility also means attempting to understand and transform the suffering that we have caused others and the unresolved suffering within ourselves. Yet if we recognize that suffering is inevitable in human relationships, we will not blame ourselves unduly for being human.

Our Bodies Are Ourselves

Not only are human beings interdependent and relational, we are also embodied. Our bodies are not flawed homes for our rational souls, nor is the flesh a "corruption" of a "more perfect" nature. To the contrary, our bodies are ourselves,[22] our mode of being in the world. All that we know, all that we suffer, all that we do, occurs in and through our bodies. The image of the earth as the body of the Goddess is a powerful symbol of embodied life. Even the Goddess knows herself and is known through her body.

Our minds are not separate from our bodies. Sensation and feeling are not the antitheses of thought: They are the essential ingredients of our knowing. Feminist Christian ethicist Beverly Harrison expresses this well:

All knowledge is rooted in our sensuality. We know and value the world, if we know and value it, through our ability to touch, to hear, to see. Perception is foundational to conception. Ideas are dependent on our sensuality. Feeling is the basic bodily ingredient that mediates our connectedness to the world. All power, including intellectual power, is rooted in feeling. If feeling is damaged or cut off, our power to image the world and to act in it is destroyed.[23]

When we are alienated from sensation and feeling, we lose the power to think clearly. The body is, as Adrienne Rich says, "the corporeal ground of our intelligence."[24]

But dualistic habits of thought have led many to discount feeling and sensation as less important than thinking. While this attitude is not prevalent in the counterculture created by the humanistic psychology movement, it remains enshrined in educational systems and in the workplace. Denial of feelings is an important aspect of the Protestant ethic and the spirit of capitalism. "Keeping a stiff upper lip" is an essential part of socialization, especially for males in northern Europe and North America. Psychotherapist J. Konrad Stettbacher names and challenges this view when he writes,

"Feelings and sensations aren't so important. It's best to forget them as quickly as you can." A person who thinks like this is a child of the times. We live in an age in which intellectual virtuosity and dazzling intelligence are showered with respect and rewards. What usually gets overlooked is the fact that, in evolutionary terms, it is only relatively recently that intellect has been raised to such a pinnacle of importance.

Stettbacher argues that feeling and sensation should be listened to and valued because they are the "guardians of life":

For millions of years . . . it was feeling and sensation that guided and directed life. . . . They are the guardians of our species, of life itself. As such, they are the most valuable asset we possess. . . . If we heed them, they keep us on track about every aspect of our lives.[25]

Attending to sensation and feeling grounds us in the body and relationship and puts us in touch with the basic energies of life.

Yet in modern societies, we are very much cut off from our bodies and from the knowledge that comes to us through our feelings and senses. Though many of us reject the view that the body is a source of sin and temptation, few of us have learned fully to value and listen to our bodies. Living in cities and suburbs, we deny ourselves renewing physical contact with plants, animals, clean air and clear water, and often even with other humans. We work so hard that our bodies are stressed, tired, and listless. When we come home from work, we often do not want to interact with other people. We expect the kids to keep quiet, our living partners not to make demands. We use television, drugs, and alcohol to cut off and deaden our feelings. The cult of physical fitness, while certainly preferable to tuning out in front of the television set, is often not a genuine communion with the physical. Rather than walking on a local hillside, swimming in a lake, or planting vegetables in our gardens, we go to gyms and work out with machines or accompanied by loud pounding music. Rather than accepting the uniqueness of our own and every other physical body, we try to remake our bodies as muscular or slim, images presented to us from outside the self.

In my own life, I spent many years working at a job that left me frustrated and dissatisfied at the end of almost every day. Then I drove home through heavy traffic on a freeway, talked over the day with my husband, had dinner and a glass of wine, and watched television until I fell asleep. Not until I started spending my summers in a Greek village where I could see the sun every day and the moon every night, walked to get where I was going, and swam in the sea, did I begin to realize how little I had allowed myself to experience joy in my body in my daily life.

Still, it was years before I listened to what my body was telling me. I had been conditioned to believe that the American way of life is far superior to any other and that the way I lived was the "best I could hope for." After all, I had a good job, a beautiful big house (and a huge mortgage), a shiny red car (and a substantial car payment). The American dream. And yet my body kept telling me that something was wrong, that the joy I experienced when my senses were fully alive was not present in my normal routines.

The Power of the Erotic

In the ground-breaking essay "Uses of the Erotic: The Erotic as Power," womanist poet and theorist Audre Lorde named "the erotic" as a power that can awaken us from the numbness of alienation from our bodies. According to Lorde, we can experience the power of the erotic in sexual passion as well as in any "physical, emotional, psychic, or intellectual" exchange. It is "an internal sense of satisfaction to which, once we have experienced it, we know we can aspire," and "a question of how acutely and fully we can feel in the doing."[26]

Lorde stated that in suppressing the erotic, our culture cut us off from the source of our deepest nonrational knowledge. She argued that only when we allow our deepest feelings and sensations to surface within us are we fully alive:

> *When we begin to live from within outward, in touch with the power of the erotic within ourselves, and allowing that power to inform and illuminate our actions upon the world around us, then we begin to be responsible to ourselves in the deepest sense. For as we begin to recognize our deepest feelings, we begin to give up, of necessity, being satisfied with suffering and self-negation, and with the numbness which so often seems like their only alternative in society.*[27]

The erotic is a transformative power because we have been taught that we should not expect to feel good. Once we recognize that we do have the right to satisfaction and joy, we will begin to change the way we have lived in "suffering and self-negation" or in "numbness."

Because we are cut off from the erotic in our daily lives, many of us identify the erotic primarily with spontaneous sexual expression. But the power of the erotic can be felt in swimming in the sea, watching the sun set, laughing with friends, holding a child, petting a cat, painting a wall, cooking a meal, in any job well done. As we learn to experience the power of the erotic in all that we do, we understand that sexuality is only one of many gates to spiritual and physical satisfaction. Nonetheless, sexuality can be a powerful expression of our connection to others and to all beings in the web of life. Sexual energy can be an almost irresistible force drawing us to connect with another human body. Sexual experience can be ecstatic, taking us out of our ordinary selves, opening up our deepest feelings, connecting us to the soul as well as the body of another, expanding the limited boundaries of the ego. Sexuality can make us intensely aware of our immersion in the rhythms of the universe, our ties to the whole web of life. For us, sexuality can also become a mode of deep communication, a profound expression of intelligent embodied love. All sexual relationships, whether homosexual or heterosexual, monogamous or nonmonogamous, have this potential. But when we use our sexuality to dominate or violate, when we take our own pleasure without concern for the other, when we create children we cannot nurture, we rupture the web of life.

Feminist theorists have pointed out that the control of female sexuality is one of the requirements of the patrilineal family, where name and inheritance are passed though the father. Only if a woman has sex exclusively with her husband can a man be certain that his wife's children are "his." In a patrilineal system, female sexuality is a threat to male dominance and control. With the rise of dualism, female sexuality is also perceived as a threat to "man's" attempt to free himself from the bonds of nature. The existence of female bodies calls attention to the fact that man does not spring full-grown from the head of Zeus. Since dualistic thinking arises within patriarchal societies, it is not surprising that woman is demonized and that her sexuality is viewed as "the devil's gateway" or the cause of the "evil impulse" in man. As long as such views remain normative, violence against women will seem justified, and both women and men will be alienated from the body and the knowledge it holds.

Female and Male

Sexual differentiation is one of the obvious facts of our bodily existence. However, though sexual difference is recognized in every society, the meanings given to being female or male are very much a product of cultures. In small-scale, not highly militarized societies, female and male roles are generally viewed as complementary: Women and men are each recognized for what they contribute to the tribe or clan, and motherhood and caring for children are valued.[28] In contrast, in patriarchal warlike societies, the role of the dominant male is more highly valued: Women's role is defined as motherhood, and motherhood is said to be less important than military, intellectual, spiritual, or other male pursuits. In Christian theology, it was asserted that woman must become "like a man" (which in this case means more "rational" or "spiritual" than is her "nature") in order to come into relationship with God (who was understood to be rational, spiritual, and "male"). According to Adrienne Rich, such views have made the body "so problematic for women that it often seemed easier to shrug it off and travel as a disembodied spirit."[29]

Women and men are different in significant ways, but the valuations given to our differences in the classical dualisms are false. Moreover, the differences between women and men are not as great as we usually think. Women have breasts, vaginas, ovaries, and uteruses, while men have penises and testes. Besides these obvious (or "primary") biological sex differences, scientists have been unable to agree on any other characteristics that definitively separate women and men. And even here, matters are not so clear. Though only women can give birth, not all women are able or choose to do so. And though no woman can give birth without the contribution of a man, not all men can or do father children. The assertion of primary sexual differences between males and females is further complicated by the existence of individuals whose sexual morphology and/or gender identity is not clearly female or male.

All "secondary" sex-related characteristics fall within a continuum. In general, men have more testosterone (the so-called masculine hormone) whereas women have more estrogen (the so-called feminine hormone) from puberty through the middle years of life. But all of us have both estrogen and testosterone, and before puberty and after middle life, the levels of these hormones are not significantly different in females and males. Other differences, such as physical strength and height, also fall within a continuum. Generally, men are taller than women, but some women (like me) are taller than most men. Similarly, some women have greater physical strength than most men. So-called sex-related differences in temperament between women and men, such as that men are "more aggressive" than women or that women are "more nurturing" than men, are even more difficult to define and test and are very much subject to cultural conditioning. They have not been definitively proved and are a subject of intense debate within academic and scientific circles. We all know some women who are more aggressive than some men, and some men who are more nurturing than some women.

It is important to affirm that all differences between women and men, other than (or perhaps even including) the strictly biological differences in our reproductive systems, fall on a continuum. But if our bodies are ourselves, the differences in our bodies probably do have some effect on the way we experience the world. The biological fact that women get pregnant and give birth, combined with the biological-cultural fact that women are usually primarily responsible for the care of infants and young children, may make it easier for women to understand that life is embodied, relational, and interdependent and to recognize the human connection to nature. Such differences in perception and body wisdom, if they exist, are subtle, difficult to measure, and not absolute. If we want to make it easier for men to understand that they, too, are embodied, relational, interdependent, and connected to nature, we can make it possible for them to be present at the birth of children[30] and to devote considerable time to caring for children and other living things.

Recognizing that there are or may be differences between men and women does not negate the basic qualities we share. Both women and men are embodied. Both men and women are relational and interdependent. Both give and receive love and nurture. Both have created technologies. Both reflect on their lives and on the lives of other beings. These qualities are neither female nor male. In the most significant ways, we are alike.

Sexual orientation also seems to fall on a continuum. Sexual "preference" can be divided into the three components of social behavior, erotic feeling, and genital sexuality. Most people in the world, including those most opposed to homosexuality, are predominantly homosocial, which means that they socialize most frequently with their own sex. Traditional societies divide the world into men's and women's spheres, and most people spend most of their time with those of their own sex. In the conventional American family, men play or watch sports together and go to bars or country clubs to socialize or drink with other men, whereas women belong to church groups, babysitting collectives, and women's clubs. At family gatherings, women congregate together to talk about their homes and children while men go to another room to talk about sports, politics, and ways to make money. Even though women have entered the work force in increasing numbers, women and men still seem to have different communication styles and interests. Most people are both homoerotic and heteroerotic, which means they have deep feelings for and express physical affection for people of both the same and the other sex. Even genital sexual expression seems to fall on a continuum. Many people prefer the other sex, some prefer the same sex, and others fall somewhere in between. What is important is that we express intelligent embodied love in all our relations.

Communities and Societies, Cultures and Social Institutions

Human relationships are embedded in communities and societies, cultures and social institutions. Ideally, communities are groups of people who come together to support each other in work, in relaxation, and in celebration of the meaning of life. Societies are larger-scale communities.

Communities are the creators of cultural meaning. In the earliest human communities, people who were gatherers and hunters traveled together in small groups, sharing the work of child care and gathering, joining together in the hunt. They had symbols and rituals and stories that helped them understand the patterns in their way of life, articulate their values, and orient themselves to the great powers of the universe. That is to say, they had religion, culture, and elementary social and economic structures.

After people settled down and learned to farm, symbols, rituals, and stories continued to guide their lives, which now centered around the process of nurturing food in the fertile earth, herding animals, pottery-making, and weaving. In small-scale groups, traditions were passed down orally in the course of everyday life and at times of communal ritual celebrations. As communities developed into larger and more complex societies, values were codified in the institutions of culture: in written records, law, religion, education, politics, economics, medicine, arts, communications, and the military.

Culture and social institutions shape our lives from the moment of birth, telling us whether the first person to hold an infant will be the mother, a grandmother, a midwife, a doctor, a nurse, the father, a nanny, a sister. When someone first speaks to an infant, they do so in language that has encoded within it culturally constructed understandings. Language tells us what it means to be a self, how we are related to others and to nature, what it means to be male and female. The English language, for example, dictates that we speak and act differently to boys and girls. Girls are sweet and delicate and must be spoken to softly. They like dolls, bunnies, and books. Boys are stronger and more active. They like loud noises and being jostled. They prefer balls, baseball gloves, and guns. Parents and others who try to break these stereotypes find it difficult. When my mother and I bought my nephew a boy doll for Christmas the year he was two, he was thrilled. But when he came back from putting his doll to bed, my brothers taunted him with language. "You are a girl," they said. He never played with his doll again.

Those who study linguistics have discovered that western languages emphasize the separate self in ways that some other languages do not. When Susan Griffin writes that "we are nature weeping" or Paula Gunn Allen writes that "we are the land," we are jarred because these constructions are unfamiliar in our languages. We have been taught that nature is to be controlled by man and that the land is the place where we live. When we hear that "She is a new creation," we are shocked because the conventions of our language tell us that God is male. The power of language has been a consistent theme in this book, but language is only one example of the ways in which our lives are constructed by cultural and social institutions. Other institutions, such as education, economics, politics, medicine, law, arts, communications, the military, and of course religion, encode cultural values, telling us who we are and how to live.

The industrial revolution and the migrations to cities that followed it led to the breakdown of traditional communities that had sustained life for millenia. Many of those living in modern cities and suburbs are as alienated from community as they are from nature. The mobility of modern life, touted as a symbol of freedom, has brought with it loneliness and isolation. Even in political democracies, many feel that impersonal elites make the important decisions that affect social life. As cities break down and homelessness and violence spread, some long for the safety and security of small-town communities.

It is important not to romanticize the past. I grew up in a small town where there was a sense of neighborhood and community. When we moved there, the town was absorbing a great influx of outsiders who had moved into the tract homes built when the orange groves were cut down. My brothers and I played Mother-May-I and Hit-the-Bat with the other kids on our street, and my family knew all the families on the block and most of the other families in town. I also experienced the narrowness and prejudice of small-town life. Though I did not question it at the time, I did not learn anything positive about the Mexicans who lived in an adjacent town. The only Girl Scout troop in my school refused to take newcomers, including me. As the smartest and tallest girl in my class, I never "fit in" to the social world of my high school. I breathed a sigh of relief when I left my small town. Female friends who grew up in Greek villages also speak of the restrictions in their lives in small communities.

We could not return to the past even if we wanted to. Yet we need community to survive and thrive as human beings. We really cannot live alone. Something very basic is lost when we are afraid to walk in the streets where we live. We need communities to support us in work and play and to help us bring up children. We feel better when we are part of groups that speak a common language, share our values, and help us understand our place in the universe. We must work with others if we are to influence the decisions that are made in our societies. All of this underscores the need to create new communities to replace those that have been lost.

Diversity and Difference in the Human Community

One of the greatest temptations in human life is to limit the sphere of our love and concern to ourselves or to those closest to us, to members of our own family, community, or society. In the modern Greek language, for example, the words *ksénos* and *kséni*, which mean "stranger" or "foreigner," can be applied to anyone who is not from one's own village and even to those from one's village to whom one is not related by recognized family ties. Greeks have a much-praised tradition of offering hospitality to the "stranger."[31] On the other hand, the stranger stands outside the system of duties and ethical obligations that are owed to "one's own." The failure to include "the other" within one's system of ethical values is found in the experience of most groups, communities, and societies.

In traditional western thought, the way to widen our sphere of concern is to replace "particularistic" thinking with "universal" values. If we can recognize that we all share a universal human nature, it is said, then we can rise above our sexual, ethnic, cultural, and historical differences. Recently, this way of thinking has been criticized by women and members of ethnic groups who are not certain that we want to give up the distinctiveness and difference of our particular identities. We have argued that the "universal" values we are being asked to embrace look suspiciously like those of dominant white males.

Goddess thealogy affirms that we all come from one source while stating that diversity is the great principle of the earth body. In this view, difference is not antithetical to unity. We are both different and related in the web of life. Not only the differences of species but the difference of cultures and ethnic groups can be affirmed as contributing to the richness of the earth body. How boring it would be if there were only one kind of songbird. How boring it would be if there were only one season. How boring it would be if there were only one culture.

But we have been taught to fear human differences. This fear is in part an inheritance of the dominator cultures that defined the peoples they conquered as inferior, savage, barbarian. If the two poles of superior and inferior, civilized and savage, are the only options for the interpretation of difference, then it is no wonder we fear it. If those who are different are "uncivilized" or "barbarian," then they must be violent and our fear of them is justified. If we allow ourselves to appreciate the otherness of the other while maintaining a dualistic framework, then we must negate ourselves. A sense of self-hatred and guilt is evoked. This in turn evokes a defensive reaction of self-affirmation.[32] A vicious cycle is created.

If we can learn to appreciate differences within nature without categorizing them as higher or lower, better or worse, perhaps we can also begin to accept and appreciate differences between and among ourselves as human beings. Audre Lorde suggested that "the power of the erotic" can help us appreciate difference: "The sharing of joy, whether physical, emotional, psychic, or intellectual, forms a bridge between the sharers that . . . lessens the threat of their difference."[33] This brings us back to the traditional Greek villagers with whom we began this discussion. Although they err in not including the other within their system of ethical duties and obligations, their delight in sharing food, drink, conversation, song, and dance with the stranger can teach us a great deal about how we might learn to perceive difference as enriching.

Technology

Human technology arises from within nature and is an aspect of human culture. For millennia, human technologies had a limited impact on the web of life.[34] But for several thousand years, human technologies have had a much greater capacity to alter the course of life than those of other animals. This has been increasingly true since the industrial revolution. In recent years human technologies have also contributed to a sense of alienation from nature and other beings in the web of life.

The earliest human tools were sticks and stones used for digging and hunting and for preparing food, shelter, and clothing. These technologies enabled human beings to survive but did not greatly change the environment. In the Neolithic revolution, new techniques of planting and harvesting, pottery making, and weaving were discovered, and farm animals were domesticated. Agriculturalists developed irrigation systems, plows, and techniques for smelting metals: first copper, then bronze. These inventions began to change the human relation to the web of life. Still, religion emphasized the human place within the cycles of nature.

The domestication of the horse, the invention of the wheel, and the forging of bronze and iron weapons allowed warfare (and with it the control of land and human beings) to become a significant factor in human culture. Many centuries later, the industrial revolution produced the modern factory, the steam engine, electricity, the telephone, radio and television, the computer, nuclear energy. With the industrial revolution, the sense of alienation from the web of life was intensified. Indeed, many came to believe that technology enables human beings to "conquer," "control," and "rise above" nature.

Yet human beings and our technologies are part of nature. Everything we do and everything we create has a consequence within the web of life. If we divert the course of a river to build our houses where the river once flowed, we can expect that one day the river will return to flood our houses. If we build flush toilets, we cannot put our sewage into rivers and seas without eventually affecting the lives of the creatures who live in them, without polluting the water that we depend on for life. If we build cities on earthquake faults, we can expect that we will experience the effects of earthquakes, not once, but many times.

When we recognize that our technology exists, as we do, within nature and not outside of it, we can also understand that we need radically to transform our consciousness concerning the purposes and limits of technology. We must give up the idea that technology enables us to "control nature" and thereby escape finitude. We need to recognize that every technological intervention brings life for some persons or beings, death for others. We must weigh each of our technologies in a scale that includes all beings in the circle of life.

Children of Violence

Human beings living today are deeply influenced by the violence in our collective history. As fiction writer and philosopher Doris Lessing has written, those born in the twentieth century are children of violence, "conceived, bred, fed, and reared on violence."[35] Ours is a world perpetually at war, a world in which genocide has been practiced. The denial of connection to other humans and to all beings in the web of life, which is required for combat, returns home with the soldiers, manifesting itself in families and social relations. The Native Americans say that it takes at least four generations for the effects of war to be cleansed from a society.[36] Yet European society has been polluted by the violence of war for thousands of years.

Our capacities to love and understand are impaired by the violence we have experienced. It is no wonder that violent societies produce violent human beings. Nor is it surprising that societies bred of violence have produced citizens who perpetrate or are able to turn a blind eye to the institutional violence of poverty, racism, sexism, heterosexism, warfare, genocide, and the destruction of the ecosphere.

The violence experienced in the past is encoded in cultural symbols and institutions that define our sense of reality and value, shaping our lives long before we become aware of alternatives. No one reading this book invented racism, sexism, classism, heterosexism, nationalism, imperialism, or specism —nor did our parents or grandparents, teachers, or political leaders. Yet even those of us who were taught to love life by our parents are deeply affected by the violence that is structured into the symbols and institutions of culture.

Cultures, like people, can change, and when conditions and desires are strong enough, we have the ability to transform our symbol systems and institutions and create alternatives. Today, questions are beginning to be raised about value systems and institutions once perceived as necessary and inevitable.

Reflection and Moral Action: Reason for Hope?

Human beings have great capacities to heal and to harm or, in traditional terms, to do good and to do evil. Human powers of reflection and moral action, which have been said to set us apart from nature, must now be used to create a new place for human beings within the web of life. Though thinking and acting (wrongly) have created many of the problems we and the Gaia body now face, human hope can only be located in the human capacity to think and to act differently about our place in the web of life.

In Goddess religion, the source of morality is the deep feeling of connection to all people and to all beings in the web of life. We act morally when we live in conscious and responsible awareness of the intrinsic value of each being with whom we share life on earth. When we do so, we embody the love that is the ground of all being. According to social historian Lucia Chiavola Birnbaum, "justice is the central value that emerges from studying the [religions of the] earth mother."[37] When the Athenians located their first law court on the rocky outcropping near the Acropolis hill known as Aeropagos, they did so in recognition of the ancient understanding that the principles of justice arise from earth's firm foundation. This insight also led the Greeks to worship Themis as the Goddess of social order.

In the monotheistic traditions, the source of morality is the law revealed by a God who is alleged to stand outside of nature and history. In dualistic rationalist traditions, human reason is said to rise above the body and nature to contemplate transcendent ethical principles. Goddess religion, in contrast, claims no revealed law or transcendent principle of morality. Some have argued that without a transcendent basis for ethics, there can be no "critical principle of justice" at all. But this view is based in dualistic thinking: If nature is brutal and blind, then morality cannot be grounded in nature. But if nature itself is intelligent and loving, if our capacities for love and for moral judgment are found within nature, then we do not need to be obligated by a transcendent law to love.

It is often feared that an ethic based in human feeling will be "narrowly" "self-interested," "narcissistic," and "hedonistic." If human beings are encouraged to follow our feelings, it is thought, we will pursue selfish interests at the expense of concern for others. In this view, the ethical self is an isolated individual who must be motivated from without to enter into responsible relationship with others: A transcendent source must evoke a sense of "duty" or "obligation," causing us to become "altruistic," "selfless," or "self-denying." But if our interests truly are interdependent with the interests of other people and other beings, we do not need to give up self-interest, but to broaden our understanding of it.

Challenging the idea that morality must be rooted in transcendent values, philosopher Simone de Beauvoir writes, "If we do not love life on its own account and through others, it is futile to seek to justify it in any way."[38] For de

Beauvoir, morality arises from within life, and its purpose is to make life better for ourselves and others. This means that our ethical decision making will always occur within the context of the ambiguities of finite life. De Beauvoir argues that those who claim that morality must derive from a transcendent source often inflict great harm in the name of a "higher law." Believing they are motivated by abstract principles of right and wrong, they state that any means is justified to achieve their goals. Christians, Marxists, and twentieth-century terrorists claiming to be chartered by God have done great harm in the name of absolute principles. Wouldn't we be better off, de Beauvoir cautions, to ground our ethics in the life we know?

I agree with de Beauvoir that ethics must be grounded in our love for life. When we are in touch with our feelings, we know that our joy in living can only exist in interdependence with the joy of other people and all beings. If I feel a sense of peace or elation when I see the colors of a sunset or when I am embraced by the sea, I also feel violated when the sky is eclipsed by heavy brownish yellow pollution or when the sea in which I swim is filled with plastic bags. If I am happy when I am at one with my body-mind-spirit, I am diminished when others are not in touch with the life force in them. Life involves conflict, pain, and loss. But each of us experiences a greater sense of well-being when others are fulfilled. It is only when our feelings are deadened that we can take pleasure at the expense of others.

But if this is so, what went wrong? What about Hitler and others who attempt genocide? Why is warfare considered the way to resolve conflict? Why are our streets filled with violence? Why does racism persist? How can people walk past the homeless living in their cities? Why are so many of our most intimate relationships defined by psychological and physical violence? Why is modern society filled with so many people who believe that it is their right to take whatever they think they need by any means necessary? Why do we continue to build nuclear weapons? Why do wealthy nations exploit the people and resources of the poorer nations? Why do we pollute the earth? Why do we destroy our bodies with cigarettes, alcohol, drugs, and overwork?

It sounds simple to say that when we are not loved, we do not love, and that when life is not respected in us, we do not respect life in others. Yet I believe that this is true. The physical, psychological, and sexual abuse of children is widespread the world around. Abusive parents are not created by the devil or by some mysterious principle of evil inside them. They are created by their parents and by their societies. The ethos of domination and the poisonous pedagogy of control encourage parents and others to think that they are only doing what is expected when they abuse children.

According to J. Konrad Stettbacher, "a longing for death and pleasure in killing are caused by a hostility to life inculcated in childhood."[39] Victims of childhood abuse, both physical and psychological, often engage in self-destructive behaviors, including suicide attempts, self-mutilation, self-starvation (anorexia), and binging and purging (bulimia). Many turn their rage outward, beating their wives or children or attacking the lives and property of strangers. Others deflect their hostility onto "socially acceptable" targets like the poor, homosexuals, or unwed mothers. Alice Miller has shown that severe childhood abuse shaped the personalities of architect of genocide Adolf Hitler and sadistic Romanian dictator Nicolae Ceausescu.[40] Their avid followers were also probably abused in some fashion as children, given that the poisonous pedagogy of control was (and is) widespread in families and schools in Europe (and America).

To transform the cycle of violence, we must proceed simultaneously on several levels: We must change ourselves and our intimate relationships, especially those with our children; we must transform the deepest values of our culture; and we must reconstruct our social institutions. As we set about the work of moral transformation, we must also recognize the limits of all human thinking and decision making. We are finite, and our perspectives will always be incomplete. We live in a world that includes death and disease, earthquakes and floods, among the conditions of life. We have been shaped by our families and the symbol systems and institutions of our culture. We carry the violence of our past within us and may never fully free ourselves from it. There are many situations in life that individual or communal hard work and good intentions cannot change, at least not in the way or in the time that we imagine they can be changed.

Knowledge of the limitations of our intelligence and moral will is deeply sobering. But recognizing limitations can also be freeing. As we come to understand all the forces that have shaped us as individuals and as societies, we can stop demanding perfection from ourselves and others. As we acknowledge the tremendous effort it takes to change ourselves and the social structures that shape our lives, we may gain greater appreciation for each small step that individuals, groups, communities, and societies take to create a world in which the powers of love and life can be more fully experienced.

Insofar as each of us has managed to survive while bearing the weight of violence in our personal and collective pasts, we have each experienced the power of intelligent love that grounds all beings in the web of life. This can become the basis for morality and moral transformation. None of us is perfect, nor can we be expected to be. What is asked of us as we work to heal the web of life is that we return the love and nurture given to us and that we try to contribute just a little bit more to the lives of all people and all beings than those who came before us. If we value our feelings of deep connection, if we love life on its own account and through others, and if we find the courage to act together on what we know, then maybe, just maybe, we can build a better future for ourselves, our children, and all the other children of earth.

❦ 8 ❦

Ethos and Ethics

We live in a time when humanity has developed the capacity to destroy itself and most of the other species with which we share the planet. Warfare is perpetual. The gap between the rich and the poor widens. Mothers and children around the world live in poverty and violence. Rivers and streams, the sea and the dry land, and the air we breathe are being poisoned and polluted. Forests are being destroyed. The end result of the course we are on will be a world radically less beautiful, radically less diverse, and radically less full of life than it is now. The moral challenge of our time is whether human beings can find ways to live in greater harmony with each other and all beings in the web of life. Goddess religion offers a mythos and an ethos that inspire us to hope that we can create a different world.

Mythos and Ethos

A mythos is a culturally shared system of symbols and rituals that defines what is real and valuable. An ethos is a way of life expressed in the everyday activities, customs, social institutions, and moral sensibility of a culture. A mythos supports an ethos, telling us that certain ways of living and acting are appropriate because they put us in touch with what is real and valuable. Conversely, the living of an ethos reinforces the sense that the mythos to which it is connected is true. The deep values and the way of life of a culture, its mythos and its ethos, are interdependent, as anthropologist Clifford Geertz has taught us to see.[1]

A mythos is more than a rational system of values: Symbols speak to both the conscious and unconscious mind, uniting rational awareness with our deepest nonrational knowledge; rituals enhance the power of symbols because they involve the body, the source of our deepest feeling. Rituals and symbols play an important role in human life because, as Zsuzsanna Budapest writes, "that which is not celebrated, that which is not ritualized, goes unnoticed, and in the long run . . . will be devalued."[2]

In cultures experiencing social transformation, new values and new ways of living are made possible and become validated through changes in mythos. Conversely, new ways of living and new values legitimate a new mythos. Today, as patriarchal dominator values and ways of living are being challenged, the authority of patriarchy's Gods is called into question, and a new ethos is emerging. But before considering the ethos of Goddess religion, it is important to have a clear understanding of the ethos that shapes modern societies.

Mythos and Ethos of Dominator Cultures

Rooted in the ethos of the warrior, modern societies have been described as "dominator cultures" by cultural historian Riane Eisler."[3] The ethos of dominator cultures states that power stems from control. Dominators are taught to control women, nature, children, animals, other men, their own bodies, and their feelings and sensations. The ethos of domination denies or disparages human embodiment, relationship, and interdependence. In the ethos of dominator cultures, finitude, vulnerability, and limitation are called "weakness."

The ethos of domination is genderized. Men are expected to dominate and control women. As the "weaker sex," women are permitted to express feelings of dependence and vulnerability, are taught that nurturing erotic connections is their sphere, and are sometimes told to accept abuse as their lot in life. Though women have been victims of the ethos of domination, many women have acted as dominators in relationships with children or people of races, nations, or ethnic groups defined as inferior or subordinate.

The values of dominator cultures are legitimized through mythos or symbols, stories, and rituals. When the values of patriarchal warrior societies were becoming established, the power of ancient Goddesses was denied and new Gods were enthroned. "Our sense of dependence upon and unity with the orders and processes of nature"[4] was shattered as the new Gods proclaimed their power by slaying the great powers of the natural world. Goddesses and women were raped by the Gods, and myth named violence as an acceptable mode of "relation" between the sexes. The new Gods led armies into battle, legitimating wars of conquest and domination.

Continuous ritual enactment of patriarchy's myths serves to convince us that they are true. In religion, education, and the arts, as well as in politics and economics, the values of dominator cultures are continually reaffirmed. Military training serves as a powerful ritual of initiation in dominator cultures. It is the key means by which dominator societies define masculinity and power.[5] The military thus shapes the fundamental values of our cultures.

In the highly ritualized context of military discipline, soldiers are denied contact with women, children, and men who are not warriors. Training exercises are designed to produce physical and mental exhaustion, so that when "defenses" (deep feelings of connection with other people and other beings in the web of life) are "broken down," the soldier will submit to "authority." In this way, a soldier is prepared to kill other people on command.

Feminist political scientist Judith Hicks Stiehm points out that an essential aspect of the ritual of military training is that it is performed on young men. In this sense it is a classic initiation rite.

> Note that [military training] is done mostly to 18-year-olds—men who are most vulnerable if doubts about their manhood are the issue. It may be that one reason men are not drafted at 30 when their physique remains strong but their judgment has matured, is that older men who are likely to be more secure in their manhood, simply would not go.[6]

Because they are at a vulnerable age, young men cannot easily resist being molded into the image of domination.

Any soldier who questions or refuses military "training" is called "weak," a "sissy," a "girl," or a "woman," epithets that indicate how deeply hatred of women is interstructured with the ethos of domination.

> The appeal to manhood is very much part of military training. From the familiar, "This is my rifle, this is my gun [pointing to the penis]; one is for killing, one is for fun," to "The marines need a few good men," pride of manhood is part of recruitment and training. When an institution tries to organize and control large numbers of unruly young men . . . it is helpful to be able to tell them that they are, by nature, better than half the population.[7]

It is said that the military turns "boys" into "men." What is less frequently recognized is that "manhood" is equated with the denial of the eros of connection and its replacement by the ethos of domination, control, and violence. The effects of this ritual of initiation into manhood are not shed when the soldier returns home and exchanges a uniform and weapons for civilian clothes.

The ethos of domination continues to be ritualized and performed in daily life. It is celebrated on national holidays, when we call out the troops for military parades and remember those who died fighting for their country. The sadness and anger of those who have lost loved ones in war is transformed into patriotism. The cry "never again" is suppressed, and a climate is created in which we are taught to equate love of country, honor, and respect for the dead, as well as bravery and manhood, with the willingness to kill. This association is made again and again in ritual reenactment (as well as in plays, movies, novels, and television programs) until we come to believe it is true.

Military service, and preferably "heroism" ("success" in killing "the enemy"), is considered one of the most important qualifications for leading a nation. This is why women, as a group, have had little success in gaining entry into the highest levels of national leadership and decision making. A historical approach suggests that the very idea of a nation-state (as distinct from a community, an ethnic group, or a people) is bound up with warfare and domination. "Nations" with "national boundaries" came into existence when warrior groups defeated local populations and installed their military leaders as kings and "protectors" of the land and people they had conquered.[8]

The military ethos has permeated many other institutions of culture as well. Parents and teachers who enforce the poisonous pedagogy of control and expect to be obeyed unquestioningly act like military officers. Is it any wonder that some of us remember home and school as being like military camp? Rituals of initiation in many professions, most notably medicine but also law and higher education, require students to submit to the authority of superiors and frequently induce physical and mental exhaustion as techniques of control. Training for competitive sports often resembles boot camp. Films, television, and music glorify competition and violence. Domination and control are enshrined in hierarchical and authoritarian power structures in all the institutions of society, including business, law, politics, medicine, education, arts and media, and religion. Women and others who seek to enter these institutions discover that they must adopt the attitudes of the dominator to move up in the hierarchy. In these and other rituals of daily life, we reenact the lessons of "basic" training.

From its beginnings, the military has been terribly destructive of life. Besides the obvious devastation of people and other beings in warfare, military buildup drains the resources of societies. The trees that were felled to sail to Troy contributed to the deforestation of the Greek islands. The time and money spent on all aspects of the military today, including military-related expenses and the cost of repairing the damage caused by war, consume a large proportion of the world's production. What if all that energy and all that money were devoted to the nurturing of life?

The symbols and rituals of Judaism and Christianity are sometimes understood to be opposed to the ethos of domination. But images of God in Jewish and Christian traditions all too often embrace the ethos of domination. Many religious groups require their adherents to submit to a "higher" authority who claims to be God's emissary on earth. Rather than providing a consistent countervailing force to the ethos of domination, Christianity and Judaism all too frequently reinforce it.

Though the ethos of domination structures the deepest values of our cultures, this does not mean that we do not experience love and joy. If we did not experience love and kindness, we could not survive. Novelist Anne Tyler writes, "Really it's kind of . . . heartening, isn't it? How most human beings do try. How they try to be as responsible and kind as they can manage."[9] I agree with Tyler that in our private lives most of us really do try. We do the best that we can, given our limitations. With daily acts of kindness, with intelligent and embodied love, we sustain the web of life.

Denial of Alternatives to Domination

One of the most pernicious lies of dominator cultures is their assertion of cultural superiority. Dominators portray ancient Goddess cultures and all preconquest societies, such as those of Native Americans or tribal Africans and Australians, as "primitive," "barbarian," and "bloodthirsty." With this lie they justify their own brutal and bloody conquest of other peoples in the name of civilization and progress. Further, they make it almost impossible for those within the dominator cultures to imagine alternatives to their own "superior," "advanced," and "civilized" way of life. As we begin to unmask the lie of superiority on which dominator cultures are based, we are freed to begin to imagine that we can create a different social order.

While we can learn from ancient prepatriarchal and other more recent tribal and clan-based societies, we cannot recreate them. The world in which we live has a much larger population and greater technological complexity than the worlds of tribal and clan-based societies. Reducing world population is a desirable goal, but it is a long-range one. And though sober assessment of its real costs may induce us radically to transform our relation to and dependence on technology, it is unlikely that most people will want to give up all modern technology. We must therefore imagine and create ways to live in harmony with other people and the web of life in a very different material situation than that faced by ancient and more recent tribal and clan-based peoples. In addition, we must confront the weight of the past, centuries of violence to other people and to the environment. Still, knowledge that there was a time when human beings lived in peace with each other and the web of life suggests the possibility that we could do so again.

Mythos and Ethos in Goddess Religion

Goddess religion, like all religions, is a mythos, a system of symbols and rituals, that shapes an ethos, providing a sense of what is real and establishing patterns of action. The insight that all beings in the web of life are deeply connected is the central ethical vision of Goddess religion. Native American teacher Dhyani Ywahoo expresses this conception: "The wisdom of our ancestors wherever they came from, basically points to one truth: everything is in relation to you. Native Americans say, 'all my relations,' acknowledging . . . connection to everything that is alive."[10] This vision is the antithesis of the illusion of dominators that they are superior to other beings and other people.

Those of us who have grown up in dominator cultures must learn again to value the experience of connection. The rituals and symbols of Goddess religion provide this link, bringing experience and deep feeling to consciousness so that they can shape our lives; helping us broaden and deepen our understanding of our interdependence to include all beings and all people; binding us to others and shaping communities in which concern for the earth and all people can be embodied.[11]

The symbols and rituals of Goddess religion celebrate our connection to the cycles of the moon and the seasons of the sun and our participation in the mysteries of birth, death, and renewal. They encourage us to appreciate diversity and difference: Darkness and light, springtime and winter, all people and all beings are sacred. Goddess symbols honor the body of the Goddess and our own bodies, calling us to embrace embodied life and to care for the earth body. They affirm the sacredness of the earth in its concrete particularity, naming the ground on which we stand as holy. Goddess images resacralize the female body, enabling women to take pride in our female selves, encouraging men to treat women and children with respect and to acknowledge their own connection to the life force. This is the ethos, the sense of what is real and valuable, created by the mythos of Goddess religion.

Ethics is grounded in an ethos, the way of life of a culture, which in turn is shaped by a mythos. Individual choices, such as what to do when a child throws a tantrum or whether to buy a car, are important. But just as crucial are the decisions we make as societies about how we support the nurturers of life and whether public transportation is available. This means that we must always think about the larger context, the mythos and the ethos, in which decisions are made. The larger context in which the ethics of Goddess religion is emerging is shaped by the mythos and ethos of domination. Our ethical decision making thus takes place "within a broken web."[12] We are children of violence and this limits our ability to act as we might choose.

One of our tasks is to create a new mythos and a new ethos that can help us resist the values of dominator cultures. Through symbols and rituals we name our values and strengthen our commitment, creating alternatives to the images presented in both higher education and mass media. Changing consciousness will not magically transform the structures of society, as some New Age philosophers imagine. But we will not be able to change the structures of society if we continue to celebrate a mythos that supports the ethos and the structures of domination.

Even if we succeed in creating a new mythos and a new ethos, our capacity for moral reasoning will still be rooted in our bodies. We cannot pretend to have universal knowledge. We can only say how it seems to us when we take the widest perspective we can. Since moral decision making occurs within a world that is constantly changing and where all interests cannot be harmonized, decisions are rarely between right and wrong. More often than not, we must choose to do the best we can in a given situation, knowing that some harm may be done. Moral action always takes place within the context of the "ambiguity" of life.[13] Thus Goddess religion cannot provide us with a new Ten Commandments or with universal ethical principles.

Still, we must ask whether Goddess religion can offer us any guidance as we attempt to live its vision in our world. In my life, I have discovered nine *touchstones* that can help to translate the mythos of Goddess religion into an ethos, a way of ethical living.[14] A touchstone is different from a principle or a commandment. Like a beautiful pebble on the shore of the sea, a touchstone is discovered by attending to the concrete. It does not derive from a source outside ourselves, but rather is discovered within the web of life. A touchstone can be consulted for guidance, but it does not tell us precisely what to do in any concrete situation. A touchstone is one among many. Ethical guidelines can never be reduced to a perfect and complete list. They are relative to the situations in which we live. New touchstones can be added as they are discovered. Those that have outlived their usefulness can be discarded.

The touchstones I have found are applicable to individuals, communities, and societies. These nine touchstones of the ethics of Goddess religion are:

- *Nurture life.*
- *Walk in love and beauty.*
- *Trust the knowledge that comes through the body.*
- *Speak the truth about conflict, pain, and suffering.*
- *Take only what you need.*
- *Think about the consequences of your actions for seven generations.*
- *Approach the taking of life with great restraint.*
- *Practice great generosity.*
- *Repair the web.*

To nurture life is to manifest the power of the Goddess as the nurturer of life. To honor, respect, and support mothers and children. To recognize all people and all beings as connected in the web of life. To embody the intelligent love that is the ground of all being. There are many ways to nurture life: caring for children; tending a garden; healing the sick; creating a hospice for the dying; helping women gain self-esteem; speaking the truth about violence; replanting forests; working to end war. How different our world would be if we made nurturing life the criterion of all that we do. What if we asked ourselves every night: How does what I did today nurture life? Midwife and healer Arisika Razak names the radical implications of putting nurture first: "If we begin with loving care for the young, and extend that to social caring for all people and personal concern for the planet, we would have a different world."[15] An ethic based in the nurturing of life has a great deal in common with the "ethic of care" described by psychologist Carol Gilligan as a female mode of ethical thinking.[16] I believe that if men were more involved with the nurturing of life in all its aspects, we would recognize the ethic of care as a human mode of moral behavior.

To walk in love and beauty is to appreciate the infinite diversity of all beings in the natural world, including ourselves and other human beings, and to sense that everything wants to be loved. This understanding has been conveyed to us in Navajo chants and in the words of Martin Buber, Susan Griffin, and Alice Walker. When we walk in love and beauty, we open our hearts to the world, to all our relations. We are stunned by beauty, and our hearts fill up and spill over with love. A song by Libby Roderick gives a sense of the loss we suffer when those around us do not walk in love and beauty:

How could anyone ever tell you
You are anything less than beautiful?
How could anyone ever tell you

You are less than whole?
How could anyone fail to notice
that your love is like a miracle?
How deeply you're connected to my soul. [17]

The melody to this song is like a lullaby. As it is sung to us, we sense the healing that could occur if we all learned to walk in love and beauty.

To trust the knowledge that comes through the body means to take seriously that our bodies are ourselves and that sensation and feeling are the guardians of life. To experience the joy and pain that come to us through the body. To allow the power of the erotic to lead us to question the denial of pleasure and satisfaction that is inherent in the ethos of domination. To ground ourselves in the earth and to acknowledge our interdependence in the web of life. Trusting body experience also means never giving ourselves over to any authority—no wise man, no guru, no spiritual teacher, no spiritual tradition, no politician, no wise woman, no one. The ethos of domination has encouraged us to put our faith in external authorities, and this has led to great suffering and harm. A prayer called the Charge of the Goddess counters this pattern, reminding us: "If that which you seek you find not within yourself, you will never find it without."[18] Not trusting authorities does not mean that we cannot learn from others. Learning from those who have gone before us is part of interdependent life. But nothing should be accepted unquestioningly. Everything must be tested in our own experience.

To speak the truth about conflict, pain, and suffering means not idealizing life. Not denying the realities of our personal and social lives. For many of us, childhood and other traumas have been intensified because conflict was denied and we were not allowed to feel our pain. Denial is also a social phenomenon. Americans can continue to assert that we live in the "greatest society on earth" only if we deny the violence and ecological destruction that is occurring all around us. Many in Hitler's Germany denied the reality of the gas chambers. Denial is only possible when we sever our minds from our bodies. When we trust the knowledge that comes through our bodies, we feel our own joy and suffering and the suffering and joy of others and the earth body.

Taking only what you need and thinking about the consequences of your actions for seven generations are touchstones that come from the Native Americans.[19] The first acknowledges that conflict—taking the lives of other beings—is inherent in human life and thus encourages restraint. The second affirms interconnection and asks us to consider not only our own needs, but those of all our relations for seven generations as we take and give back to the circle of life. Seven generations is a very long time. It is about as far into the future as the human imagination can stretch. We are not asked to hold ourselves to impossible models of perfection, but to consider the consequences of our actions on a scale we can comprehend.

Approaching the taking of life with great restraint is implicit in taking only what we need. I have made it a separate touchstone because those of us who live in industrialized countries take so much more than we really need without thinking of the lives that are lost. And because as individuals, communities, and societies we so readily resort to violence and warfare to resolve personal, ethnic, and national conflicts.

The "spirit of great generosity" advocated by Dhyani Ywahoo is an important guide as we work to transform our cultures and societies. According to Ywahoo, generosity begins with ourselves. If we are to gain the power to act, we must acknowledge that no one of us can take on all the burdens of the world. As we recognize our strengths and forgive our limitations, we can begin to approach others with a generous spirit. Ywahoo asks us to always "speak the best of one another and perceive the best in everything." She adds that "it is a strenuous discipline in these times to practice this."[20] We must speak the truth about the harm dominator societies are doing to ourselves, other people, and the web of life. Yet it requires great discipline to understand the harm that white people have done to Native Americans and other people of color without concluding that all white people are mean and that white culture has nothing of value in it. Or to acknowledge the evils of sexism without deciding that all men and everything they have ever done is bad. Or to learn of the roles of Christianity and Judaism in the suppression of Goddess religion and the ethos of interdependence without coming to believe that Judaism and Christianity express no positive ethical values. Or to see the threat that national conflicts present to the human race and the web of life without stating that all of our political leaders are evil. Though great harm has been done, very few people or groups have nothing to commend them. When we polarize situations, we make it difficult for our "adversaries" to change, and we begin to perceive ourselves unrealistically as "all good."

The last touchstone, repair the web, reminds us that we are living in a world where the bonds of relationship and community are broken by violence. Stemming from the Jewish commandment to "repair the world,"[21] it calls us to transform our personal relationships, our social and cultural institutions, and our relation to the natural world. In our time, the nurturers of life must work to establish greater harmony, justice, and peace for all beings on earth.

These nine touchstones define the ethos of Goddess religion, providing a framework for ethical decision making but not a blueprint for action. There are still hard decisions which we must make as individuals, communities, and societies. The touchstones of Goddess religion can be embodied in different lifestyles and ethical choices. They do not tell us whether individuals or groups are ever justified in resorting to force to defend themselves. Nor do they tell us whether we "need" to eat meat or whether we "need" flush toilets and electricity. But clearly there is no license to justify violence as the ordinary way to defend personal, national, or other interests, to take what others need, or to deplete the earth. Our needs must always be weighed in relation to the needs of other people and other beings for continued life and survival. It is not possible to live in perfect harmony with all people and all beings in the web of life. We cannot live without taking the lives of other living creatures, and we cannot live with other human beings without some degree of conflict. Our choices are always between relative degrees of healing and harming other people and the web of life.

But once we recognize the possibility and value of a life lived in reverence and respect for other people and life in all its diverse forms, it becomes painfully obvious how far modern societies have deviated from this vision. While it may not be easy to decide exactly what "taking only what we need" means in modern technological societies, it is certain that in dominator societies we have been taught that it is our right to take far more than we really need in disregard for the needs of other people and other beings. The violent behavior of individuals and groups and nations is taking too great a toll on human bodies, the body politic, and the earth body. While we may disagree on strategies and priorities for change, if we value the ethos of interdependence, we can agree that those of us living in dominator societies must make radical changes in the way we live.

Changing the Patterns of Domination

Change begins in our daily lives. Individual action is important, especially when we understand that every act we perform has the power to influence the web of life for seven generations. Our acts not only affect the other people and beings whose lives we touch, but they also enter into the collective memories of our communities and will possibly have an influence for healing or harm far beyond anything we can imagine.

As individuals, we can begin to value the erotic in our own lives. We can create time and space to commune with nature and other people, to allow the life force to flow through us, to experience the joy of embodied life. We can pay more attention to our feelings so that we learn to distinguish true joy from empty pleasure. We can view our relationships with other people and with plants, animals, and other beings not as leisure activities, relegated to Saturdays and Sundays, but as the stuff of which life is made. We can end the violence that is embedded in our most personal and intimate relationships so that every child and every adult will know the power of intelligent embodied love that connects us to one another and to all beings in the web of life. We can examine how our actions influence the quality of life for ourselves and others in our own time and for seven generations.

As we make even small changes in our personal lives, we recognize that modern societies are deeply structured to deny the power of intelligent embodied love. If we are expected to work at a job we do not enjoy for forty, fifty, or even sixty or more hours a week and we come home tired, or if we live in poverty and our children are hungry, how can we find the time and space to enjoy life, let alone to think about how each of our actions will affect all beings in the web of life for seven generations?

Every change we make in our lives eventually forces us to confront the structures of the dominator society. For example, a woman may start to think about how she experienced violence in her own family and vow not to reenact the patterns she learned from her parents in the lives of her children. She seeks help in transforming the pain she holds within herself. She treats her children with greater kindness and respect. But as her son grows up, she learns that other kids will call him a sissy if he doesn't learn to fight back. She begins to understand that change cannot occur solely on a personal level because we are affected by our culture. Still, she talks to her son about the values expressed by the other boys, tries to help him resist the notion that he must become violent to become a man.

To change the environment that shapes her son's life, she works to change school curricula, supports candidates who favor peaceful solutions to international problems, and attends peace demonstrations. But if she pays taxes, her tax dollars will still be used to support the military and the arms race, which remains the largest single item in the budgets of most nations. And her sons and daughters may be drafted into the army.

A man who understands that racism is wrong may resolve to overcome it in his personal and business relationships with people of color. His acts may enable a black or Hispanic man to get a job that otherwise would have gone to a less-qualified white man. But he soon realizes that his consciousness is not shared by many others, whose views of people of color have been shaped by the racist consciousness that permeates our culture. If he challenges the views of his superiors too strongly, he may jeopardize his own job. He begins to see that he cannot overcome racism in his workplace as long as racist structures dictate that people of color are less likely to go to college than white people, that people of color earn less money than white people, and that the many children of color are raised in poverty. And if he does not also recognize that the sexism that shapes his relationship with his wife and daughters and with his female co-workers of all races is as wrong as racism, he will only have begun to eradicate the ethos of domination from his life.

A woman who sees that environmental pollution diminishes the quality of life for herself, other people, and other creatures may sort her garbage and take it to a recycling center, but only if such a center exists and only if it is open at hours when she is not at work. As her time is consumed in the process of recycling, she wonders why recycling, like all "housework," is considered women's work. She concludes that recycling would be much easier and would become more widespread if more cities established separate curbside pickups for glass, paper, aluminum, plastic, and other garbage. She questions the methods for disposing of garbage that is not recycled. She becomes angry that companies continue to produce products that are intended to be thrown out rather than repaired, encasing them in packaging that is not biodegradable. She asks herself if she really needs all the things she buys, reassessing priorities in her own life, gradually cutting back on her desires for things she doesn't really need. She recognizes that the advertising that makes us feel we need so many things that are not necessary must also be addressed. She comes up against the capitalist system.

The ethos that prods us to consume more and more every year must be challenged. In my own life, I have found that it is both easier and more difficult to give up consumerism than I had imagined. When I lived in the United States, I was a typical shopper, furnishing a big house and buying clothes for work and play. My job was often unsatisfying, and when I felt tired and empty and there was nothing on television, I would go to the mall to buy something, hoping to make myself feel better. When I first moved to a Greek village, I did not have a lot of money to spend. In addition, there were few shops to spend it in. I had no television to tell me I needed more than I had. No one else had a lot of things. I discovered that beauty in nature and in my home were important to me. I spent more time with people. And I found that I could live happily with far less than I had thought possible. However, when I moved to Athens and bought a television, I found myself slipping back into my old habits of consumerism, although less compulsively. It is not so hard to live with less, but it requires great discipline to do so when city life cuts us off from sustaining connections with nature and other people and when we are bombarded constantly by advertising.

My experiences as a university professor forced me to confront the difficulties of making changes in established systems. Because I learned from teachers who changed my life, I always tried to use the model of embodied thinking in my classes. This sometimes led to conflict with students and other faculty who followed the model of objective thinking. The university required that I teach large classes where individual attention to every student was impossible. I was expected to give hour-long objective examinations that tested the knowledge of facts, but not their integration. When I gave essay questions, I received a call from the dean, who explained that some of my students had complained that "they didn't understand what was expected of them." Once the dean even called to tell me that another professor had become angry because my students left the chairs in a circle and he couldn't "control" his students if the chairs were not in rows when they entered his classroom.

In the summer program of the Aegean Women's Studies' Institute, I was able to experiment more boldly. In addition to reading women's literature and books about the Goddesses, my students and I shared our personal stories of despair and joy, growth and transformation.[22] Many of us were deeply moved by this experience, and some of us changed our lives as a result of it. I enjoyed teaching more. Returning from Greece to my teaching position at a large state university, I vowed to imbue my classroom with a similar feeling. Though I was successful in some ways, I was ultimately frustrated by the institutional structures in which I worked. In addition, the personal reflection about the ethos of domination that my classes provoked meant that my office hours were filled with students who told me stories of incest, rape, and beating. I was not prepared to handle the stress of listening to so many students tell me so many painful stories, and eventually my own health suffered.

Working to change institutional structures that were often hostile to me and to my visions wore me out. Tired, stressed, and diagnosed with the early stages of cancer, I felt I had to change my life. As I see many of my friends developing stress-related or stress-activated diseases, I wonder if they, too, are suffering from working too long and too hard in the wrong ways. Carol Lee Sanchez explains how this occurs:

> Many activists maintain a negative attitude, a continued focus on everything that is wrong, that is harmful and hurtful to self, creatures, and the environment. Over a period of time many activists suffer "burnout," long for a different world, and drop out because they accurately perceive themselves to be "out of balance."

Recognizing that this had happened to her, Sanchez vowed to "focus on the beauty and positive aspects of my life while at the same time accepting my human responsibilities to *do* something—to find another way."[23] Such decisions are sometimes interpreted as "copping out" or "dropping out." But this is a mistake. Sanchez is still working to change the world, but in a way that feels more grounded.

If we trust the power of the erotic, then we must listen to our bodies when they tell us that something is wrong. If we do not love life on its own account and through others, our activism is not rooted in its source. Despite the patterns of domination, the world is still a beautiful place, and we can experience joy in living. Love for life is the wellspring of our desire to transform the structures of domination and our sustenance as we go about doing it.

Each of these stories illustrates that while change can begin on the personal level, it will not take root unless we transform all of the institutions of culture, including education, politics, law, medicine, communications, the arts, media, economics, and religion. Sometimes we are made to feel that only if we take explicitly political action are we really doing something to transform our society. But once we understand that the ethos of domination affects every aspect of life, we can see that there are many ways to work for change.

Building Community

As our individual actions bring us up against seemingly immovable structures, we come to understand the importance of building community. Actions that take root in relationships and in communities do make a difference and may affect the circle of life for seven generations. Communities, which may be made up of as few as several people or may be much larger, provide the support that is necessary when we attempt to make changes in our personal and social lives, especially those that bring us into conflict with friends, family, or co-workers. Communities are places where we can share values and envision a different world. Communities enable us to work together to change structures.[24]

Reflecting on her experience as a Native American living in an American city, Carol Lee Sanchez suggests that building communities that will live in reverence for life requires acknowledging the community's connection to a land base and affirming the diverse histories that have brought the group together.[25] While communities are drawn together by perceptions of common goals and interests, they often break down when differences emerge. It must be recognized from the beginning that differences will inevitably emerge among people within a group. If difference is positively affirmed as an aspect of the diversity that enriches the whole, then structures can be developed to honor and resolve conflict.[26] It is important for individuals within groups not to get bogged down in theoretical disputes that prevent them from acting together on goals they really do hold in common.[27] Communities take time and space to build, as those who have tried to form them learn by experience. But they are worth the effort, as no single action can transform the ethos of domination into the ethos of interdependence.

My experience demonstrates the importance of community in work for social change. When I first began graduate study in theology at Yale, I was the only woman in my classes. My attempts to challenge the ethos of domination by calling attention to Martin Buber's view of the I-Thou relation and Paul Tillich's vision of God as the ground of being were dismissed as signs that I had not yet learned to think clearly. I questioned myself and my abilities. When Judith Plaskow entered the program the next year, we were wary of each other, perhaps wondering if in fact there was room for more than one "exceptional" woman in the program.

When we finally met and really talked, the walls came tumbling down. We found that we shared similar interests and perspectives. Together we went to the meetings of the first women's liberation group at Yale and found our experience named and affirmed by other women. With other women, we protested in front of a university-sponsored all-male club and lobbied for the admission of women to Yale as undergraduates. In our "community" of two, we supported each other and found the strength to challenge the structures of domination in the field of theology more effectively. In time, we organized other women to protest the ways women were treated in the male-dominated Religious Studies' Program. We joined with women in other parts of the university to bring the Department of Health, Education, and Welfare to investigate Yale for sex discrimination. Later, we helped organize the women in the American Academy of Religion, the professional organization in our field. The Women and Religion Section was established, and women's studies gained a toehold in the field. We also helped to found the New York Feminist Scholars in Religion, a small group that was still meeting more than twenty years later. Together we edited *Womanspirit Rising* and *Weaving the Visions*, which brought our research to a wider audience. Judith founded the *Journal of Feminist Studies in Religion* with Elisabeth Schüssler Fiorenza, and I served on its board. Our work bore fruit in the creation of communities we did not share, for Judith, B'not Esh, a Jewish feminist spirituality community, and for me, Rising Moon, a women's spirituality group in California, and the Minoan Sisterhood, formed by participants in Goddess pilgrimages to Crete.[28]

Besides making small changes in our larger world, Judith and I developed friendships that have literally been life-sustaining with each other and with other women who have shared our work. We have shared meals and wine. We have laughed and cried together. We have assisted or witnessed major transitions in each other's lives: marriages, births, the publication of books, divorces, commitment ceremonies, moves across the country and around the world. We have been there for each other over the years. When we begin to speak the truths that come from the deepest places in ourselves, we know that there are others who can "hear us into speech."[29]

None of the community building Judith and I have done arose from a sense of external obligation or duty. Rather, it grew out of "the power of the erotic," the satisfaction we experienced in our work and our friendship. We formed communities because we needed them to support our spirits and our work, not out of a desire to do good or to help others. We understood intuitively (and developed theory to support our understanding) that we really are interdependent with other people.

But it would be false to say there have never been conflicts between us and within the larger women's community in which our work is anchored. When I moved out of Christianity into Goddess religion, I wondered why Judith and others didn't come with me. Judith often felt that I was throwing the baby out with the bath water. I accused her of clinging to a patriarchal religion, and she countered that there was no principle of justice in Goddess religion. Sometimes these conflicts were extremely painful. They were also being acted out in the organizations we had helped to form. There were long periods of time when I was paralyzed by a renewed sense of isolation. Conflict surfaced everywhere in the women's movement. Charges of anti-Semitism, anti-paganism, racism, classism, and homophobia were added to the mix.

When these conflicts emerged, none of us had theories that could explain them. Heady with the discovery of commonality and community where before we had felt alone, we imagined that women shared not only common experiences, but also common visions. We viewed difference as a threat to relationship, a severing of community. Somehow, we persevered in our friendships and in our work. Out of our struggles, theories that provided positive understandings of diversity and difference and recognized conflict as part of relationship and community emerged.[30] All of the wounds women inflicted on one another have not been healed, but we and the women's movement as a whole are rooted in a more realistic and fruitful base of understanding.

Despair, Hope, and Prayer

I know I have made important changes in my life and in the communities of which I am a part, but when I consider the whole web of violence and domination in which we are immersed, I often feel overwhelmed, hopeless, and powerless. There are so many whose suffering my work has not touched or diminished. As environmental destruction proceeds, I wonder how much more time we have left before life as we know it will no longer be possible. Nothing that I can do, it seems, can possibly be enough to change structures that seem to go on and on, no matter how hard we work to change them. I feel even more hopeless when I recognize, as I am sometimes forced by others to do, that the structures of oppression are not only outside me, but within me as well.

Though I believe that it is possible for human beings to live in greater peace, harmony, and justice with each other and all beings in the web of life, I also recognize the enormous power of force and violence, the fragility of good. Once a cycle of violence is begun, it is very difficult to stop it. When domination is enforced by violent power, it is very hard to find a different way. And yet Martin Luther King and Mohandas Gandhi and the people who walked with them brought about major transformations of their societies through the power of nonviolent resistance. Though much remains the same, the worldwide women's movement has made enormous changes in women's lives. The web of life continues to be destroyed at a stunning rate, but environmental issues are now being discussed the world around. Necessity is a powerful teacher. Who can say when the balance will shift?

If we focus on the beauty around us, if we love life on its own account and through others, if we trust the knowledge that comes to us through our bodies, we will find the strength to continue the work of personal, cultural, and social transformation. If we speak the best of ourselves and others while at the same time speaking the truth about the harm that has been done, perhaps we all will recognize that it is in our own best interest to care about the survival of the web of life. Then we can begin again to create communities and societies that live in greater harmony and justice with other people, all our relations, and the earth body.

*

May be the Goddess join Her strength to our strength.
May the earth in infinite beauty and diversity survive.
Blessed be.

*

Epilogue:
What Was Lost?

Because most of what I have written about in this book comes from the experience of women, I would like to end with a story that provides an opening to men. Daniel Cohen, its author, writes,

> Men who have been influenced by feminism see how greatly men's strength, including their own, has been used in abusive and oppressive ways. We often respond by denying our strength completely. Perhaps this is a necessary step for most of us, but it ends up being harmful. What is needed is an understanding of how we can use strength (and knowledge, and other aspects of our being) in nonoppressive ways, in ways which not only serve humanity, but go further to act in service of the earth and its creatures. My stories are partly about ways of doing this.[1]

In his retelling of the story of Iphigenia, Cohen suggests that new images of male strength will be created only after men have faced the lies that have been told in history and acknowledged what men have done in the name of those lies. The real story begins where Cohen's ends, when men who have looked the monster other men have created in the eye, turn within and tell us what they find hidden there, in the darkness.

Iphegenia: A Retelling
by Daniel Cohen

This is the tale of the first death in the Trojan war.

The Greek army was gathered in Aulis. Men had come from many towns and islands. Some were there with dreams of glory, some with dreams of gold. Others were there only because their chief had demanded their presence, and either loyalty to the chief or fear of him had brought them.

The fleet was waiting and the soldiers were ready to embark. But for weeks now the wind had been blowing from the wrong direction, and the men were getting restless at waiting so long. They were beginning to think of the harvest—they had expected that the war would be won long before harvest time—but that was now so close that many men were making ready to go home, and some had already gone.

Agamemnon, the leader of the Greek army, was fearful that the conquest and glory he sought would escape him if the winds continued contrary. And so he consulted the seer Calchas. After much searching the seer replied "The Goddess Artemis sends you a warning. If you wish to make war against Troy, you will have to kill your daughter."

So Agamemnon sent for his daughter Iphegenia, pretending to her and her mother, that he planned to marry her to the hero Achilles. When she arrived an altar was built to Artemis, and she was bound to the altar. Her mother, Clytemnestra, pleaded with Agamemnon for the life of their child, but he would not listen. Agamemnon raised the sacrificial knife, but as it descended a mist came down. When the mist cleared, Iphigenia had vanished, and a deer lay sacrificed on the altar. Shortly after, the wind changed, and the army set sail for Troy, but the rest of that tale is not part of our story.

So now you know who was the first to die in the war of the Greeks against Troy. "But no," you reply, "I had thought it would be Iphigenia, but since she vanished, I have no idea who it can be." Do you truly have no idea? Then I will give you a clue.

When this tale is told nowadays, men talk in horrified tones of the old blood-thirsty goddesses, of Artemis who demanded that Agamemnon sacrifice his daughter. These same men speak approvingly of the god of Abraham and Isaac, who called Abraham to sacrifice his son just to prove that he feared his god and would obey.[2] They do not see that Artemis demanded no sacrifice. She simply gave Agamemnon a warning that his acts would have consequences.

But Agamemnon could think only of what he called glory and fame—he did not care if the cost of these was the death of many daughters and mothers, sons and fathers. Even when the goddess tried to make him see this cost by asking if he was prepared to see his own daughter killed, he was so blinded by his ambitions that this did not seem important. . . . He remained deaf to the pleas of his wife and daughter, regardless of what his daughter's sacrifice would do to his family and himself, regardless of what war would do to others. He thought of himself as a great man, he thought that a great man should look only to his own fame and ignore others, he thought that compassion was fit only for women and was no concern of his.

Now do you see who it was who first died? Surely those women who [hear] this tale know the answer by now. For you men who still do not know I will give one further clue. Look into yourself—look into your heart. Do you see who it is who lies there, in a sleep near to death, a sleep that has lasted for centuries, a sleep from which only you can awaken her? Now do you know the answer to my question? Do you know? Do you?[3]

Notes

Preface

1. Marija Gimbutas, *The Language of the Goddess* (San Francisco: Harper and Row, 1989), p. 318.
2. It is difficult to know the number of those who have been deeply influenced by the emerging symbol of the Goddess. The Goddess movement is not institutionalized and there are no membership lists. Rituals may be private or with groups, spontaneous or planned. Some who have not participated in rituals nonetheless find that the symbol of the Goddess helps them understand the meaning of their lives. The symbols and rituals of the movement have been widely disseminated in books and magazines. To the joy of some and the dismay of others, books on the Goddess have been among the best-selling titles in the women's studies' trade market for two decades. The figure "hundreds of thousands" is not high if all who have been deeply moved by Goddess images and literature are counted.
3. I use *we* in this book, in an attempt to evoke the community that grounds the vision I describe. Sometimes *we* is inclusive of all beings in the web of life, sometimes only of humans, sometimes of those influenced by the values of western culture, sometimes of women and men, sometimes of women, sometimes of feminists, sometimes of those who share my vision of the Goddess. The meaning should be clear from the context. I hope readers will find my use of *we* inviting rather than excluding. I hope that everyone who reads this book will want to be see themselves in the most inclusive *we* that names our deep connection and interdependence with all beings in the web of life.
4. Quotation marks here and elsewhere often mark words and patterns of understanding found in traditional philosophy and theology that are challenged in this book.

5. In the Preface, I spell *thea-logy* and its derivatives with a hyphen to call attention to the newness of its meaning. In other chapters I omit the hyphen. The word *thealogy* may have been coined by Naomi Goldenberg in *Changing of the Gods: Feminism and the End of Traditional Religions* (Boston: Beacon Press, 1979), p. 96.

6. See the *American Heritage Dictionary*, 3rd ed. (Boston: Houghton Mifflin, 1992), pp. 1525, 2111, 2121.

7. Starhawk's influential 1979 book, *The Spiral Dance* (San Francisco: Harper and Row), is subtitled *A Rebirth of the Ancient Religion of the Great Goddess*. Recently scholars not in the movement have begun to concur. See Cynthia Eller, *Living in the Lap of the Goddess: The Feminist Spirituality Movement in America* (Boston: Beacon Press, 1995), p. 39; and Susan Starr Sered, *Priestess, Mother, Sacred Sister: Religions Dominated by Women* (New York: Oxford University Press, 1994). Eller's book is a phenomenological study of feminist spirituality by a sympathetic outsider. Starr Sered's is a fascinating comparative anthropological study of religions in various cultures that are created and led by women.

8. Jane Ellen Harrison, *Prolegomena to the Study of Greek Religion* [1903] (London: Merlin Press, 1962, p. vii. Harrison considered the works of Hesiod and Homer to be theological because they presented fully formed views (rather than experiences in process) of the Gods and Goddesses.

9. Michael Novak's *Belief and Unbelief: A Philosophy of Self-Knowledge* (New York: New American Library, 1965) strongly influenced my understanding of what theology could and should be.

10. Carol P. Christ, *Odyssey with the Goddess: A Spiritual Quest in Crete* (New York: Continuum, 1995). Also see my earlier book, *Laughter of Aphrodite: Reflections on a Journey to the Goddess* (San Francisco: Harper and Row, 1987).

Chapter 1

1. Carol P. Christ, *Laughter of Aphrodite: Reflections on a Journey to the Goddess* (San Francisco: Harper and Row, 1987), p. 21.

2. See Starhawk, "Witchcraft and Women's Culture," in Carol P. Christ and Judith Plaskow, eds., *Womanspirit Rising: A Feminist Reader in Religion* (San Francisco: Harper & Row, 1979), p. 263.

3. The phrase "to hear into speech" was coined by Nelle Morton to express the sense that women gained the power to speak because other women were there to hear and affirm their words. See Nelle Morton, *The Journey Is Home* (Boston: Beacon Press, 1985, pp. 17–18.

4. See M. Esther Harding, *Women's Mysteries: Ancient and Modern* [1935] (New York: G.P. Putnam's Sons, 1971); Jane Ellen Harrison, *Prolegomena to the Study of Greek Religion* [1903] (London: Merlin Press, 1962); G. Rachel Levy, *Religious Conceptions of the Stone Age: And Their Influence on European Thought* [1948] (New York: Harper and Row, 1963); and Helen Diner [Eckstein-Diener, Bertha], *Mothers and Amazons: The First Feminine History of Culture* [1932], edited and translated by John

Philip Ludin (New York: Anchor Books, 1973). See *WomanSpirit* magazine, published quarterly by Jean Mountaingrove and Ruth Mountaingrove for ten years, from 1974–1984 (back issues available from 2000 King Mountain Trail, Sunny Valley, OR 97467, USA); Z. Budapest, *The Holy Book of Women's Mysteries* (Oakland, CA: Wingbow, 1989) [originally published as *The Feminist Book of Lights and Shadows*, edited by Helen Beardwoman (Los Angeles: Susan B. Anthony Coven #1, 1975); Hallie Austen Iglehart, *Womanspirit: A Guide to Women's Wisdom* (San Francisco: Harper and Row, 1983) and her articles in *WomanSpirit* magazine under the name Hallie Mountainwing; Merlin Stone, *When God Was a Woman* (New York: Dial Press, 1976); Elizabeth Gould Davis, *The First Sex* (New York: G.P. Putnam's Sons, 1971); Marija Gimbutas, *The Gods and Goddesses of Old Europe, 7000–3500 BC: Myths, Legends, and Cult Images* (Berkeley: University of California Press, 1974) [republished in 1982 with the author's original title, *The Goddesses and Gods of Old Europe*]; Charlene Spretnak, *Lost Goddesses of Early Greece: A Collection of Pre-Hellenic Myths* [1978] (Boston: Beacon Press, 1984); and Starhawk, *The Spiral Dance: A Rebirth of the Ancient Religion of the Great Goddess* (San Francisco: Harper and Row, 1979). Z. Budapest claims to be the founder of the contemporary Goddess movement, but Cynthia Eller, *Living in the Lap of the Goddess: The Feminist Spirituality Movement in America* (Boston: Beacon Press, 1995), concludes that "Though Z. Budapest was a ground-breaking figure in the feminist move to neo-paganism, she was not alone" (p. 58).

5. A chant I first learned from Z. Budapest.
6. For the phrase *dissident daughter*, see Sue Monk Kidd, *The Dance of the Dissident Daughter: A Woman's Journey from Christian Tradition to the Sacred Feminine* (San Francisco: HarperSanFrancisco, 1996).
7. See Christ, *Laughter of Aphrodite*, pp. 183–205.
8. My mother's dying and my coming to integrate the insight I received are described in greater detail in *Odyssey with the Goddess: A Spiritual Quest in Crete* (New York: Continuum, 1995), especially pp. 18–26.
9. Eller's *Living in the Lap of the Goddess* provides an interesting overview of the Goddess movement, its participants, its origins, its practices, and its beliefs.
10. Downing identifies this old man as Martin Buber, who was the subject of her dissertation. Letter dated August 15, 1995.
11. Christine Downing, *The Goddess: Mythological Images of the Feminine* (New York: Crossroad, 1981), p. 3.
12. Luisah Teish, *Jambalaya* (San Francisco: Harper and Row, 1985), p. 40.
13. Ibid., p. 39.
14. Ibid., pp. 40–41. The image of listening "to my head" reflects the Afro-*Voudou* understanding that the particular God or Goddess who rules, directs, or influences your life "sits on your head" and communicates through an opening in the head. It does not mean that Teish was instructed to trust exclusively in the powers of "rational" thought that Europeans locate in the head.
15. Ibid., p. 40.

16. Ibid., pp. 39–41.
17. Nelle Morton, *The Journey Is Home* (Boston: Beacon Press, 1985), p. 157.
18. Lynn Gottlieb, *She Who Dwells Within: A Feminist Vision of a Renewed Judaism* (San Francisco: HarperSanFrancisco, 1995), p. 16.
19. Ibid., p. 17.
20. Jess Hayden, letter dated May 14, 1996.
21. Jess Hayden, conversation in Plaka, Athens, in early 1996; and letter dated May 14, 1996.
22. Caz Love, *Ariadne's Thread* 4 (1996): 4.
23. Ralph Metzner, *The Well of Remembrance: Rediscovering the Earth Wisdom of Northern European Myths* (Boston: Shambhala, 1994), p. 13.
24. Ibid., p. 12.
25. Ibid.
26. Downing, *The Goddess*, p. 4. Downing's play on words is inspired by Adrienne Rich's poem "Transcendental Etude."
27. Anne L. Barstow, "The Prehistoric Goddess," in Carl Olson, ed., *The Book of the Goddess* (New York: Crossroad, 1983), p. 8.
28. Anne L. Barstow, "The Uses of Archaeology for Women's History: James Mellaart's Work on the Neolithic Goddess at Çatal Hüyük," *Feminist Studies* 4/3 (1978): 16.
29. Adrienne Rich, *Of Woman Born: Motherhood as Experience and Institution* [1976] (New York: W.W. Norton, 1986), pp. 93–94.
30. Marija Gimbutas, *The Language of the Goddess* (San Francisco: Harper and Row, 1989), p. 321.
31. The descriptions of these images are based on the understanding of the "language of the Goddess," as deciphered by Marija Gimbutas, and on my own intuition of their meanings. The names and titles at the end of the descriptions are in some cases derived from Gimbutas, in others are products of my imagination.
32. See Carol P. Christ, "Why Women Need the Goddess" in Christ and Plaskow, *Womanspirit Rising*, pp. 273–87.
33. Alice Walker, *The Color Purple* (New York: Pocket Books, 1983), pp. 176, 177.
34. Marcia Falk, "Notes on Composing New Blessings," in Judith Plaskow and Carol P. Christ, eds., *Weaving the Visions: New Patterns in Feminist Spirituality* (San Francisco: Harper and Row, 1989), p. 132.
35. Judith Plaskow, *Standing Again at Sinai: Judaism from a Feminist Perspective* (San Francisco: Harper and Row, 1990), pp. 128–34. Also see Carol P. Christ, "Yahweh as Holy Warrior," in *Laughter of Aphrodite*, pp. 73–81.
36. Exodus 15:3–4.
37. This is a common image in the prophets. See, for example, Hosea 8, Jeremiah 5, Isaiah 24, and passim.
38. Timothy Ware, *The Orthodox Church* (London: Penguin, 1991), pp. 24–25.
39. Ibid., pp. 67–69.

40. Robert N. Bellah, "Civil Religion in America," in *The Religious Situation 1968* (Boston: Beacon Press, 1968), pp. 331–55.

41. This kind of thinking is prominent in the new Christian fundamentalism. Many of its adherents imagine that the world will be destroyed in a final battle that will begin in the Middle East. Some of the most Orthodox Jews resist the establishment of the state of Israel, which they say must be established by God. For the connection between apocalyptic thinking and the founding of America, see Catherine Keller, "The Breast, the Apocalypse, and the Colonial Journey," *Journal of Feminist Studies in Religion* 10/1 (Spring 1994): 53–72.

42. See, for example, "Selections from *The Inclusive Language Lectionary*," in Plaskow and Christ, eds., *Weaving the Visions*, pp. 163–69. The complete volumes are published by the Division of Education and Ministry of the National Council of Churches in the U.S.A.

43. For a survey of the various arguments, see Christ, *Laughter of Aphrodite*, pp. 135–59.

44. Judith Plaskow, "The Right Question Is Theological," in Susannah Heschel, ed., *On Being a Jewish Feminist* (New York: Schocken Books, 1983), p. 230.

45. Starhawk, *Truth or Dare: Encounters with Power, Authority, and Mystery* (San Francisco: Harper and Row, 1987), p. 21.

46. Ntozake Shange, *for colored girls who have considered suicide/when the rainbow is enuf* (New York: Macmillan, 1976), p. 63.

47. These words are taken from Clifford Geertz's definition of religion, which will be discussed in the next chapter.

48. Charlene Spretnak, *States of Grace: The Recovery of Meaning in the Postmodern Age* (San Francisco: HarperSanFrancisco, 1991), p. 108.

49. Patricia Allott Silbert, letter dated February 19, 1995, reprinted in *Ariadne's Thread* 2 (1995), p. 2.

50. Alice Walker, *In Search of Our Mother's Gardens* (New York: Harcourt, Brace, Jovanovich, 1983), p. 241.

51. Rachel Bagby, "Daughters of Growing Things," in Irene Diamond and Gloria Feman Orenstein, eds., *Reweaving the Web of Life: The Emergence of Ecofeminism* (San Francisco: Sierra Club Books, 1990), pp. 231–48.

52. Starhawk, "Ritual as Bonding," in Plaskow and Christ, eds., *Weaving the Visions*, pp. 329–35, chants on pp. 330, 331, 332, quote on 334. Originally published in Starhawk, *Dreaming the Dark: Magic, Sex, and Politics* (Boston: Beacon Press, 1982).

53. The issue of nonnatives' use of Native traditions is discussed in Chapter 2.

54. Carol P. Christ, *Odyssey with the Goddess: A Spiritual Quest in Crete* (New York: Continuum, 1995), pp. 118–19.

55. Starhawk, "Witchcraft and Women's Culture," in Christ and Plaskow, eds., *Womanspirit Rising*, pp. 278–79.

56. Rituals geared to the phases of the moon and the shifting of the seasons have been practiced by traditional cultures the world around. The Goddess movement

initially drew on and adapted the practices of the contemporary neopagan or witchcraft movement. See Eller, *Living in the Lap of the Goddess*, pp. 49–61.

57. Budapest, *The Holy Book of Women's Mysteries*; and Starhawk, *The Spiral Dance*. Also see Noreen Penny, ed., *Women's Rites: An Alternative to Patriarchal Religion* (Waikuku, New Zealand: self-published, 1994), which translates the seasonal rituals for those living in the southern hemisphere.

Chapter 2

1. See Evelyn Fox Keller, *Reflections on Gender and Science* (New Haven: Yale University Press, 1985).

2. Carol Gilligan, *In a Different Voice: Psychological Theory and Women's Development* (Cambridge: Harvard University Press, 1982).

3. Alfred North Whitehead, *Science and the Modern World* (New York: Free Press, 1925), p. 48.

4. Mary Daly, *Beyond God the Father* (Boston: Beacon Press, 1973), pp. 11–12.

5. See Thomas S. Kuhn, *The Structure of Scientific Revolutions* (Chicago: University of Chicago Press, 1962).

6. The ideas that follow are influenced by Michael Novak, *Belief and Unbelief* (New York: New American Library, 1965); Martin Buber, *I and Thou*, trans. Walter Kaufman (New York: Charles Scribners' Sons, 1970); and Audre Lorde, *Sister Outsider* (Trumansburg, NY: Crossing Press, 1984). Also see Carol P. Christ, "Embodied Thinking: Reflections on Feminist Theological Method," *Journal of Feminist Studies in Religion* 5/1 (1989): 7–15.

7. See Chapter 1.

8. Note the use of the personal voice in Christine Downing's *The Goddess: Mythological Images of the Feminine* (New York: Crossroad, 1981) and Karen McCarthy Brown's *Mama Lola: A Vodou Priestess in Brooklyn* (Berkeley: University of California Press, 1991), among many others.

9. This point is also made in Rita Gross, *Feminism and Religion: An Introduction* (Boston: Beacon Press, 1996), p. 51.

10. Carol P. Christ, *Laughter of Aphrodite: Reflections on a Journey to the Goddess* (San Francisco: Harper and Row, 1987).

11. See Chapter 1.

12. Audre Lorde, *Sister Outsider*. "Uses of the Erotic: The Erotic as Power," in Judith Plaskow and Carol P. Christ, eds., *Weaving the Visions: New Patterns in Feminist Spirituality* (San Francisco: Harper and Row, 1989), p. 208.

13. "The ground of being," a metaphor for the divine power found in the work of Protestant theologian Paul Tillich, is particularly appropriate in a Goddess theology. The metaphor of the ground of being suggests that divine power is not "above," "outside," or "beyond" the cycle of life and death, but "beneath" or "within" all things as their support or foundation.

14. Starhawk, *The Spiral Dance: A Rebirth of the Ancient Religion of the Great Goddess* (San Francisco: Harper and Row, 1979); and Zsuzsanna E. Budapest, *The Holy Book of Women's Mysteries*, Part 1, ed. Helen Beardwoman (Los Angeles: Susan B. Anthony Coven #1, 1979).

15. I do not intend this statement to be read as a blanket judgment of the meaning of spell casting and divination in the lives of others.

16. See Vincent Scully, *The Earth, the Temple, and the Gods: Greek Sacred Architecture*, rev. ed. (New Haven: Yale University Press, 1979).

17. Carol Lee Sanchez, "New World Tribal Communities," in Judith Plaskow and Carol P. Christ, eds., *Weaving the Visions: New Patterns in Feminist Spirituality* (San Francisco, Harper and Row, 1989), p. 346.

18. See Robert Bellah, "Civil Religion in America," in *The Religious Situation 1968* (Boston: Beacon Press, 1968), pp. 331–55.

19. Carol Lee Sanchez, "Animal, Vegetable, and Mineral," in Carol J. Adams, ed., *Ecofeminism and the Sacred* (New York: Continuum, 1993), pp. 222–24.

20. As I wrote in *Laughter of Aphrodite*, I left the church as much because of its anti-Judaism as its sexism.

21. See Judith Plaskow, "Christian Feminism and Anti-Judaism," *Cross Currents* 28 (1978): 306–9, and Annette Daum, "Blaming Jews for the Death of the Goddess," *Lilith* 7 (1980), pp. 12–13..

22. See Clifford Geertz, "Religion as a Cultural System," in *The Interpretation of Cultures: Selected Essays* (New York: Basic Books, 1973), pp. 87–125, esp. 90, 93. Also see his "Ethos, World View, and the Analysis of Sacred Symbols" in the same volume, pp. 126–41.

23. Gordon D. Kaufman, *Theology for a Nuclear Age* (Philadelphia: Westminster Press, 1985), p. 28.

24. Gordon D. Kaufman, *In Face of Mystery: A Constructive Theology* (Cambridge, MA: Harvard University Press, 1995), p. xi.

25. Paul Tillich, *Dynamics of Faith* (New York: Harper Torchbooks, 1957), p. 43.

Chapter 3

1. Merlin Stone, *When God Was a Woman* (New York: Dial Press, 1976), p. 1. Stone's book contains some inaccuracies that have been challenged and corrected by other scholars; her book nonetheless brought the history of the Goddess into contemporary consciousness at a critical moment.

2. Three books that synthesize the research that has followed the publication of *When God Was a Woman* are Anne Baring and Jules Cashford, *The Myth of the Goddess: Evolution of an Image* (London: Viking Arkana, 1991), the longest and most detailed; Peg Streep, *Sanctuaries of the Goddess: The Sacred Landscapes and Objects* (Boston: Little, Brown, 1994); and Elinor Gadon, *The Once and Future Goddess* (San Francisco: Harper and Row, 1989).

3. See "On Its Own Two Feet," *Time* (August 28, 1995): 40–42. Discoveries in 1995

by Meave Leakey and Alan Walker indicate that hominoids learned to walk upright about four million years ago. "Lucy" lived about three and a half million years ago.

4. See C.C. Lamberg-Karlovsky, "Introduction," in *Hunters, Farmers, and Civilizations: Old World Archaeology: Readings from* Scientific American (San Francisco: W.H. Freeman, 1979, p. 5. Also see Mircea Eliade, *A History of Religious Ideas,* vol. 1: *From the Stone Age to the Eleusinian Mysteries,* trans. Willard Trask (Chicago: University of Chicago Press, 1978), pp. 8–13.

5. See Eliade, *History,* vol. 1, pp. 9–10. Burial in a fetal position suggests returning to the Mother.

6. Ibid., chap. 1.

7. G. Rachel Levy, *Religious Conceptions of the Stone Age* (New York: Harper and Row, 1963). First published as *The Gate of Horn* (London: Faber and Faber, 1948).

8. See Andre Leroi-Gourhan, "The Evolution of Paleolithic Art," in *Hunters, Farmers, and Civilizations,* p. 39.

9. See Bogdan Rutkowski, *The Cult Places of the Aegean* (New Haven, CT: Yale University Press, 1986), chap. 4.

10. The Orthodox icon consistently portrays the birth of Jesus as having occurred in a cave—not, as the western Church imagines, in a stable.

11. Susan Griffin, *Woman and Nature: The Roaring Inside Her* (New York: Harper and Row, 1978), pp. 159–60. Also see Carol P. Christ, *Odyssey with the Goddess: A Spiritual Quest in Crete* (New York: Continuum, 1995), pp. 45–47.

12. See Sally R. Binford and Lewis R. Binford, "Stone Tools and Human Behavior," in *Hunters, Farmers, and Civilizations,* p. 20.

13. See Francis Dahlberg, *Woman the Gatherer* (New Haven, CT: Yale University Press, 1981).

14. Adrienne Rich, *Of Woman Born: Motherhood as Experience and Institution* [1976] (New York: W.W. Norton, 1986), p. 94.

15. See Lamberg-Karlovsky, "Introduction" (to "Neolithic Villagers and Farmers"), in *Hunters, Farmers, and Civilizations,* pp. 85–90. Parallel and apparently unrelated developments occurred in the Americas and in Asia.

16. Ruby Rohrlich-Leavitt, "Women in Transition: Crete and Sumer," in Renate Bridenthal and Claudia Koontz, eds., *Becoming Visible* (Boston: Houghton Mifflin, 1977), p. 38. See Eliade, *History,* vol. 1, p. 40. For a discussion of women's contributions to the development of agriculture, also see Margaret Ehrenberg, *Women in Prehistory* (Norman: University of Oklahoma Press, 1989), chap. 3; and Patty Jo Watson and Mary C. Kennedy, "The Development of Horticulture in the Eastern Woodlands of North America: Women's Role," in Joan M. Gero and Margaret W. Conkey, eds., *Engendering Archaeology: Women and Prehistory* (Cambridge, MA: Blackwell, 1991), pp. 255–75.

17. See Ehrenberg, *Women in Prehistory,* pp. 82–83.

18. Elizabeth Wayland Barber, *Women's Work: The First 20,000 Years: Women, Cloth, and Society in Early Times* (New York: W.W. Norton, 1994).

19. Rita P. Wright, "Women's Labor and Pottery Production in Prehistory," in Gero and Conkey, eds., *Engendering Archaeology*, pp. 194–223.
20. See Ehrenberg, *Women in Prehistory*, pp. 99–107. Her theories are discussed in greater detail later in this chapter.
21. Ehrenberg, p. 79.
22. Watson and Kennedy in *Engendering Archaeology* argue that men as hunters have been perceived as active, whereas women as gatherers have been perceived as passive. They argue that this (mis)perception has led to the downplaying of women's active contributions to the discovery of agriculture.
23. Marija Gimbutas, *The Language of the Goddess* (San Francisco: Harper and Row, 1989), p. 321.
24. Marija Gimbutas, "Women and Culture in Goddess-Oriented Old.Europe," in Judith Plaskow and Carol P. Christ, eds., *Weaving the Visions: New Patterns in Feminist Spirituality* (San Francisco: Harper and Row, 1989), p. 63.
25. Gimbutas, *Language*, p. xxi.
26. Marija Gimbutas, *The Civilization of the Goddess* (San Francisco: Harper and Row, 1991), p. 222.
27. These terms, which represent the deciphering of the "language of the Goddess," are taken from the table of contents in Gimbutas, *Language*.
28. Miriam Robbins Dexter makes this assertion in *Whence the Goddess: A Source Book* (New York: Teachers College Press, 1990), chap. 1.
29. See Gimbutas, *Civilization*, pp. 331–41, 352, 357–401.
30. See Gimbutas, *Civilization*, chap. 9, esp. pp. 324, 331, 334, 342–49; quote from p. 349.
31. James Mellaart, "A Neolithic City in Turkey," in *Hunters, Farmers, and Civilizations*, p. 131. Also see his *Çatal Hüyük* (New York: McGraw-Hill, 1967) and *Earliest Civilizations of the Near East* (New York: McGraw-Hill, 1965).
32. Mellaart, "Neolithic City," p. 130.
33. Anne L. Barstow, "The Uses of Archaeology for Women's History: James Mellaart's Work on the Neolithic Goddess at Çatal Hüyük," *Feminist Studies* 4/3 (1978): pp. 7–18, was one of the first feminists to call attention to Mellaart's work; her essay was published in somewhat different form as "The Prehistoric Goddess," in Carl Olson, ed., *The Book of the Goddess* (New York: Crossroad, 1983), pp. 5–28. A long section is devoted to Çatal Hüyük in Baring and Cashford, *Myth of the Goddess*, pp. 82–93; and a chapter in Gadon, *Once and Future Goddess*, pp. 25–37.
34. See Brian Fagan's critique of Gimbutas, "A Sexist View of Prehistory," *Archaeology* 45/2 (March–April 1992): 14–18, where he cites a study of the pre-Hispanic Sausa society of the Andes.
35. See Eleftherios Pavlides and Jana Hesser, "Women's Roles and House Form and Decoration in Eressos, Greece," in Jill Dubisch, ed., *Gender and Power in Rural Greece* (Princeton, NJ: Princeton University Press, 1986), pp. 68–96.
36. See Ernestine Friedl, "The Position of Women: Appearance and Reality," in

Dubisch, ed., *Gender and Power in Rural Greece*, pp. 42–52.

37. Peggy Reeves Sanday, *Female Power and Male Dominance: On the Origins of Sexual Inequality* (Cambridge, MA: Cambridge University Press, 1981), p. xv.

38. Ibid., p. 5.

39. See *Myth, Religion, and Mother Right: Selected Writings of J.J. Bachofen* [1954], ed. Rudolf Marx, trans. Ralph Manheim (Princeton, NJ: Princeton University Press, 1967).

40. See Ruby Rohrlich, "State Formation and the Subjugation of Women," *Feminist Studies* 6/1 (1980): 78–102.

41. Daniel McCall, "Mother Earth: The Great Goddess of West Africa," in James J. Preston, ed., *Mother Worship: Theme and Variations* (Chapel Hill: University of North Carolina Press, 1982), pp. 306, 308. McCall is commenting on the relevance of Durkheim's theory that religion reflects society.

42. See Rita Gross, *Feminism and Religion* (Boston: Beacon Press, 1996), pp. 188–89.

43. See Gimbutas, *Civilization*, chap. 10; and Ehrenberg, *Women in Prehistory*, pp. 99–107. For a critical yet not entirely unsympathetic evaluation of several versions of this argument, see Gross, *Feminism and Religion*, chap. 5. Gross also uses Ehrenberg and Sanday to amplify and correct simpler and less accurate versions of the argument about peaceful matristic cultures in the Neolithic.

44. Ehrenberg, *Women in Prehistory*, pp. 99–107.

45. Ibid., p. 105.

46. Eliade, *History*, vol. 1, p. 187.

47. L. Luca Cavalli-Sforza, cited in Louise Levathes, "A Geneticist Maps Ancient Migrations," *New York Times*, July 27, 1993: B1, B6. Also see L. Luca Cavalli-Sforza, "Genetic Evidence Supporting Marija Gimbutas' Work on the Origin of Indo-European People," in Joan Marler, ed., *From the Realm of the Ancestors: Essays in Honor of Marija Gimbutas* (Manchester: Knowledge, Ideas, and Trends, 1977); and his *The Great Human Diasporas* (New York: Addison-Wesley, 1995).

48. Robert DeMao, cited in Riane Eisler, *Sacred Pleasure* (San Francisco: HarperSanFrancisco, 1995), pp. 92–96.

49. Rohrlich, "State Formation and the Subjugation of Women."

50. Some believe that the use of rape as a "tool" of war began in the 1990s in the war in the former Yugoslavia. But rape as the "spoils of war" is testified to in the Bible and the *Iliad* and has been practiced in almost all wars. What is new about the situation in the former Yugoslavia is that the world community, as represented by the International War Crimes Tribunal in The Hague, recognized rape as a war crime.

51. Sanday, *Female Power and Male Dominance*, p. 89.

52. Jane Ellen Harrison, *Prolegomena to the Study of Greek Religion* [1903] (London: Merlin Press, 1962), p. 285. The comment is technically only about Hesiod.

53. The only complete version of the *Enuma Elish* is late Assyrian and was found in the seventh-century library at Nineveh. Other fragments are dated no earlier

than c. 1000 B.C.E. But scholars believe that the myth dates to 1200 B.C.E. or earlier. See Tikva Frymer-Kensky, "Enuma Elish," in *The Encyclopedia of Religion*, vol. 5, (New York: Macmillan, 1987) pp. 124–26; N.K. Sandars, *Poems of Heaven and Hell from Ancient Mesopotamia* (Baltimore: Penguin Books, 1971); and Barbara C. Sproul, ed.,. *Primal Myths: Creating the World* (San Francisco: Harper and Row, 1979). Since I view patriarchy as an evolving ideology, I am hesitant to assume that a late version of its texts reflects earlier sources.

54. Sandars, *Poems from Heaven and Hell*, p. 83. Sandars describes Tiamat as "the Old Hag, the first mother" (p. 83 and *passim*). Linguist Miriam Robbins Dexter informs me that a more accurate translation is "Mother Hubur, fashioner of all things." She notes that "some Western male translators have a more negative feeling about Tiamat than the Babylonians did" (personal communication).
55. Sandars, *Poems of Heaven and Hell*, pp. 90–91.
56. Paul Roche, trans., *The Orestes Plays of Aeschylus* (New York: New American Library, 1962), p. 159. It is noteworthy that Aeschylus rewrites the history of the succession of deities at Delphi, imagining a peaceable takeover.
57. Pierre Chantraine, *Dictionnaire Etymologique de la Langue Greque* (Paris: Editions Klincksieck, 1966–1970), p. 261.
58. Ioanna K. Konstantinou, *Delphi: The Oracle and Its Role in the Political and Social Life of the Ancient Greeks* (Athens: Hannibal, no date), pp. 28–29.
59. Thelma Sargent, trans., "To Pythian Apollo," in *The Homeric Hymns* (New York: W.W. Norton, 1973), p. 23.
60. *Homeric Hymns*, p. 24.
61. See Konstantinou, *Delphi*, p. 29.
62. See R.M. Frazer, trans., *The Poems of Hesiod* (Norman: University of Oklahoma Press, 1983), pp. 83–85; also see Robert Graves, *The Greek Myths*, vol. 1 (Baltimore: Penguin, 1955), pp. 44–47; and Maria S. Brouscaris, *The Monuments of the Acropolis* (Athens: General Direction of Antiquities and Restoration, 1978), pp. 62–63; the frieze of the defeat of the Amazons is on the west metope, which means that it would be seen immediately on entry to the acropolis; the defeat of the Amazons is a common theme in Greek temple art.
63. Paul Roche, trans., "The Eumenides," *The Orestes Plays of Aeschylus*, p. 190.
64. Ibid., p. 186.
65. See Martha Lee Osborne, ed., *Woman in Western Thought* (New York: Random House, 1979), p. 46, quote from Aristotle's *Metaphysics*.
66. See Walter Burkert, *Greek Religion*, trans. John Raffan (Cambridge: Harvard University Press, 1985), pp. 131–35.
67. *The Poems of Hesiod*, "Theogony," pp. 34–37 (the birth of Aphrodite); "Theogony," pp. 64–67, and "Works and Days," pp. 97–100 (Pandora).
68. The myth of the slaying of the Goddess is alluded to in Psalms 74:13–14, Isaiah 27:1, Psalms 89:9–10, and Job 26:12–13.
69. This and other quotations from the Bible are from the Revised Standard Version.

70. See Raphael Patai and Robert Graves, *Hebrew Myths: The Book of Genesis* (New York: McGraw-Hill, 1964), pp. 21–28; also see Cyrus H. Gordon, *Ugaritic Manual* (Rome: Pontificum Institutum Biblicum, 1955), p. 332.

71. Stone, *When God Was a Woman*, chap. 10. Also see J.A. Phillips, *Eve: The History of an Idea* (San Francisco: Harper and Row, 1984). For an alternate reading, see Phyllis Trible, "Eve and Adam: Genesis 2–3 Reread," in Carol P. Christ and Judith Plaskow, eds., *Womanspirit Rising* (San Francisco: Harper and Row, 1979), pp. 74–83. Trible's reading, while internally consistent, is not convincing to me because it does not mention that the snake, the naked woman, and the sacred tree are well-known symbols of Goddess religion and because it does not offer reasons for their use in the biblical story.

72. See Friedrich Heinrich Wilhelm Gesenius, ed., *Hebrew and Chaldee Lexicon to the Old Testament Scriptures* [1846], trans. S.P. Tragelles, (Grand Rapids, MI: Eerdmans, 1949), p. 264. The title "Mother of All the Living" is found in Genesis 3:20.

73. See Phillips, *Eve*, pp. 29-30.

74. See Elisabeth Schüssler Fiorenza, *In Memory of Her: A Feminist Reconstruction of Christian Origins* (New York: Crossroad, 1983), pp. 234–35.

75. There are different versions of the nature of the first sin, the two most common being "disobedience to the Word of God" and "concupiscence," or sexual desire. However sin is described, Eve's less rational or more carnal nature is usually implicated.

76. Phillips, *Eve*, p. 76, quoting Tertullian, "On the Apparel of Women," in *The Ante-Nicene Fathers*, vol. 4 (Grand Rapids, MI: Eerdmans, 1948), p. 14.

77. Quoted in Marina Warner, *Alone of All Her Sex: The Myth and Cult of the Virgin Mary* (New York: Alfred A. Knopf, 1976), pp. 59–60, from St. Justin Martyr, *A Dialogue with Trypho*.

78. The title of Warner's book, *Alone of All Her Sex*, is taken from a poem by Caelius Sedulius, see p. xvii.

79. See Zella Bardsley, "The Many Pieces of Spirituality," in *Woman's Way: The Path of Empowerment* 2/3 (Winter 1994–1995): 11.

80. Naomi R. Goldenberg, "A Theory of Gender as a Central Hermeneutic in the Psychoanalysis of Religion," in Jacob van Belzen, ed., *Hermeneutic Approaches to the Psychology of Religion* (Amsterdam: Editions Rodopi, 1996).

81. Gimbutas, *Language*, pp. 318–20.

82. Thelma Sargent, trans., "To Aphrodite," in *The Homeric Hymns*, p. 46.

83. Mary Barnard, *Sappho: A New Translation* (Berkeley: University of California Press, 1958), #42.

84. Ibid., #37.

85. Ibid., #37.

86. Ibid., #38.

87. Costis Davaras, *Guide to Cretan Antiquities*, 3d ed. (Athens: Eptalofos, 1976), pp. 124–25.

88. Gloria Anzaldua, "Entering into the Serpent," in Plaskow and Christ, *Weaving the*

Visions, p. 77. Also see Preston, ed., *Mother Worship*, pp. 5–50, articles "The Virgin of Guadalupe and the Female Self-Image" by Ena Campbell and "The Tonantsi Cult of the Eastern Nahua" by Alan R. Sandstrom.

89. Mary Condren, *The Serpent and the Goddess: Women, Religion, and Power in Celtic Ireland* (San Francisco: Harper and Row, 1989), pp. 66–67.

Chapter 4

1. Moses Finley, "Archaeology and History," *Daedalus* 100 (1971): 168–86, quoted in Sarah B. Pomeroy, *Goddesses, Whores, Wives, and Slaves* (New York: Schocken, 1975), p. 14.

2. Walter Burkert, *Greek Religion* (Cambridge, MA: Harvard University Press, 1985), pp. 11–12.

3. Most prominent female critics of the Goddess hypothesis and the work of Marija Gimbutas are Margaret Conkey and Ruth Tringham, "Archaeology and the Goddess: Exploring the Contours of Feminist Archaeology," in A. Stewart and D. Stanton, eds., *Feminisms in the Academy: Rethinking the Disciplines* (Ann Arbor: University of Michigan Press, 1995), pp. 199–247; and Lynn Meskell, "Goddesses, Gimbutas and 'New Age' Archaeology," *Antiquity* 69 (1995):74–86. For another view, see Carol P. Christ and Naomi Goldenberg, eds., *The Legacy of the Goddess: The Work of Marija Gimbutas*, a collection of essays in *Journal of Feminist Studies in Religion* 12/2 (Fall 1996). Also see Joan Marler, ed., *From the Realm of the Ancestors: An Anthology in Honor of Marija Gimbutas* (Manchester, CT: Knowledge, Ideas, and Trends, 1997).

4. Sarah B. Pomeroy, *Goddesses, Whores, Wives, and Slaves*, p. 15.

5. These are the terms used in the first paragraph of Meskell's essay, "Goddesses, Gimbutas and 'New Age' Archaeology."

6. See Elisabeth Schüssler Fiorenza, *In Memory of Her: Feminist Theological Reconstruction of Christian Origins* (New York: Crossroad, 1983), especially chap. 2.

7. Burkert, *Greek Religion*, p. 10.

8. Ibid., pp. 14–15.

9. See Marija Gimbutas, *The Language of the Goddess* (San Francisco: Harper and Row, 1989), p. xv.

10. See Naomi Goldenberg, "Marija Gimbutas and the King's Archaeologist," *Journal of Feminist Studies in Religion* 12/2 (Fall 1996), pp. 67–72, who recalls an academic conference where the arguments of "the king's archaeologist" about the activities of prehistoric priests were far more readily accepted than Gimbutas's arguments about the prehistoric Goddesses.

11. Margaret Miles, *Image as Insight* (Boston: Beacon Press, 1985).

12. Jane Ellen Harrison, *Prolegomena to the Study of Greek Religion* [1903] (London: Merlin Press, 1962), p. 285.

13. Burkert, *Greek Religion*, p. 4.

14. The complete story is told in the *Works and Days*. See *The Poems of Hesiod*, ed.

R.M. Frazer, (Norman: University of Oklahoma Press, 1983), pp. 97–100 (lines 47–105).

15. Harrison, *Prolegomena*, pp. 276–85.
16. Samuel Noah Kramer, *History Begins at Sumer* (New York: Doubleday, 1958).
17. See *The Epic of Gilgamesh*, trans. N.K. Sandars, (Baltimore: Penguin, 1964), pp. 83–85.
18. Merlin Stone, "9978: Repairing the Time Warp and Other Related Realities," *Heresies* 5 (September 1978): 124–26.
19. See Anne L. Barstow, "The Uses of Archaeology for Women's History: James Mellaart's Work on the Neolithic Goddess at Çatal Hüyük," *Feminist Studies* 4/3 (October 1978): 10, and Merlin Stone, *When God Was a Woman* (New York: Dial Press, 1976), pp. xvii–xxiv, for citation and discussion of scholarly prejudice against the Goddesses.
20. Ruby Rohrlich, "State Formation in Sumer and the Subjugation of Women," *Feminist Studies* 6/1 (1980): 91–92.
21. The exhibit opened in March 1996 and ran for a year. The accompanying book, *Neolithic Culture in Greece* (Athens: Nicholas P. Goulandris Foundation/Museum of Cycladic Art, 1996), was edited by George A. Papathanassopoulos, who coordinated the exhibit as well.
22. The Greek word *ánthropos* means "human being," not "man." But the word itself is gendered as male by its article and ending. I have recently heard Greek feminists propose that the feminine article be used with the masculine word ending to create a truly both-gendered word for "human being": *i ánthropos*.
23. Papathanassopoulos, ed., *Neolithic Culture in Greece*, figs. 30–33, 37–39, on pp. 96–99, 136–38.
24. Christina Marangou, "Figurines and Models," in Papathanassopoulous, *Neolithic Culture in Greece*, p. 146. The translator of the essays from Greek to English was also a woman!
25. This section is condensed from a longer version published as "Mircea Eliade and the Feminist Paradigm Shift in Religious Studies," *Journal of Feminist Studies in Religion* 7/2 (Fall 1991): 75–94,
26. Mircea Eliade, *A History of Religious Ideas*, vol. 1, trans. Willard R. Trask (Chicago: University of Chicago Press, 1978); vol. 2 (1982).
27. Ibid., vol.1, p. 20.
28. Ibid., p. 40.
29. Ibid., p. 187.
30. Ibid., p. 188.
31. Ibid., p. 189.
32. Ibid., p. 250.
33. Ibid., p. xiii.
34. Ibid., p. xiv.
35. Ibid., p. 4.
36. Ibid., p. 6.

37. Ibid., p. 21.
38. See, for example, vol. 2, p. 404, where Eliade writes, "In the language of theology, it could be said that, integrated into a Christian scenario, a number of archaic traditions gain their 'redemption.'"
39. Ibid., p. 41.
40. Ibid., p. 40–44. The association of sacred trees with female symbolism and Goddesses is widespread in later periods in the Near East and Mediterranean (for example, on Cretan seal rings, in the association of Inanna with the date palm, in the reverence of Asherah in the form of the sacred tree [pole]) and probably lies behind the Genesis 2–3 story of Eve. For matrilocation and the burial of female bones in the dwellings, see Barstow, "Uses of Archaeology for Women's History," pp. 7–18; and James Mellaart, *Çatal Hüyük* (New York: McGraw-Hill, 1967). For temples as images of the body of the Goddess, see Marija Gimbutas, *Language*.
41. Eliade, *History*, vol. 1, p. 45.
42. Ibid., pp. 45, 47, 49, 50.
43. Ibid., p. 53.
44. Ibid., p. 36.
45. Ibid., p. 271.
46. Ibid., p. 268.
47. Jane Ellen Harrison's *Prolegomena* relies on vase paintings to construct a very different picture of Greek religion and the Greek Goddesses than Hesiod. In the lecture presented at the 1989 meeting of the American Academy of Religion, Ursula King argued that the work of women scholars in the field of religion has been systematically excluded from the scholarly canon; Harrison was one of her examples.
48. Vincent Scully, *The Earth, the Temple, and the Gods: Greek Sacred Architecture*, rev. ed. (New Haven, CT: Yale University Press, 1979) begins with a discussion of the importance of the landscape in Greek sacred architecture, moves from there to a consideration of the Goddess in Minoan and Indo-European Mycenean temples, followed by chapters on Hera, Demeter, Artemis and Aphrodite, and finally Apollo, Zeus, Poseidon, and Athena.
49. Eliade, *History*, vol. 1, p. 250.
50. Ibid., pp. 253, 254.
51. Ibid., p. 250.
52. Ibid., p. 262, italics in original text.
53. Ibid., p. 274.
54. For a summary, positive evaluation, and critique of Jung's ideas as they affect religion and women's studies, see Naomi R. Goldenberg, *Changing of the Gods: Feminism and the End of Traditional Religions* (Boston: Beacon Press, 1979), pp. 46–71.
55. These views are racist as well as sexist; see the discussion of light and darkness in Chapter 5.
56. Erich Neumann, *The Great Mother: An Analysis of an Archetype* [1955], trans. Ralph Manheim (Princeton, NJ: Princeton University Press, 1963).

57. Erich Neumann, *The Origins and History of Consciousness* [1949], foreward by C.G. Jung, trans. R.F.C. Hull (Princeton, NJ: Princeton University Press, 1971).
58. See Joseph Campbell, *The Hero with a Thousand Faces* [1949] (Princeton, NJ: Princeton University Press, 1972); *The Masks of God*, 3 vols. (Princeton, NJ: Princeton University Press, 1959, 1961, 1964); and *The Hero's Journey: Joseph Campbell on His Life and Work*, ed. Phil Cousineau (San Francisco: HarperSanFrancisco, 1990).
59. Campbell, *The Hero with a Thousand Faces*, quoted in *The Hero's Journey*, p. 78.
60. Campbell, *The Hero's Journey*, p. 92.
61. See Joseph Campbell, *Masks of God*, Foreword to *The Language of the Goddess*, pp. xiii–xiv..
62. Robert Graves, *The White Goddess: A Historical Grammar of Poetic Myth*, rev. ed. (New York: Farrar, Straus, and Giroux, 1966), pp. 9–10. Also see his *The Greek Myths*, 2 vols. (Baltimore: Penguin, 1955, 1960); and with Raphael Patai, *Hebrew Myths: The Book of Genesis* (New York: McGraw-Hill, 1966).
63. See Martin Seymour-Smith, *Robert Graves: His Life and Work* (London: Hutchinson, 1982; Miranda Seymour, *Robert Graves: Life on the Edge* (New York: Henry Holt and Co., 1995); and the three-volume biography by Richard Perceval Graves (London: Weidenfeld and Nicolson, 1986, 1990, and 1996).

Chapter 5

1. See Christine Downing, *The Goddess* (New York: Continuum, 1981), p. 139; translation by Charles Boer.
2. "Firm of foundation" is Thelma Sargent's translation of the words that were translated as "hard as rock" by Boer. See *The Homeric Hymns: A Verse Translation* (New York: W.W. Norton, 1973), p. 79.
3. This line is from Adrienne Rich's poem "Transcendental Etude" in her *Dream of a Common Language: Poems, 1974–1977* (New York: W.W. Norton, 1978), p. 77.
4. This chant was taught to the women on a Goddess pilgrimage to Crete by Lorraine Tartasky in the spring of 1996.
5. It has been argued (especially by Christians) that there is a connection between "paganism" and national fascism. While fascists have invoked the metaphor of "blood and soil" and invoked the gods and goddesses in the cause of ethnic purity and nationalism, this is an obvious misunderstanding of the connection of the Goddess to the earth.
6. Sallie McFague, *The Body of God: An Ecological Theology* (Minneapolis: Fortress Press, 1993), p. 19.
7. Ibid., p. 16.
8. One searches in vain in *The Body of God* for reflection on the body of God as female. This is odd since in an earlier work, *Models of God: Theology for an Ecological, Nuclear Age* (Philadelphia: Fortress Press, 1987), McFague proposes the metaphor of God as Mother. I can only conclude that McFague recognizes the threat

that the image of the earth as the body of God the Mother presents to the traditional Christian audience she hopes will adopt her ecological agenda, and thus
she chooses not to mention "Her."

9. These questions were called to my attention by process theologian John Cobb.
10. Marija Gimbutas, *The Language of the Goddess* (San Francisco: Harper and Row,
1989), p. 141.
11. See Paula Gunn Allen, *The Sacred Hoop: Recovering the Feminine in American Indian
Traditions* (Boston: Beacon Press, 1986), p. 29.
12. For a discussion of some of the issues involved in the debate over so-called essentialism, see Carolyn Merchant, ed., *Ecology: Key Concepts in Critical Theory* (At-
lantic Highlands, NJ: Humanities Press, 1994), pp. 12–13; and the essay in that
volume by Elizabeth Carlassare, "Essentialism in Ecofeminist Debate," pp.
220–34. Carlassare notes that "essentialism" is not part of the self-definition of
feminist thinkers dismissed by means of that label, and she concludes that the
term has been used "in the interest of privileging the position of social/ist ecofem-
inists" (p. 228).
13. Zsuzsanna E. Budapest, "Self-Blessing Ritual," in Carol P. Christ and Judith
Plaskow, eds., *Womanspirit Rising: A Feminist Reader in Religion* (San Francisco:
Harper and Row, 1979), p. 271.
14. This point is discussed more fully in Chapter 7.
15. Quoted in Elizabeth Wayland Barber, *Women's Work: The First 20,000 Years: Women,
Cloth and Society in Early Times* (New York: W.W. Norton, 1994), p. 29.
16. See Peggy Reeves Sanday, *Female Power and Male Dominance* (Cambridge: Cambridge University Press, 1981); Margaret Ehrenberg, *Women in Prehistory* (Norman: University of Oklahoma Press, 1989); and Gunn Allen, *Sacred Hoop*.
17. See Chapter 1.
18. Matthew Fox, *Original Blessing: A Primer in Creation Spirituality* (Santa Fe, NM:
Bear, 1993), p. 309.
19. William Anderson, with photography by Clive Hicks, *Green Man: The Archetype
of Our Oneness with the Earth* (San Francisco: HarperCollins, 1990), but note the
specter of dualism in the emphasis on speech and logos.
20. See Starhawk, *The Spiral Dance: A Rebirth of the Ancient Religion of the Great Goddess*
(San Francisco: Harper and Row, 1979), chap. 6.
21. William G. Doty, *Myths of Masculinity* (New York: Continuum, 1993); and Jan
Henning and Daniel Cohen, *Hawk and the Bard Reborn: Revisions and Renewals of
Old Tales* (London: Wood and Water, 1988).
22. Robert Bly, *Iron John* (Reading, MA: Addison-Wesley, 1990).
23. Ariska Razak, "Toward a Womanist Analysis of Birth," in Irene Diamond and Gloria Feman Orenstein, eds., *Reweaving the World: The Emergence of Ecofeminism* (San
Francisco: Sierra Club Books, 1990), p. 172.
24. Delores Williams, "Sin, Nature, and Black Women's Bodies," in *Ecofeminism and the
Sacred*, p. 28. Also see Delores Williams, *Sisters in the Wilderness: The Challenge of
Womanist God-Talk* (Maryknoll, NY: Orbis Books, 1993).

25. Luisah Teish, *Jambalaya* (San Francisco: Harper and Row, 1985); and Gloria Anzaldua, *Borderlands/La Frontera: The New Mestiza* (San Francisco: Spinsters Aunt Lute, 1987).

26. Carol Lee Sanchez, "Animal, Vegetable, and Mineral," in *Ecofeminism and the Sacred*, ed. Carol J. Adams, (New York: Continuum, 1993), p. 209.

27. See Martin Bernal, *Black Athena: The Afroasiatic Roots of Classical Civilization*, vol. 1: *The Fabrication of Ancient Greece 1785–1985* (New Brunswick, NJ: Rutgers University Press, 1987); vol. 2: *The Archaeological and Documentary Evidence* (New Brunswick, NJ: Rutgers University Press, 1991). Bernal's theories have provoked scholarly controversy. Many have criticized details and factual errors in his arguments. Historian Glen Bowersock comments, "Mr. Bernal's mistakes should not be taken as an excuse to ignore the larger issues he raised, particularly modern ideas of the origins of Western civilization as they have evolved over the last three centuries." See "Rescuing the Greeks," *New York Times Book Review*, Feb. 25, 1996.

28. See Gimbutas, *Language*.

29. Miriam Robbins Dexter argues that the polarization of night and day, dark and light, was less extreme in India than in Europe. See her *Whence the Goddess: A Source Book* (New York: Teachers College Press, 1990), p. 38.

30. Emile Saillens, quoted in Leonard W. Moss and Stephen C. Cappannari, "In Quest of the Black Virgin," in James J. Preston, ed., *Mother Worship: Theme and Variations* (Chapel Hill: University of North Carolina, 1982), p. 68.

31. See Carol P. Christ, *Odyssey with the Goddess: A Spiritual Quest in Crete* (New York: Continuum, 1995), pp. 45–47 and *passim*.

32. See Wolfgang Lederer, *The Fear of Woman* (New York: Greene and Stratton, 1968).

33. See, for example, Nancy E. Auer Falk, "Feminine Sacrality," in *The Encyclopedia of Religion* (New York, Macmillan, 1987) vol. 5, pp. 302–12.

34. This view was frequently expressed by students at the California Institute of Integral Studies when I taught there in 1994.

35. See Elinor Gadon, *The Once and Future Goddess: A Symbol for Our Time* (San Francisco: Harper and Row, 1989), p. 83.

36. Christine Downing, *Women's Mysteries: Toward a Poetics of Gender* (New York: Crossroad, 1992), pp. 147–78.

37. In Dexter, *Whence the Goddess*, p. 19.

38. Ibid. It is an irony of history that this is one of the few ancient poems to the Goddess attributed to a woman, the priestess Enheduanna.

39. Downing, *Women's Mysteries*, p. 176.

40. Nancy Falk, "Feminine Sacrality," p. 309.

41. Plato, *The Symposium*, trans. Walter Hamilton (Baltimore: Penguin, 1951), pp. 93–94. It is one of the ironies of history that this view, which has been understood in profoundly anti-female ways, is attributed by Plato to the "woman of Mantinea, called Diotima" (p. 79), whom Plato said taught it to Socrates.

42. Plato, *Symposium*, p. 95.

43. Hallie Iglehart Austen, "The Heart of the Goddess," *Woman of Power* 15 (Fall–Winter, 1990): 88.

44. Mara Lynn Keller, "Wholistic Philosophy from Feminist and Other Natural Resources," unpublished essay. My view perhaps differs from Keller's in being somewhat more critical of thinking in pairs.

45. Quoted in Bill Moyers, *Healing and the Mind* (New York: Doubleday, 1993), p. 189 and in Marcia Lee Falk, *The Book of Blessings: New Jewish Prayers for Daily Life, the Sabbath, and the New Moon Festival* (San Francisco: HarperSanFrancisco, 1996), p. 6.

46. See Van A. Harvey, *A Handbook of Theological Terms* (New York: Macmillan, 1964), pp. 127–28, 172–73, 235–36, 242–43.

47. Fox, *Original Blessing*.

48. See John B. Cobb, *God and the World* (Philadelphia: Westminster Press, 1969) and *Is It Too Late? A Theology of Ecology* (Beverly Hills, CA: Bruce, 1972). Also see Sheila Greeve Davaney, ed., *Feminism and Process Thought* (New York: Edwin Mellen, 1981).

49. Martin Buber, *I and Thou*, trans. Walter Kaufmann (New York: Charles Scribner's Sons, 1970).

50. See Rosemary Radford Ruether, *New Woman/New Earth: Sexist Ideologies and Human Liberation* (New York: Seabury/Crossroad, 1975) and *Gaia and God: An Ecofeminist Theology of Earth Healing* (San Francisco: HarperSanFrancisco, 1992). Also see Lynn Gottlieb, *She Who Dwells Within: A Feminist Vision of a Renewed Judaism* (San Francisco: HarperSanFrancisco, 1995).

51. Matthew Fox was silenced by the Catholic Church for a year, and he eventually resigned from his order and the Roman Catholic priesthood. Many Jewish thinkers find Martin Buber insufficiently Jewish because his theology is not based on observance of Jewish law. The "RE-Imagining" conference held in Minneapolis in 1993 as part of the Ecumenical Decade in Solidarity with Women of the World Council of Churches in which Sophia (Wisdom) was invoked with images reminiscent of the Goddess provoked an outpouring of condemnation by traditionalists. Lynn Gottlieb's right to live her vision of Judaism has been challenged.

52. Nelle Morton, "The Goddess as Metaphoric Image," in Judith Plaskow and Carol P. Christ, eds., *Weaving the Visions: New Patterns in Feminist Spirituality* (San Francisco: Harper and Row, 1989), p. 111. Also see *The Journey Is Home* (Boston: Beacon Press, 1985).

53. Morton, "Goddess as Metaphoric Image," p. 116.

54. Starhawk, "Power, Authority, and Mystery: Ecofeminism and Earth-based Spirituality," in Irene Diamond and Gloria Feman Orenstein, eds., *Reweaving the World: The Emergence of Ecofeminism* (San Francisco: Sierra Club Books, 1990), p. 73.

55. Starhawk, *Dreaming the Dark* (Boston: Beacon Press, 1982), p. 74.

56. Sometimes her position seems more like pantheism; at others, panentheism.

57. Process philosophy is a school of thought associated with Alfred North White-

head and his followers, the most important of whom is Charles Hartshorne, whose thinking has influenced mine. Students of process theology will note that while I draw on what might be called the basic insights of process theology, I do not accept all of the philosophical theories of Whitehead and Hartshorne, the major proponents of process philosophy and theology. Whitehead's explanation of experience as a series of discrete events, for example, seems overly atomistic to me. As an introduction to the process view of God, I find most provocative Charles Hartshorne's *The Divine Relativity* (New Haven, CT: Yale University Press, 1982). See also Davaney, ed., *Feminism and Process Thought;* and the works of Christian theologian John Cobb and that of his female students, Marjorie Suchocki and Catherine Keller, who have developed Whitehead's philosophy in feminist directions.

58. See J.E. Lovelock and L. Margulis, "Gaia and Geognosy," in M.B. Rambler, ed., *Global Ecology: Towards a Science of the Biosphere* (London: Jones and Bartlett, 1984); and J.E. Lovelock, *Gaia: A New Look at Life on Earth* (Oxford: Oxford University Press, 1982).

59. The words *intelligent, aware,* and *alive* are taken from a quote by Paula Gunn Allen describing the earth, which is discussed in Chapter 6. The idea that God is a kind of a person with whom we stand in relation is found in Buber, *I and Thou,* especially "Third Part," pp. 123–68.

60. The metaphor of God as the "ground of being" is found throughout the work of Christian theologian Paul Tillich. I have been profoundly moved by this metaphor but interpret it differently from Tillich because I use a process ontology.

61. See Chapter 1; also see Christ, *Odyssey with the Goddess.*

62. Alice Walker, *The Color Purple* (New York: Pocket Books, 1983), p. 178.

63. Ibid., pp. 178–79.

64. See Raphael Patai, *The Hebrew Goddess* (New York: KTAV, 1967).

65. I do not mention Islam here because critique of Islam is beyond the purview of this book. This should not be read to imply that I believe Islamic monotheism is gender-neutral.

66. Theodore M. Ludwig, "Monotheism," in Mircea Eliade, ed., *The Encyclopedia of Religion* (New York: Collier Macmillan, 1987), pp. 68–69.

67. Paul Tillich, *The Dynamics of Faith* (New York: Harper and Row, 1957).

68. Karen McCarthy Brown, personal conversation.

69. See Downing, *The Goddess,* pp. 22–29.

70. Falk, "Notes on Composing New Blessings," in *Weaving the Visions,* p. 128; also see her *Book of Blessings.*

71. Ibid., p. 129.

72. This chant is attributed to Z. Budapest.

73. Ludwig, "Monotheism," p. 71.

74. Ibid.

75. Downing, *The Goddess,* p. 5.

Chapter 6

1. Martin Buber, *I and Thou*, trans. Walter Kaufmann (New York: Charles Scribner's Sons, 1970), pp. 58–59.
2. Ibid., p. 60.
3. Ibid., p. 58.
4. Paula Gunn Allen, *The Sacred Hoop: Recovering the Feminine in American Indian Traditions* (Boston: Beacon Press, 1986), p. 119.
5. Susan Griffin, *Woman and Nature: The Roaring Inside Her* (New York: Harper and Row, 1978), p. 227
6. Griffin refers to Plato's vision in the cave in the early pages of *Woman and Nature*, and I read this passage as a refutation of it.
7. Griffin, *Woman and Nature*, p. 219.
8. Alix Kates Shulman, *Drinking the Rain: A Memoir* (New York: Farrar, Straus, Giroux, 1995), pp. 55–56.
9. Griffin, *Woman and Nature*, p. 219.
10. See "Songs from a Goddess Pilgrimage to Crete" (Blacksburg, VA: Ariadne Institute for the Study of Myth and Ritual, 1996); I adapted the words from "A Traditional Navajo Prayer," trans. Gladys A. Reichard, in Jane Hirshfield, ed., *Women in Praise of the Sacred: 43 Centuries of Spiritual Poetry by Women* (New York: Harper-Collins, 1994), p. 201, and Jana Ruble set them to music. Also see Lisa Theil, "On the Trail of Beauty," in Kate Marks, ed., *Circle of Song* (Amherst, MA: Full Circle Press, 1995).
11. Carol P. Christ, *Diving Deep and Surfacing: Women Writers on Spiritual Quest* [1980] (Boston: Beacon Press, 1995). In this book, I argued that women might be particularly open to these kinds of mystical experiences. In this chapter, I focus on their availability to all.
12. Gunn Allen, *Sacred Hoop*, p. 60.
13. Griffin, *Woman and Nature*, p. 219.
14. Elisabet Sahtouris, *Gaia: The Human Journey from Chaos to Cosmos* (New York: Pocket Books, 1989), p. 126.
15. Ibid., p. 90.
16. Ibid., p. 91.
17. Ibid., p. 90.
18. Griffin, *Woman and Nature*, p. 226.
19. Buber, *I and Thou*, p. 58.
20. *I and Thou* was originally translated into English by Ronald Gregor Smith in 1937. See the note to Kaufmann's translation of "Er leibt mir gegenüber" on p. 58 of his book; also see p. 45.
21. Sahtouris, *Gaia*, p. 91.
22. See Exodus 3:5: "for the place on which you are standing is holy ground."
23. Carol Lee Sanchez, "New World Tribal Communities," in Judith Plaskow and Carol P. Christ, eds., *Weaving the Visions: New Patterns in Feminist Spirituality* (San

Francisco: Harper and Row, 1989), p. 345.

24. Susan G. Worst, letter dated May 11, 1995.

25. Sanchez, "New World Tribal Communities," p. 345.

26. See Chapter 1.

27. Sanchez, "New World Tribal Communities," p. 355.

28. Gordon Kaufman, *The Theological Imagination: Constructing the Concept of God* (Philadelphia: Westminster Press, 1981), p. 226.

29. Ibid., p. 225. Kaufman's own recent work repudiates the view he describes here. See his *In Face of Mystery: A Constructive Theology* (Cambridge, MA: Harvard University Press, 1993).

30. See Dorothy Dinnerstein, *The Mermaid and the Minotaur: Sexual Arrangements and Human Malaise* (New York: Harper and Row, 1976).

31. *Of a Like Mind*, Candlemas 9995 [1995], inside cover. I have not quoted all of the affirmations, and I have listed them in a different order than they appear in the original.

32. But the medical intervention that prolonged my grandmother's death was wrong.

33. There is little doubt that Greek mourning rituals have pre-Christian roots; see Loring M. Danforth, *The Death Rituals of Rural Greece* (Princeton, NJ: Princeton University Press, 1982). Greek mourning rituals have a patriarchal aspect, with stricter expectations for women's mourning than for men's, assuming that a woman's mourning for a husband will last the rest of her life.

34. Joanna Macy, *Despair and Personal Power in the Nuclear Age* (Philadelphia: New Society Publishers, 1993).

35. It is beyond the purview of this book to speculate about a time when the sun will become cold and the Gaia body as we know it will cease to exist. But if the universe is the body of the Goddess, even then the processes of birth, death, and renewal will continue.

36. Ruth M. Underhill, *Red Man's Religion: Beliefs and Practices of the Indians North of Mexico* (Chicago: University of Chicago Press, 1965), p. 116.

37. Though not if we are buried in a metal coffin encased in concrete.

38. Though the view I take is different from hers, my thoughts in this section were provoked by reading Kathleen M. Sands, *Escape from Paradise: Evil and Tragedy in Feminist Theology* (Minneapolis: Fortress Press, 1994).

39. See, for example, Sophocles, *Oedipus at Colonus*, trans. and ed. David Greene and Richard Lattimore. *Greek Tragedies*, vol. 3 (Chicago: University of Chicago Press, 1960), pp. 166–67, lines 1211–48.

40. See Simone Weil, *The Iliad or the Poem of Force*, trans. Mary McCarthy (Wallingford, PA: Pendle Hill, 1956).

41. See John Cobb's Ingersoll Lecture on Immortality at Harvard Divinity School in 1987, published as "The Resurrection of the Soul," *Harvard Theological Review* 80/2 (1987): 213–27; Cobb writes that "every cellular event in our bodies lives on in God just as does every personal experience" (p. 227).

42. See Carol P. Christ, *Odyssey with the Goddess: A Spiritual Quest in Crete* (New York: Continuum, 1995), p. 22.

43. John Cobb, in "The Resurrection of the Soul," also imagines a sort of conditional life after death. However, he interprets it differently than I do.

Chapter 7

1. Susan Griffin, *Woman and Nature: The Roaring Inside Her* (New York: Harper and Row, 1978), p. 226.

2. For a sampling of the recent literature on intelligence in animals, see Jeffrey Moussaieff Masson and Susan McCarthy, *When Elephants Weep: The Emotional Lives of Animals* (New York: Delacorte Press, 1995); Stephen Hart, *The Language of Animals* (New York: Henry Holt, 1996); and Alexander F. Skutch, *The Minds of Birds* (College Station: Texas A & M University Press, 1996).

3. Frans de Waal, *Good Natured: The Origins of Right and Wrong in Humans and Other Animals* (Cambridge MA: Harvard University Press, 1996).

4. *Athens News*, May 4, 1966: 4.

5. Martin Buber, *I and Thou*, trans. Walter Kaufmann (New York: Charles Scribners' Sons, 1970), p. 62.

6. Ibid., p. 78. Buber is struggling with language in this passage, de-forming and re-forming the language of philosophy in which the self has been understood.

7. J. Konrad Stettbacher, *Making Sense of Suffering: The Healing Confrontation with Your Own Past*, trans. Simon Worall (New York; Meridian, 1993), p. 89.

8. Karen McCarthy Brown, "Women's Leadership in Haitian Vodou," in Judith Plaskow and Carol P. Christ, eds., *Weaving the Visions: New Patterns in Feminist Spirituality* (San Francisco: Harper and Row, 1989), p. 233.

9. Stettbacher, *Making Sense of Suffering*, p. 91.

10. See Carol P. Christ, *Odyssey with the Goddess: A Spiritual Quest in Crete* (New York: Crossroad, 1995).

11. Stettbacher, *Making Sense of Suffering*, p. 96.

12. Alice Miller's enormously influential and important work is built on her own recognition of the source of her suffering in late middle age after two unsuccessful psychoanalyses and years of working as a psychoanalyst. Miller acknowledges a debt to Stettbacher and wrote the introduction to the American edition of his book *Making Sense of Suffering*. See her *Breaking Down the Wall of Silence: The Liberating Experience of Facing Painful Truth*, trans. Simon Worrall (New York: Meridian, 1993); *Thou Shalt Not Be Aware: Society's Betrayal of the Child*, trans. Hildegarde Hannum and Hunter Hannum (New York: Meridian, 1986); and *For Your Own Good: Hidden Cruelty in Child-rearing and the Roots of Violence*, trans. Hildegarde Hannum and Hunter Hannum (New York: Noonday Press, 1990).

13. Kate Millett, *Sexual Politics* (Garden City, NY: Doubleday, 1970), p. 155.

14. See Delores Williams, "Women's Oppression and Life-line Politics in Black

Women's Religious Narratives," *Journal of Feminist Studies in Religion* 1 (Fall 1985): esp. 60, 65–68.

15. Carol P. Christ, *Laughter of Aphrodite: Reflections on a Journey to the Goddess* (San Francisco: Harper and Row, 1987), p. 204.

16. Christ, *Odyssey*, pp. 105, 147.

17. Heinrich Kramer and James Sprenger, *The Malleus Maleficarum* [c.1496], trans. Montague Summers (New York: Dover, 1971).

18. See Barbara Ehrenreich and Deirdre English, *Witches, Nurses, and Midwives: A History of Women Healers* (New York: Feminist Press, 1973).

19. Ginette Paris, *Pagan Meditations: Aphrodite, Hestia, Artemis* (Dallas: Spring Publications, 1986), pp. 142–43.

20. See Zsuzsanna E. Budapest, *The Grandmother of Time: A Women's Book of Celebrations, Spells and Sacred Objects for Every Month of the Year* (San Francisco: Harper and Row, 1989), pp. 127, 187–88.

21. Brown, "Women's Leadership," p. 233.

22. This phrase is the title of an important and popular feminist book on women's health, *Our Bodies, Ourselves* by the Boston Women's Health Collective (New York: Simon and Schuster, 1973).

23. Beverly Harrison, "The Power of Anger in the Work of Love," in Plaskow and Christ, *Weaving the Visions*, p. 218.

24. Adrienne Rich, *Of Woman Born: Motherhood as Experience and Intuition* [1976] (New York: W.W. Norton, 1986), p. 40.

25. Stettbacher, *Making Sense of Suffering*, p. 111.

26. Audre Lorde, "Uses of the Erotic: The Erotic as Power," in *Weaving the Visions*, pp. 209, 210.

27. Ibid., p. 58.

28. See Peggy Reeves Sanday, *Female Power and Male Dominance: On the Origins of Sexual Inequality* (Cambridge: Cambridge University Press, 1981).

29. Rich, *Of Woman Born*, p. 40.

30. See Arisika Razak, "Toward a Womanist Analysis of Birth," in Irene Diamond and Gloria Feman Orenstein, eds., *Reweaving the World: The Emergence of Ecofeminism* (San Francisco: Sierra Club Books, 1990), pp. 165–72.

31. In ancient Greek, the word *ksénos* took on the connotation of "guest-friend."

32. In the United States, many liberals suffer from self-hatred and guilt for being members of dominant groups, whereas conservatives defensively assert "traditional" (dominator) values.

33. Audre Lorde, "Uses of the Erotic," p. 212.

34. Ecological historians debate this subject. For some, the agricultural revolution marks the time when humans began to destroy their environment. Others choose later dates. It also appears that other animals have the capacity to destroy the environment in which they live. It is possible that the dinosaurs or other species ate themselves out of existence.

35. *Children of Violence* is the title of Doris Lessing's five-volume series of novels about the life of Martha Quest, who was conceived during the First World War, came of age during the Second, and raised her children under the cloud of nuclear holocaust. The quote is from *Landlocked* (New York: New American Library, 1970), p. 195.
36. This is reported as the view of native people of Vancouver Island in Anne Cameron's fictionalized account, *Daughters of Copper Woman* (Vancouver, British Columbia: Press Gang Publishers, 1981), p. 121.
37. Lucia Chiavola Birnbaum, *Black Madonnas: Feminism, Religion, and Politics in Italy* (Boston: Northeastern University Press, 1993), p. 23.
38. Simone de Beauvoir, *The Ethics of Ambiguity*, trans. Bernard Frechtman (New York: Philosophical Library, 1948), pp. 135–36.
39. Stettbacher, *Making Sense of Suffering*, p. 109.
40. See Miller, *Breaking Down the Wall of Silence*, pp. 81–113; and Miller, *For Your Own Good*, pp. 142–197.

Chapter 8

1. See Chapter 1; and Clifford Geertz, "Religion as a Cultural System," and "Ethos, World View and the Analysis of Sacred Symbols," in Clifford Geertz, *The Interpretation of Cultures: Selected Essays* (New York: Basic Books, 1973), pp. 87–125 and 126–41.
2. Zsuzsanna E. Budapest, *The Grandmother of Time* (San Francisco: Harper and Row, 1989), p. xxi.
3. See Riane Eisler, *The Chalice and the Blade* (San Francisco: Harper and Row, 1987). Eisler proposed the term *dominator culture* as a description of what others had called "patriarchal culture." *Dominator culture* has the advantage of making it clear that men also dominate other men in patriarchal societies.
4. Gordon Kaufman, *The Theological Imagination: Constructing the Concept of God* (Philadelphia: Westminster Press, 1981), p. 226.
5. See Judith Hicks Stiehm, "Women, Men, and Military Service: Is Protection Necessarily a Racket?" in Ellen Boneparth, ed., *Women, Power, and Politics* (New York: Pergamon, 1982), pp. 282–93.
6. Ibid., p. 289.
7. Ibid., p. 288.
8. Jonathan Schell, in *The Fate of the Earth* (New York: Avon, 1982), argues that national sovereignty is incompatible with world peace.
9. Anne Tyler, *The Accidental Tourist* (New York: Berkeley Publishing, 1986), p. 338.
10. Dhyani Ywahoo, "Renewing the Sacred Hoop," in Judith Plaskow and Carol P. Christ, eds., *Weaving the Visions: New Patters in Feminist Spirituality* (San Francisco: Harper and Row, 1989), p. 275.
11. For depictions of the rituals of Goddess religion, see Starhawk, *The Spiral Dance*,

2d ed. (San Francisco: Harper and Row, 1989); and Budapest, *Grandmother of Time.*
Also see Carol P. Christ, *Laughter of Aphrodite: Reflections on a Journey to the Goddess*
(San Francisco: Harper and Row, 1987), especially chap. 11, and *Odyssey with the
Goddess* (New York: Continuum, 1995). Also see Chapter 1 of this book.

12. See Catherine Keller, *From a Broken Web: Sexism, Separation, and Self* (Boston: Beacon Press, 1986).

13. Simone de Beauvoir, *The Ethics of Ambiguity* [1948], trans. Bernard Frechtman (New York: Citadel Press, 1970), discussed in Chapter 7.

14. The idea of moral touchstones is taken from Maurice Friedman, *Touchstones of Reality: Existential Trust and the Community of Peace* (New York: Dutton, 1972). My touchstones are different from his.

15. Ariska Razak, "Toward a Womanist Analysis of Birth," in Irene Diamond and Gloria Feman Orenstein, eds., *Reweaving the World: The Emergence of Ecofeminism* (San Francisco: Sierra Club Books, 1990), p. 172.

16. Carol Gilligan, *In a Different Voice: Psychological Theory and Women's Development* (Cambridge, MA: Harvard University Press, 1982).

17. Libby Roderick, from the song "How Could Anyone Ever Tell You" on her album entitled "If You See a Dream" (Turtle Island Records).

18. See Starhawk, *Spiral Dance*, p. 91. The Charge of the Goddess has been attributed to Doreen Valiente; see Cynthia Eller, *Living in the Lap of the Goddess: The Feminist Spirituality Movement in America* (Boston: Beacon Press, 1995), p. 51.

19. See Ywahoo, "Renewing the Sacred Hoop," p. 276. Also see Brooke Medicine Eagle, *Buffalo Woman Comes Singing: The Spirit Song of a Rainbow Medicine Woman* (New York: Ballantine, 1991).

20. Ibid., p. 275.

21. See Judith Plaskow, *Standing Again at Sinai: Judaism from a Feminist Perspective* (San Francisco: Harper and Row, 1990), chap. 6, esp. pp. 218–20.

22. This teaching method is described in more detail in the introduction to the second edition and in the Afterword to the latest edition of my book *Diving Deep and Surfacing* (Boston: Beacon Press, 1980, 1986, 1995).

23. Carol Lee Sanchez, "New World Tribal Communities," in Plaskow and Christ, *Weaving the Visions*, p. 347.

24. Starhawk's *Truth or Dare* (San Francisco: Harper and Row, 1987) is an important resource for building communities; also see Brooke Medicine Eagle, *Buffalo Woman Comes Singing.*

25. Sanchez, p. 346.

26. See Starhawk, *Truth or Dare*, esp. chap. 10.

27. See Sharon Welch, "Idealogy and Social Change," in Plaskow and Christ, *Weaving the Visions*, pp. 336–43.

28. See Plaskow, *Standing Again at Sina;* Martha Acklesberg, "Spirituality, Community, and Politics: B'not Esh and the Feminist Reconstruction of Judaism," *Journal of Feminist Studies in Religion* 2 (Fall 1986): 109–20; Christ, *Laughter of Aphrodite*, esp. pp. 202–3; and *Odyssey with the Goddess.* The newsletter *Ariadne's Thread* docu-

ments the Minoan Sisterhood. Information on Goddess Pilgrimages to Crete, Women's Spiritual Quest in Lesbos, and other educational programs is available from Ariadne Institute for the Study of Myth and Ritual, Ltd., 1306 Crestview Dr., Blacksburg, VA 24060 USA.

29. This phrase is Nelle Morton's. See her *The Journey Is Home* (Boston: Beacon Press, 1985, pp. 17–18).

30. The fruits of the theories generated by these conflicts are reflected in this book.

Epilogue

1. Jan Henning and Daniel Cohen, *Hawk and the Bard Reborn: Revisions and Renewals of Old Tales* (London: Wood and Water, 1988), p. 1.

2. Abraham's God intervened to prevent the sacrifice, as Artemis did in Euripides's version of the story.

3. Cohen stated in an afterword, "There are many possible ways of answering the question I ask"; see *Hawk and the Bard Reborn*, p. 89.

Acknowledgments

This book has had a very long gestation. It was begun during a year spent as a lecturer in the Women and Religion program at Harvard Divinity School. Helpful comments on an early version were given by Ellen Boneparth, Judith Plaskow, Mara Lynn Keller, Christine Downing, Alexis Masters, and Marie Cantlon. Several years later, Candace Chase asked to publish an earlier version of Chapter 2 in *Metis*, unwittingly sparking me to rewrite the entire manuscript. My writing group, the Athens Circle, helped unlock my energy and prodded me to write more clearly and more beautifully. The Goddess pilgrimages I lead in Crete and the women who participate in them have deeped my understanding of the Goddess. The Greek people have helped me root the Goddess in the land.

Jana Ruble, Patrick Simpson, and Marie Cantlon read the new version as I wrote it; Sue Camarados and Chris Lavadas read it soon after it was finished; Judith Plaskow, Miriam Robbins Dexter, Christine Downing, Marie Cantlon, John Cobb, Gordon Kaufman, Susan Worst, Mara Lynn Keller, and Naomi Goldenberg offered thoughtful suggestions for revision. My editor at Addison Wesley Longman, Liz Maguire, who approached the manuscript "interested but skeptical and found herself seduced and persuaded," has been a sensitive reader in the book's final stages. I am grateful to Susan Swan for introducing me to my agent, Kim Witherspoon, and to Kim Witherspoon for believing in my work. Finally, special thanks to Christine Lavadas and Daniel Cohen for permission to use their works as prologue and epilogue.

Carol P. Christ
Athens, Greece
September 21, 1996

Permissions Acknowledgments

Parts of Chapters 2 and 4 appeared in different form in "Toward a Paradigm Shift in the Academy and in Religious Studies," in *The Impact of Feminist Research in the Academy*, ed. Christie Farnham (Bloomington: Indiana University Press, 1987), pp. 53–76.

The discussion of the work of Mircea Eliade in Chapter 4 is condensed from "Mircea Eliade and the Feminist Paradigm Shift," *Journal of Feminist Studies in Religion* 7/2 (1991): 75–94.

Some parts of "Rethinking Theology and Nature," *Weaving the Visions: New Patterns in Feminist Spirituality* (San Francisco: Harper and Row, 1989), pp. 314–25, and "Embodied Thinking: Reflections on Feminist Theological Method," from *Journal of Feminist Studies in Religion* 3/1 (1989): 7–15, found their way into this book.

An earlier version of Chapter 2 appeared as "Thealogy Begins in Experience," in *Metis* 1/1 (Spring 1996): 25–41.

Excerpts from earlier versions of Chapters 5 and 7 were printed in *SageWoman* 32 (Winter 1995): 50–53 and *SageWoman* 35 (Fall 1996): 54–56.

Permission to use "Evrynome: A Story of Creation" granted by Chris Lavdas.

Permission to use "Iphegenia," from *Hawk and the Bard Reborn* by Jan Henning and Daniel Cohen, granted by Daniel Cohen.

Permission to reprint photographs of images of the Goddesses granted as follows:

Figure 1, Figure 8: Courtesy of © Naturhistorisches Museum Wien.

Figure 2: Permission of Musée de l'Homme, Paris, France.

Figure 3: Courtesy of the collection of the Musée d'Aquitaine-Bordeau, France; tous droits resérvés.

Figure 4: Courtesy of the Anatolian Museum, Ankara, Turkey. The Goddess is displayed in the Anatolian Civilizations Museum. All rights belong to the Museum.

Figure 5, Figure 11: Courtesy of the Greek Archaeological Services; from the Heracleion Museum.

Figure 6, Figure 9: From the collection of Marija Gimbutas, used by permission; from the Museum of Stara Zagora and the National Archaeological Museum of Bucharest, Romania.

Figure 7: Courtesy of the Greek Archaeological Service; from the National Archaeological Museum.

Figure 10: Courtesy of the Heracleion Museum; from the Heracleion Museum.

Figure 12: Courtesy of Miriam Robbins Dexter and Gregory Dexter, used by permission; from the Vatican Museum, Rome, Italy.

Index

Made in the USA
Middletown, DE
23 January 2021